Haunting Experiences

Ghosts in Contemporary Folklore

Haunting Experiences

Experiences

Ghosts in Contemporary Folklore

Diane E. Goldstein

Sylvia Ann Grider

Jeannie Banks Thomas

Utah State University Press
Logan, Utah

Utah State University Press
Logan, Utah 84322-7200

Manufactured in the United States of America
Printed on recycled, acid-free paper

ISBN: 978-0-87421-636-3 (paper)
ISBN: 978-0-87421-681-3 (e-book)

Portions of chapter 5 were previously published in Sylvia Grider, 1999, The haunted house in literature, tradition, and popular culture: A consistent image, *Contemporary Legend, New Series* 2:174–204.

Portions of chapter 2 were previously published in Diane E. Goldstein, 1991, Perspectives on Newfoundland belief traditions: Narrative clues to concepts of evidence, in *Studies in Newfoundland folklore: Community and process*, eds. G. Thomas and J. D. A. Widdowson, 27–40 (St. Johns, Newfoundland: Breakwater Books).

Library of Congress Cataloging-in-Publication Data

Goldstein, Diane E.
   Haunting experiences : ghosts in contemporary folklore / Diane E. Goldstein, Sylvia Ann Grider, Jeannie Banks Thomas.
      p. cm.
   Includes bibliographical references.
   ISBN 978-0-87421-636-3 (pbk. : alk. paper)
   1. Ghosts. 2. Supernatural. 3. Haunted places. I. Grider, Sylvia Ann. II. Thomas, Jeannie B. III. Title.
   GR580.G65 2007
   398'.47–dc22

                              2007025178

For their support and encouragement, dedicated to John Banks and Dorothy Pingree, Rochelle Goldstein, the folks at I.S.C.L.R., and to Rowdy Grrlz everywhere.

Contents

Illustrations

Acknowledgments

Without the help of a great many friends, we three authors would never have been able to manage the logistics and complexities of putting this book together. Spread across the continent from Newfoundland to Utah to Texas, e-mail served us well, but our friends made the book happen. We would like to thank the following people: Joan Alessi for her haunted house photograph; John Alley and Utah State University Press for their preternatural patience; John Ashton for the book title; the nameless bar in Edinburgh where we conjured up the topic; Nancy Banks for accompanying Jeannie on ghost tours and through the infamous Winchester Mystery House; Ian Brodie for technical assistance with the electronic versions of the photographs; Bill Ellis for his prescient reading of an earlier version of the manuscript; Burt Feintuch for technical assistance with PhotoShopping; Janet Langlois for serving as discussant on our AFS panel at which we introduced some of this material; Carl Lindahl for his photographs at the San Antonio railroad tracks; Lynne McNeill for photographs, bibliographical assistance, and for participating in our AFS panel on this topic in 2003; Wayne Smith for photography and technical assistance; Madison and Rio Thomas for their artwork; and the International Society for Contemporary Legend Scholarship for bringing the three of us together.

FIGURE 1: Bottle chimes, Winchester Mystery House gift shop. San Jose, California. (Photo by Jeannie Banks Thomas)

Introduction

Old Spirits in New Bottles

Bottle Trees and Cell Phones

Bright wind chimes composed of enticing, candy-colored, pastel bits of glass are for sale at the Winchester Mystery House gift shop (figure 1). Some of the glass is formed into colorful bottles reminiscent of those in the southern supernatural tradition of bottle trees, a custom depicted in movies such as *Ray* (2004), a biopic about African American musician Ray Charles, or *Because of Winn-Dixie* (2005), a children's film about a beloved dog. The famous southern writer Eudora Welty photographed them. A contemporary southern author, Dennis Covington, describes them: "If you happen to have evil spirits, you put bottles on the branches of a [bare] tree in your yard. The more colorful the glass, the better, I suppose. The evil spirits get trapped in the bottles and won't do you any harm. This is what Southerners in the country do with evil spirits" (1995, xv).

Bottle trees are a product of southern African American culture. Jim Martin says that glassblowing and bottle making existed as early as the ninth century in Africa. The practice of hanging objects from trees to ward off evil spirits is also African, and the bottle tree itself is Kongo-derived. He adds that as the wind moves the tree, the spirits in the bottles moan (1988, 495). Martin maintains this type of bottle tree is less common today than in the past. However, certain variants for "upscale neighborhoods" have come into vogue: for example, sculpted metal trees are sold

1

in nurseries, and rural and urban sophisticates alike place their empties—mainly wine bottles—on them (Marquez 2004). The idea of bottle trees is appealing: they capture spirits that frighten or could harm us while still bravely keeping them in front of us. Right before our own doorsteps the bottles flash color and light, and then moan testimony to the uncanniness of both nature and the supernatural at the same time. Bottle trees are arresting, beautiful, and bizarre reminders that unseen forces move in the world.

Ghost stories are like these bottle trees. The stories contain spirits; they capture them for us and keep them before our eyes, scaring us but containing that fright in narrative form, which captures our attention and also reminds us of the variegated hues and shapes of the numinous world. Like the spirit-bottle chimes for sale in the Winchester Mystery House gift shop, contemporary ghost lore—while rooted in tradition—is also wedded to and embedded in mass culture. Ghost narratives and supernatural beliefs are the ancestors of mass-mediated forms such as the *Scooby Doo* cartoons (1969–1972) mentioned in chapter 4—but today they are marketed as mass media's creation, its offspring. However snarled their genealogies, mass culture ghosts and folk ghosts are clearly family and despite generations of rationalism and the influence of the enlightenment (Motz 1998), consumers still buy into the supernatural (see chapter 6).

Consumption is a hallmark of contemporary American culture, and the other darling of the age is technology. Consider the cell phone, for example. It is a "superartifact" (Ascher 1999, 335), a ubiquitous object indicative of the time and culture from whence it has sprung. It flaunts its high-tech nature as it brings unseen voices into every space of life. Technology accomplishes what we once thought only the supernatural could. However, the cell phone has an intriguing relationship to the supernatural. A few years ago, a member of the Society for Psychical Research in England asserted that cell phones were to blame for a decrease in ghost sightings. According to Tony Cornell, ghostly visitations have dropped dramatically since the introduction of the cell phone; he maintains, "With the introduction of mobile phones

15 years ago, ghost sightings began to decline to the point where now we are receiving none." His theory is that the "electrical noise" produced by cell phones drowns out ghosts (FarShores ParaNews, 2005a). Even if one were to accept Cornell's theory, however, one might still have to conclude that the exiled ghosts may beat cell phones by joining them. Now stories about ghostly voices on cell phones—much like earlier narratives about haunted telephones—circulate both orally and on the Internet, and numerous games with ghostly motifs have been developed for cell phones.

Other paranormal researchers assert that TV, not the cell phone, is behind the spectral decline. Steve Parsons, of the Parascience Society of Wirral, England, argues that the drop in ghost sightings is due to the decline in the number of supernatural-themed television programs, such as *The X-Files* (1993–2002). He says, "In the run-up to the year 2000 there was loads of stuff on the telly about the paranormal and that made the public more aware. But now people may have an experience and not realise that it's of a paranormal nature. And, anyway, we use lots of high-tech equipment in our research and that has no effect. Good, solid, reliable ghosts are there, and they are as hard as ever to catch" (Weaver 2001). Parsons's assertion demonstrates how the mass media and the supernatural are linked; other studies also argue that television has an impact on belief (Forbes 1997). His comments about the use of high-tech equipment by ghost research societies show that those deeply engaged with the supernatural realm avidly embrace technology.

Both the gussied-up spirit bottles and the stories about cell-phone ghosts indicate that rationalism, consumerism, and technology have not exorcised ghosts, in spite of earlier attempts to disprove their existence. For example, in eighteenth-century England, the Royston Dissenting Book Club (whose members included clergymen, lawyers, doctors, and successful tradesmen and their wives) debated the question, "Is there any foundation in fact for the popular belief of ghosts and apparitions?" Fifteen members said yes; twenty-six said no—a fact that prompted nineteenth-century historian Alfred Kingston to marvel with distaste

and shock that even fifteen "educated people" could believe in
ghosts (Jones-Baker 1977, 85). Kingston would have been duly
horrified had he lived to learn that according to Gallup, three
out of four Americans in the early twenty-first century have some
sort of paranormal belief, which includes at least one of the following: "extra sensory perception (ESP), haunted houses, ghosts,
mental telepathy, clairvoyance, astrology, communicating with
the dead, witches, reincarnation, and channeling. There are no
significant differences in belief by age, gender, education, or
region of the country" (Moore 2005; see chapter 6). Of course,
the paradox is that no one knows for sure whether any of these
things actually exist, but that doesn't stop us from going on ghost
tours, visiting haunted houses, and telling ghost stories.

GHOSTS, FOLKLORE, AND POPULAR CULTURE

Haunting Experiences focuses on the dynamic relationship in contemporary society between ghosts in folklore and ghosts in popular
culture. While folklore resembles popular culture in that both rely
upon conventional content, genres, and styles of communication
as well as traditional formulas, folklore is transmitted, intimately,
face to face or in small groups, while popular culture tends to
be mediated through a channel that provides a greater degree
of anonymity between producers on a mass scale and a wider
audience. While undeniably linked in contemporary culture, the
interaction between folklore and popular culture has historically
been less discussed but no less significant. For example, consider
the widespread dissemination of broadside ballads in the eighteenth and nineteenth centuries, the use of traditional narratives
to sell patent medicines within the medicine show tradition, and
the historical identification of inter-cultural appropriation and
the use of culture brokers throughout history. Mass transmission,
responses to new media and new technologies, appropriation, and
commodification are part and parcel of contemporary culture but
they are not new and neither are they responsible, as critics have
so often predicted, for the death of traditional culture. Intricately
woven together, popular culture uses folklore continuously to tap

into traditional cultural values and to satisfy audience expectations. But just as popular culture appropriates folklore, folklore too appropriates popular culture. Children's cartoon characters such as Casper the Friendly Ghost,[1] movies such as *The Shining* (1980), and television talk shows such as *The Oprah Winfrey Show* (1986–2007) all feed themes, motifs, and descriptive details back into the small-group intimate transmission of traditional ghost narratives, modernizing the details and incorporating contemporary issues, language, and concerns (see chapter 4). As Narváez and Laba argue, folklore and popular culture are "related rather than disparate," best understood as spanning a continuum of artistic communication in "different sized groups in which communications are transmitted via various configurations of . . . technological media" (Narváez and Laba 1986, 1).

The media and the technology associated with popular culture continually create change, but are also responsible for the vigorous sustaining of vernacular traditions. As Linda Dégh argues,

> The phenomenon we identify as folklore permeates all society assisted by mass media; it is not ruled out as folklore simply because its bearers manipulate new instruments to fit the needs of modern consumers. Folklore blossoms and proliferates before our eyes as it emerges from new conditions more vigorously and forcefully, empowered with more authority and prestige, than ever before. (1994, 1)

It is this relationship between folklore and popular culture, the mutual borrowing, dynamism and constancy in contemporary contexts that informs this volume. In the chapters that follow, readers will find two-hundred-year-old folktales discussed on the same page, and perhaps in the same vein, as an episode of the television show *The Addams Family* (1964–1966) or a discussion of Moaning Myrtle in J. K. Rowling's *Harry Potter* series (1999a, 2000, 2005). The combination is neither accidental nor a result of quirky personal associations. Contemporary tradition is deeply rooted in vernacular culture and interwoven with television, movies, the Internet, and cell phones. Not a book on popular culture and not a book on traditional ghost lore, *Haunting Experiences* is meant to reflect the effortless comingling of ancient tradition and contemporary mass and commodified culture in quotidian reality. This is the world our children inhabit. It is the world *we*, as adults—as rationalists and romanticists, believers and disbelievers, consumers and commodifiers—inhabit.

†††††

Collections of ghost stories have long been publishers' staples, along with literary ghostly tales commonly known as gothics. Contemporary horror literature and movies continue to top the consumer popularity charts. Such a vast literary output has, of course, resulted in an almost equally large number of literary and analytical studies of the genre. Literary scholars have produced dozens and dozens of recent studies examining ghosts in American literature as metaphors for national consciousness, ranging from racism to historical memory. For example, one these studies, Renée Bergland's *The National Uncanny: Indian Ghosts and American Subjects* (2002), concentrates on early nineteenth-century American fiction which features Native American ghosts because "in American letters, and in the American imagination, Native American ghosts function both as representatives of national guilt and as triumphant agents of Americanization" (2002, 4). Yet another study of American ethnicity and literature, *Cultural Haunting: Ghosts and Ethnicity in Recent American Literature*, proposes that "cultural haunting" is a separate, contemporary genre of ethnic literature in which the ghost is an "enigmatic transitional figure moving between past and present, death and life, one culture and another" (Brogan 1998, 6). This book examines three recent American novels, each about a different ghost, in detail: Toni Morrison's *Beloved* (1987), Louise Erdrich's *Tracks* (1988), and Cristina Garcia's *Dreaming in Cuban* (1992). From the wider disciplinary perspective of sociology, Avery Gordon's *Ghostly Matters: Haunting and the Sociological Imagination* presents haunting as "a paradigmatic way in which life is more complicated than those of us who study it have usually granted. It is neither premodern superstition nor individual psychosis; it is a generalizable social phenomenon of great import" (1997, 7). He goes on to propose, "If haunting describes how that which appears to be not there is often a seething presence, . . . the ghost is just the sign, or the empirical evidence . . . that tells you a haunting is taking place" (1997, 8).

In spite of all the collections of ghost stories and myriad scholarly studies, as well as treatments in other academic disciplines, very little has been published that treats ghosts from an analytical, folkloric perspective, and even less exists which treats traditional ghost lore and popular culture materials simultaneously. Full-length, serious treatments of traditional ghost stories (as opposed to literary stories) have to some extent lagged behind popular interest. This volume is meant to begin addressing that gap. It is intended for a variety of audiences ranging from the general reader interested in the supernatural, to university students, to specialists in the fields of belief and narrative studies.

Ghosts and Folklorists

Walking into a local public or university library to find a book on ghosts is a bit like trying to find a tree in the forest. In fact, running a keyword search of the Amazon.com[2] book listings in summer 2005 produced 11,158 titles prompted by a search of the word "ghost," 45,170 titles prompted by a search of "hauntings" and a staggering 68,828 tomes triggered by the keywords "haunted house." Many of these volumes are novels, children's books, haunted house pop-up books, and Halloween guides; most are regional popular collections such as *Haunted Houses of California: A Ghostly Guide to Haunted Houses and Wandering Spirits* (May 1993) or *Haunted Castles and Houses of Scotland* (Coventry 2004), but surprisingly few of these books are authored by academics in general and even fewer are written by academically trained folklorists.

Perhaps we should not be altogether surprised by the scarcity of books on ghosts written by folklorists. The study of supernatural belief and tradition is heavily trivialized in the academy (see chapter 6). And as supernatural traditions become increasingly popular (and important) in film, television, literature, tourism, and virtually all other manner of popular culture, many academics become proportionately unwilling to view such topics as worthy of serious study. But because such traditions remain understudied in the academy, those traditions become increasingly represented *only* by popular culture. Nevertheless, no matter how little interest academics have in studying the supernatural, it is clearly a significant part of contemporary culture. As folklorist Barbara Walker noted,

> I have had students tell me of sighting Big Foot, of living and communicating for several years with a ghost who adopted the family, of first-person interactions with vanishing hitchhikers. The valley that is my home also shelters water-witches, folks who plant by the signs, a weeping cemetery statue, a canyon ghost, a haunted bridge, a house cursed by gypsies, Three Nephites, a temple where Christ has appeared, a coven of witches and a cluster of UFO watchers. I highly suspect my experience is not unique, and whether I'm skeptical or not really doesn't matter because these things are part of my immediate world regardless. (1995, 4)

Walker's students provide a useful index to the seriousness with which the supernatural is taken by at least some of the general population, despite the academy's lack of interest. Of course folklorists, as members of the academy who specialize in the study of vernacular traditions, pride themselves on having their ears to the ground and being interested in, and cognizant of, the changing and continuing concerns of a culture. Although the maintenance and dynamics of supernatural belief are a central part of that picture, the trivialization factor has undermined the number of folklorists willing to work on supernatural belief and thereby created an unusual gap in contemporary folkloristic treatment of supernatural topics. This is unfortunate because, despite individual ontological positions, supernatural belief is fundamental to cultural tradition. As Walker argues, "How groups regard the supernatural contributes to thought and behavior, and by attending to those patterns, we gather a fuller understanding of what is meaningful to the group, what gives it cohesion and animation, and thus we develop a rounder perspective of cultural nuance, both within the group and cross-culturally" (Walker 1995, 4). Popular culture is no less central to cultural meaning than are older cross-generational traditions, and yet the new wave of trendy and commodified expressions of ghost belief seem to further diminish the willingness of scholars to take on supernatural study.

But while folklorists, like their other colleagues in the academy, have not taken on the exploration of ghost belief tradition to the extent that the topic warrants, there *have* been a number of important studies that apply the vernacular perspectives of folklore to ghost tradition. The earliest folklorists working on ghost traditions in North America were collectors, indexers, and compilers of folk belief—rationalists and functionalists interested in these traditions primarily for antiquarian survivalist and romantic reasons (see chapter 6). Ghost beliefs, like supernatural beliefs in general, were understood as "quaint notions" and "idle conceits," leftovers from a previously romantic primitive culture that still retained some, albeit regressive, function. These scholars, such as Wayland Hand, were responsible for publishing huge collections of folk beliefs, containing pages and pages of beliefs about ghosts contributed by hundreds of collectors spread out within a region, and meticulously indexed according to topical themes such as "dispelling ghosts," "spirits," "warding off spirits," "haunts, " and "laying haunts." Hand's collections (both published and unpublished) are massive, containing tens of thousands of items of popular belief (Hand 1964; Hand, Casetta, and Thiederman 1981). Ray Browne published a similar collection in Alabama in 1958 of over 4,000 belief items collected from just over a hundred individuals whom Browne met while collecting local folksongs. Similarly in 1935, Harry Middleton Hyatt published a collection of over 10,000 beliefs from a single county in western Illinois.

Hand, Hyatt, and Browne were all products of a period in folklore that focused on decontextualized items of folklore, thus they brought an item orientation to the study of belief. Their collections and indexes, while invaluable in the breadth of collecting they provided, contained little information on the nature of the belief or the cultural context of its collection. Nevertheless, these collections provide important comparative information, and often provided interesting annotations that allowed the reader to piece together more complex cultural data. In Hand's *Popular Beliefs and Superstitions* from *The Frank C. Brown Collection of North Carolina Folklore, Volume 7,* for example, item 5,744 indicates that "a newspaper left close to the door or window will keep the spirits out, for they have to count every word" (1964, 146). While the piece is an interesting little tidbit on its own, it fits very nicely with one contemporary ghost tour operator's recent suggestion that the tradition in the Antebellum South of wallpapering the walls with newspaper was not solely for insulation, but rather to confuse a ghost who would have to read every word before it could hurt anyone. The ability to look up such beliefs in the Hand, Browne, or Hyatt collections allows one to establish age, variation, and geographical distribution of beliefs encountered in even the most contemporary contexts. Items from these collections provide a wealth of information on historical provenance and geography of belief traditions, antecedents of popular traditions, cultural stability and variation, as well as a variety of other research questions.

Roughly during the same period that Hand, Browne, and Hyatt were publishing collections of belief items, other North American collectors of supernatural belief materials were publishing collections with a focus on ghost narratives rather than items of belief. Working in Canada in the early-to-mid-twentieth century, Helen Creighton documented hundreds of Nova Scotian ghost stories. Creighton's collections, such as *Bluenose Ghosts* ([1957] 1994), are of interest due to her use of personal voice in her collections, her expressed respect for the supernatural stories and their narrators, and her attention to behaviors associated with female ghosts in the stories. In her books, she also frequently describes the contexts in which she heard the ghost stories.

Another prolific collector of ghost stories, contemporary with Creighton, was Ruth Ann Musick. In her *The Telltale Lilac Bush and Other West Virginia Ghost Tales* (1965) and *Coffin Hollow and Other Ghost Tales* (1977), as well as scores of articles published in various folklore journals, Musick meticulously documented the oral traditions of her native West Virginia. The venerable practice of publishing collections continues into the present day with works such as Lynwood Montell's *Ghosts Along the Cumberland* (1975), *Ghosts Across Kentucky* (2000), and *Haunted Houses and Family Ghosts of Kentucky* (2001).

Some folklorists publishing ghost materials during the middle of the twentieth century used their collections to create classification systems that would provide greater understanding of the shape and nature of specific belief traditions. Louis C. Jones, known best for his book *Things That go Bump in the Night* (1959)—a collection of 200 ghost stories found in the Archive of New York Folklore, continually used local narrative corpuses to explore motifs and patterns repeated in the tradition. Jones's *Journal of American Folklore* article "The Ghosts of New York: An Analytical Study" (1944) is a triumph in this regard, analyzing 460 ghost narratives collected between 1940 and 1944. Jones groups the material to highlight patterns in ghostly appearance, purpose and character, when and where ghosts return, activities, and folk attitudes toward ghosts. The size of the collection combined with the classification system allowed Jones to note statistical patterns as well as to come to numerous general conclusions about ghostly tradition, many of which are still reflected in both the narratives and the observations made within this volume. An excerpt from Jones's conclusion notes, for example:

> Ghostlore is still widespread and popular. There is a great range and variety of detail in the stories, some of which is very up to date. While most of the actions thought to be common among ghosts (chain clanking, cemetery haunting and so forth) can be found, they are by no means so widespread in the popular ghostlore as we have been led to expect. The ghost who is very like the living is far more

common than any other. The one universal characteristic of ghosts is the ability to vanish or fade out of sight.
Most ghosts are found to be harmless, many of them even
helpful. Violent death is frequently a factor in becoming
a ghost. The reasons for returning are varied, but most
prominent are the completion of unfinished business
and a desire to warn or inform the living. (1944, 253)

Like Creighton, Musick, and Montell, Jones was primarily a
narrative scholar. Narrative scholars added a dimension to the
study of ghosts that was not possible with the item-oriented
belief scholars. When Linda Dégh emigrated from Hungary in
the 1960s and joined the faculty of Indiana University's Folklore
Institute, she brought a new perspective to the study of American
folklore, and especially to the study of narrative. Applying her
European ethnographic training in an entirely new setting, Dégh
saw the contemporary creativity and dynamism of the American
narrative tradition, particularly the legend. Dégh was among the
first scholars to recognize the role of the Internet, as well as that
of advertising and other popular literature, in the formation and
transmission of legends. She and a whole generation of her graduate students collected and published carefully annotated and
analyzed legends, primarily in the journal she founded, *Indiana
Folklore*. As Dégh explains at length in her recent *Legend and Belief*
(2001), the legend is the narrative vehicle best suited for the
performance of stories of the supernatural, which are always disputed and analyzed by audiences because "the legend touches
upon the most sensitive areas of our existence, and its manifest
forms cannot be isolated as simple and coherent stories. Rather,
legends appear as products of conflicting opinions, expressed in
conversation. They manifest in discussions, contradictions, addi-
tions, implementations, corrections, approvals, and disapprovals
during some or all phases of their transmission, from their incep-
tion through various courses of elaboration, variation, decline,
and revitalization" (2001, 2).

Legend scholars have added greatly to the literature through
discussions of just the kind of elaboration, variation, and

revitalization mentioned by Dégh above. A perusal of the journal *Contemporary Legend* together with issues of *Western Folklore* and the *Journal of Folklore Research* reveal a number of articles on ghost legends particularly in contemporary adolescent and young adult traditions. Bill Ellis, author of a number of important articles and books on contemporary legend, has explored issues related to extraordinary phenomena (including ghosts) in everyday life in his book *Aliens, Ghosts and Cults: Legends We Live By* (2001a). Ellis's work on legendary discursive traditions as well as on legend-related cultural processes such as the phenomenon called "legend tripping" (discussed in chapters 1, 5, and 6), demonstrate the significant contemporary outgrowth of supernatural narrative scholarship. Legend-tripping, a common teenage activity, is the custom of visiting the site of a legend in hopes of experiencing a supernatural encounter there (Ellis 1983, 1991, 1993, 1996). A new volume by Elizabeth Tucker entitled *Campus Legends: A Handbook* (2005a) also explores the role of ghost legends in daily university life. In addition to providing numerous text examples, Tucker explores the academic scholarship and approaches to ghostly narratives, focusing on the layered meanings triggered by contemporary ghost lore. The legacy of narrative research as a way to explore constancy and dynamism in ghost tradition continues in legendary scholarship, adding important observations on the maintenance of belief traditions in contemporary contexts.

The item and collection orientation that characterized much of the work in folk belief studies in the first half of the twentieth century began to change in the 1960s as folklorists became more and more committed to the importance of social and cultural contextualization of folklore and to the description of culture through ethnography. Outside of their social context, items of belief appeared arbitrary—like snippets of superstition, not part of a larger cultural worldview. But situated ethnographically, those same items of belief made greater sense as integrated parts of logically constructed belief systems. Ghost beliefs reflected conceptions of the afterlife, cultural understandings about land use and home construction, concerns about morality and human responsibility, ideas about proper grieving and respect and treatment of the dead, and any manner of culturally based issues that endowed items of belief with meaning and power. Out of this new contextualism rose a different kind of belief study, one that recognized belief as dynamic, situated, variable both among cultures and within the lives of individuals. Contextual theory and ethnography inspired the "ethnography of belief," a movement toward the study of belief as complex, rational, dynamic, emergent, and intrinsically central to all individuals, at every level of society, and across cultural contexts.

Central to this move toward the ethnography of belief is the work of David Hufford, who developed what he termed the "experience-centered" approach. Hufford's work is heavily phenomenological, focused on the relationship between experience and the supernatural, and based on the premise that stable and consistent features in narrative and reported tradition may, in fact, suggest actual experiences, accurately observed and interpreted rationally. Like Louis Jones, Hufford is interested in patterns of consistency in the narratives, although Hufford's focus is much more oriented toward what those patterns might say about the nature of experience. His primary work, *The Terror That Comes in the Night* (1982b), is a study of a supernatural assault tradition called "the old hag," which describes the experience of awakening during the night, unable to move or cry out, hearing or seeing something in the room approaching the bed, and feeling pressure on the chest. Hufford collected large numbers of old hag narratives, analyzing what those narratives suggested about the primary and secondary features of the old hag experience and ultimately establishing that the descriptive features of the old hag are consistent cross-culturally and occurred in subjects with no prior knowledge of the tradition. Hufford's study indicates that at least some part of the old hag experience occurs independent of the tradition, suggesting that an experience of some kind has provided the central empirical foundation from which the supernatural tradition arose.

The Terror That Comes in the Night is not a book about ghosts *per se*, but it is a study that revolutionized the way folklorists approach belief. In his articles, "Beings Without Bodies: An Experience-Centered Theory of the Belief in Spirits" (1995a) and "The Experience-Centered Analysis of Belief Stories" (1995b), Hufford applies his theories specifically to ghost belief, but it is his general theoretical perspective on folk belief that made the greatest contribution to the study. Hufford's work fought to grant reasonableness to folk belief and folk believers, to allow for the possibility that traditional beliefs might be produced by a particular type of experience. Hufford also sought to develop a series of methodologies that would recognize traditions of disbelief as well as belief and that would apply the same questions to both traditions regardless of cultural authority. His theories and methods have been applied across a broad range of disciplines and in studies of the supernatural, folk religion, and folk medicine.

Inspired by the work of David Hufford and following in the same theoretical tradition, British folklorist Gillian Bennett has added greatly to the study of ghosts through the publication of her books *Traditions of Belief: Women, Folklore and the Supernatural Today* (1987) and the revised and reprinted version of that volume, *"Alas, Poor Ghost!" Traditions of Belief in Story and Discourse* (1999). Bennett's work explores the nature of experiential narratives, traces historical arguments concerning the supernatural, discusses connections between ghostly experiences and bereavement, and documents intricate cultural distinctions made between different types of presences and ghostly experiences. Above all, Bennett's work on the history of ghosts and visitations is unparalleled in the field, demonstrating the significance of ghost tradition in crucial religious and political arguments and tracing the changing literary images of ghosts.

In 1994, Michiko Iwasaka and Barre Toelken (also influenced by David Hufford) published *Ghosts and the Japanese* (1994), a study of belief as it is situated in and steeped in cultural context. *Ghosts and the Japanese* provides an overview of Japanese death customs and focuses on a series of Japanese ghost legends originally published in a Japanese journal, *Tabi to Densetsu* (*Travel and Legend*) from 1928–1932. With attention to the cultural contexts of the narratives, Iwasaka and Toelken demonstrate that ghost narratives reflect cultural values and simultaneously shape and maintain those values.

✝✝✝✝✝

Many of the individuals mentioned in this brief review of the literature do not (and would not) write about the type of material offered in this volume, and if they did it might be in a context of condemnation. Contemporary ghost traditions expressed in popular and commodified culture woven together with literary images and reflecting seemingly silly topical patterns appear to undermine the concern expressed in the second half of the twentieth century that folk belief be understood as rational, important, and not a laughing matter. Images of haunted houses on greeting cards, ten-buck tours of haunted locations, and ghosts that appear to be obsessed with bathroom behaviors suggest a certain silliness—a mixing of heartfelt traditions and experiences with the trivial. Certainly, the reasons for wariness are good. The serious study of belief has had a hard road, filled with paternalistic, rationalistic obstacles at every turn. But like the recent realization that folk music or folk art dubbed by academics as tacky or kitsch has been unfairly censored from the scholarly imagination and continually expurgated from collections (Binkley 2000), we oppose the *a priori* notion that folk belief expressed in popular or commodified culture is any less serious, any less important, any less rational, or any less a belief than what is expressed more traditionally. As Paul Smith once argued, "In the real world, not just a single *oral* medium of transmission is utilized to communicate folklore, but any available and relevant media" (1992, 41). In the real world haunted walking canes[3] and fruit jars in which spirits have been trapped are sold on eBay, and spirit bottle trees become trendy yard art, and none of that eliminates the potential for belief.

While the eBay haunted walking cane may be a fairly new development in the commodification, appropriation, and popularization of ghosts, the role of commodification and appropriation itself in the history of belief has been long lived and crucially important to many significant moments in culture. Bennett reminds us that ghost lore played a central role in the debates about the Reformation. While not a commodity in the strict sense of buying and selling (although that certainly was the case as well) ghost belief was highly manipulated during the Reformation for political gain. As Bennett notes, "Crudely put, if ghosts existed then so must purgatory, but if ghosts did not exist, then there was no evidence that purgatory did either" (1987, 158). Such arguments were crucial to debates over Catholic/ Protestant religious worldviews. "If," continues Bennett, "as the new Protestantism taught, the souls of the dead went straight to heaven or straight to hell, then there was no such thing as ghosts, for the blessed would not want to leave heaven and the damned would not be allowed to leave hell" (1987, 158). As Bennett notes, "Ghosts were essential weapons in very serious and bitter wars" (1987,158). Like most cultural appropriation, the ghostly Reformation debates adopted and adapted ghost tradition, ignoring the underlying folk belief and creating a superficial version of the tradition. But while the appropriation devalued the core beliefs of the original tradition, its new cultural significance was clear. The seriousness of the Reformation debates should remind us that the predetermined association of popular culture, commodification, and appropriation with trivialization of belief tradition is not only unfounded but also disturbing in its potential to dismiss some of the most momentous belief moments in cultural history.

HAUNTING EXPERIENCES

The three authors first conjured up this volume in a pub in the appropriately haunted city of Edinburgh, Scotland. The chapters cover a variety of contemporary ghostly topics ranging from haunted hotels to spook lights to "Hell House Outreach Kits" and range from a focus on traditional folklore forms to a focus on popular culture, while consistently examining the interplay between the two. All of this is the stuff of which today's spirits are made, and all of the chapters work together to document the manner in which ghosts appear in contemporary (primarily western) North American folklore. Every chapter includes examples from both folk tradition (including oral narratives, folk beliefs, and customs) and popular or mass culture (including movies, TV, popular literature, and Internet blogs).

While a worthy topic and an area in need of more research, ghost lore and nationality or ethnicity is not the focus of this book (for excellent examples of such a study, see Gaudet 1999; Iwasaka and Toelken 1994). The authors believe, however, that the volume should reflect the natural diversity of ghost tradition in terms of the narrators' age, gender, nationality, and ethnicity. Hence, the stories come from a range of groups, including children, teenagers, women, and men as well as Canadians, Americans, African Americans, Native Americans, and Latinas within the North American context.

We have divided *Haunting Experiences* into three parts. The three sections work together to explore the major tenet of this book: that ghosts in contemporary folklore—while found in new contexts, with new motifs, and communicated in new ways using new technologies—are actually not all that distinct from the ghosts of yesterday. Part I, "Taking Ghosts Seriously," explores the ways contemporary ghost stories inspire, or at least reveal, complex concerns about modernity, technology, the physical and cultural environment, and education. Too often people assume that ghost stories are simple, trivial stories that are told by unintelligent, uneducated, "superstitious," pre-modern or antimodern "folk." This assumption ignores the reality that supernatural narratives are told by people of all educational and class backgrounds. The two chapters in this section argue that ghost lore must be taken seriously because it is serious—culturally meaningful, rational, and still very much a part of our modern and technological world.

Chapter 1, "The Usefulness of Ghost Stories," argues that ghost stories are significant and useful vehicles for raising and exploring issues dealing with culture, the natural environment, and individual perception and behavior. The chapter reminds the reader that there's much more to numinous narratives than only issues of belief. The chapter uses a range of stories—from those told as true to obvious fictions—to illustrate just how much ghosts communicate. The examples in the chapter come from the oral tradition (the San Antonio train tracks), Hollywood (*The Amityville Horror* [1979, 2005]), and popular literature (the Harry Potter books [Rowling, 1998, 1999a, 1999b, 2000, 2003, 2005]).

Chapter 2, "Scientific Rationalism and the Structure of Supernatural Experience Narratives," takes issue with the academic belief that supernatural tradition is antithetical to modern thought and therefore destined for imminent demise as technology and education increase. This chapter addresses the academic dichotomy of belief and rationality, and contrasts that dichotomy with the internal reasoning demonstrated by the narrative tradition. Through the analysis of a variety of personal narratives of ghostly encounters ranging from a marine encounter with a phantom ship to an online description of a ghost in a mirror, this chapter argues that essential information about the determination and accumulation of evidential criteria is embedded in each telling of the supernatural experience.

Part II, "Narrating Socialization and Gender," explores how ghosts provide entry into cultural and developmental discourses. The chapters in this section demonstrate that ghosts articulate and sometimes challenge our perceived boundaries and provide everything from stereotypical definitions of normality to vernacular and subversive critiques of culture. Chapter 3, "Gender and Ghosts," and chapter 4, "Children's Ghost Stories," thus provide insight into both the contemporary shape of ghost lore with a group (children) and the reflected attitudes toward groups (women and men) within contemporary ghost lore. These chapters detail how the stories work developmentally and socially among children and how adult notions of gender are reflected and refracted in the tales.

Chapter 3, "Gender and Ghosts," examines the ways in which gender is represented and challenged in ghost stories. This chapter explores two ghostly gendered types, the "Extreme Guy" and the "Deviant Femme," who commonly appear in supernatural stories. In a discussion of a variety of supernatural legends including Bloody Mary and La Llorona, the chapter argues that the adult world of sexuality and domestic violence is reflected in ghost stories. Finally, the chapter discusses a third type of ghost, the "Genderless Presence." In this figure the supernatural gives us its most radical take on gender: it eliminates it entirely. In this fashion, ghost stories challenge our perceived gender boundaries and categories.

Chapter 4, "Children's Ghost Stories," begins historically and then moves to a discussion of how ghost stories function in contemporary childhood. The chapter explores the probable background of much of the ghost imagery that dominates popular culture today, especially the ephemeral sheeted ghost figure whispering "Boo." It proposes that much of the popular culture iconography of the supernatural can be traced to a lingering cultural memory of the Black Plague of the fourteenth century and the imagery of unburied corpses in winding sheets. Its hypothesis is that the macabre stories of ghosts and the living dead which are based on a panoply of adult beliefs have filtered down and lodged in the realm of contemporary childhood, and they have been trivialized in the process. For all of their silliness and incongruity, these stories nevertheless play an important role in the socialization of each new generation of children. The repeated performance of these formulaic children's ghost stories year after year, especially at Halloween, provides entertainment but also helps enculturate children into a broader supernatural belief system, as well as enhancing cognitive skill development and narrative competence.

Part III, "Old Spirits in New Contexts," explores the impact of contextual continuity and change on narrative traditions. In some instances, academic, literary, and commodified images and presentations of the supernatural have replaced the actual nature and shape of belief traditions with preconceived imagery and culture-bound notions of authenticity, folk belief, and consumerism. On the other hand, however, highly contemporary and commodified traditions show remarkable consistency with older traditions of belief. These last two chapters demonstrate that the commodification of ghost lore does not necessarily result in culturally vapid, preconceived activities and images that are devoid of belief.

Chapter 5, "Haunted Houses in Tradition and Popular Culture," deals with the stories about haunted houses rather than with the empirical reality of the houses themselves, demonstrating how the malevolent haunted house of tradition functions as both setting and antagonist in many narratives as well as literary and media productions. A careful literary, structural analysis of the haunted house of oral tradition reveals dramatic affinities with the narrative genre of the folktale rather than the legend and that the liminal staircase is the true focus of stories of haunted houses. The chapter demonstrates how the contrived, ostensive "spook houses" of Halloween (as well as the "hell houses" of the Christian Right) are material culture manifestations of the metaphoric imagery that dominates many haunted house tales of oral tradition.

Chapter 6, "The Commodification of Belief in Contemporary Culture," maintains that ghost stories are subject to forces of commercialization but are not necessarily made trivial or meaningless in the process. This chapter explores the commodification of haunted spaces through descriptions of the commercialization of haunted real estate, haunted hotels, and ghost tours. It critically explores the academic concern with authenticity, trivialization, and fragmentation perceived to be a by-product of commodification and contrasts these concerns with the experience-seeking attitudes of consumers of haunted spaces. Through interviews with ghost tour patrons, the chapter examines the role of commodification in the creation of new and different contexts for the serious exploration and expression of belief.

†††††

In sum, this book shows us that ghosts continue to haunt our daily lives. In contemporary culture, both a rogue's gallery of phantoms *and* our beloved dead still elbow their way into our stories. *Haunting Experiences* demonstrates that ghost stories can tell us something about our children, gender, and the places where we vacation, shop, and live. They can even tell us something about scholarly bias and the complex workings of trivialized narratives. The tendency toward trivializing and dismissiveness neglects to recognize the contemporary nurturing and maintenance of older, more traditional, belief forms. It is the goal of this volume to explore contemporary ghost tradition as we see it, with traditional forms deeply integrated and interwoven with new media, new technologies, new contexts, and new functions—old spirits in new bottles and new spirits in old bottles.

Part I:

Taking Ghosts Seriously

ONE

THE USEFULNESS OF GHOST STORIES

JEANNIE BANKS THOMAS

When I discuss supernatural narratives with my students, they inevitably ask me, "Do you believe in ghosts?" They're looking for some kind of vindication or refutation of the numinous. Nothing I can say will do either definitively. Sometimes I give them a poetic answer; I say that the DNA each of us carries in our bodies makes us all ghosts. This is the reverse of how we usually think about ghosts. That is, we imagine them as ethereal forms and as those who've died before us—and not as those of us who are alive today. However, our DNA makes us, in part, the ghosts of our ancestors. We embody scraps, fragments, and glimmers of our forebears. We are shadows of who they were.

This is *not* the answer that my students want to hear.

They want me to tell them unequivocally whether or not ghosts exist. Also, they secretly (or not so secretly) want me to support with tidy, scholarly facts *their* belief in either the existence or the nonexistence of ghosts. They want me, as the voice of authority, to take up and confirm the merit of their own views. But because of my training as a folklorist, making such arguments about the existence of ghosts does not interest me (see Dégh 1971). Instead, my focus is the *stories* about ghosts.[1] These stories range from funny to powerful to mundane, but all are evocative. They communicate culturally or personally significant information to their audiences. It's true that belief is powerful in some of these narratives, and regardless of what scholars assert people will go on narrating anomalous experiences and choosing to believe in scientific or supernatural explanations—or some mixture of both. In fact, it is a deep cultural desire to mix both the scientific and the supernatural. To have scientific evidence for the supernatural, the existence of ghosts, and life beyond death would answer some of the most enduring questions of human existence. Folklore research, like other forms of scholarship, cannot sate that desire. From my folklorist's perspective, providing the answer to the question "Do you believe?" belongs to the people narrating or listening to a haunting experience. They decide what to believe or even if they want to engage with the narrative in terms of belief at all. What folklorists do is take supernatural narratives and belief traditions seriously; we pay attention to them and treat them analytically (see also Houran 2004).

In this chapter, I emphasize that there is much more to the realm of the supernatural than questions of belief, and I argue that ghost stories are a useful way to come to a better understanding of the worlds we inhabit. I present several ghost stories and describe a range of ways in which the narratives help us look more closely and analytically at culture, the environment, and the personal. This approach to ghost stories can help believers, skeptics, and those anywhere in between learn more from ghost stories than they might imagine possible.[2] In making this kind of an argument, I am not attempting to explain *away* ghost stories—that is, to move from culture, nature, and the personal back into the stories to give some indication of their descriptive accuracy and credibility. Rather, I move in the opposite direction: I'm demonstrating how the stories—whatever their level of believability—can point us outward and take us into realms of interest and significance

For purposes of clarity, I separate the realms of culture, nature, and the personal from each other. I do so recognizing that ghost stories, thanks to their varying content, often differ in what they communicate. For example, some stories reveal the personal; others say more about the cultural. However, I realize that the three realms are often deeply intertwined, shape each other in lived experience, and can all be present in a given supernatural narrative. I also do not mean to imply that ghost stories tell us about only these realms. My focus on them is only meant to be suggestive, to provide a starting point for taking ghost stories seriously.

Like the other chapters in this book, this one also draws the stories from a range of contexts, including both the oral tradition and popular culture, to highlight the way ghosts materialize in contemporary times. So I present several different genres of ghost narratives—ranging from literary fiction to film to narrative (or memorate) to legend—and discuss the larger issues to which the stories direct us. I end this first section of this chapter with a ghost story from the contemporary oral tradition in order to establish some common characteristics of a story from the folk tradition. Gina, one of my students from Indiana, tells this story:

> This . . . had occurred just after we had moved into our new home. It was an old two-story home. It was dated back in the late 1800s. Our next-door neighbor was quite old and lived in her home since it was built in 1907. She said our house was there for a long time before hers was built. She remembered that, at one time, the owners had buried a horse out in the backyard. She showed us where, and from the looks of the ground, my Dad said, it was sunk in and in a perfect square-shaped hole. "Big enough to put a horse in," he said.
>
> She also told us that the owner's wife had died in that house. They only heated the house with the living room fireplace, and she froze to death one night sitting in her rocking chair.
>
> Well, we didn't pay much attention to if what she said was true or not. We went on about our business, until one night my sister and I noticed that as we went up the stairway, the attic doors that were on both sides of the stairs on the landing were wide open.
>
> I asked my sister if she had been up there; she said no, and I didn't do it [either]. We asked my brother

later on that night, and he didn't do it either. Mom and
Dad were not at home that day, so we knew they didn't
do it.

The next day, the same thing happened. This time
Mom was home, so we asked if she had been upstairs;
she hadn't. But she told us to make sure we kept those
attic doors closed because all that cold air would make it
colder upstairs if we didn't. Weeks and weeks went by, and
every day we would find those doors opened some part of
the day. We closed them; then they would be open again.
Dad finally came up to see if the latches were working.
Maybe the doors weren't latching, and the draft caused
them to come open. The only problem is that the old
carpet that was on the floor would not allow the doors to
come all the way open. You had to pull hard to get them
to come all the way back.

One night, while my sister and I were in our room,
I was doing my homework, and she was talking on the
phone; I thought I heard those doors being pulled open.
I told Sue, my sister, to shut up for a minute and listen.
I walked to our bedroom door, which was open, to get a
better look. That's when I saw the other attic door on the
opposite hall wall open. I looked back to see if Sue saw it,
and she was sitting there with her mouth wide open. She
couldn't believe it. I couldn't believe it. We both didn't
want to run past those doors to get downstairs, so we
started screaming for Mom or Dad.

Dad came stomping up the stairs, hollering for us to
quit screaming. I think he scared us worse with his yell-
ing. He told us that we were seeing things, and there was
no ghost in the house. He said it was just the wind. Well,
it took both of us a long time before we didn't have to
run past those doors. We'd run past them and hurry into
our room and shut our door. I'll never forget the feeling I had when I watched those doors being pulled open
before my eyes. It did seem that after a couple of months,
the doors quit opening. Maybe the lady who died was just

trying to see if we would leave her house, and after she found out we wouldn't, she left us alone. Who knows? (ISUFA 1995a)

Gina's story is notable because it's a good example of the manner in which ghost stories from contemporary oral tradition are frequently only *slightly* dramatic. The drama comes from the subject matter and the manner in which people tell the stories rather than from the extraordinary behavior of the supernatural beings. In the oral tradition, people commonly report merely feeling some type of "presence," a cold feeling in the room, or strange noises and nothing more (Guiley 1992, 13). The supernatural presence often does little beyond making itself known in some manner, such as opening the doors in Gina's story. These mild numinous experiences stand in contrast to most Hollywood presentations of the supernatural, as I discuss later in this chapter.

The oral accounts often reveal the importance of "rational explanations"; in Gina's story, her family speculates about faulty latches and the wind as potential causes of the disturbing and anomalous occurrences. However, for Gina and other narrators of haunting experiences, either the rational explanations are not satisfying enough or the possibility of an encounter with the supernatural is just too intriguing not to narrate. In either case, telling a ghost story marks events that do not square with a narrator's knowledge of the ordinary. Categorization and understanding of lived experience are important and expected components of everyday life. When events evade such analysis, they haunt us, and we try to give them some sort of conceptual frame. In some cases, we class them as ghost stories. To draw on the metaphor used in the introduction of this volume, just as some Southerners trap spirits in bottles, we all use a variety of cultural materials—from commodified forms (such as popular fiction, movies, and the ghost tours mentioned in chapter 6) to oral narratives—both to contain these anomalous experiences and also to keep them tantalizingly before us in hopes they'll impart glimmers of meaning. That ghost stories are still frequently told indicates that understanding all the events of everyday life can be difficult, elusive, indefinite, and sometimes impossible. As a type of narrative, the ghost story reminds us how much is awfully and deliciously indeterminate in life. Just as Gina says at the end of her memorate, metaphorically ghost stories also say, "Who knows?"

GHOSTS AND CULTURE: BATHROOMS AND DEBTS

One of the most common ways that the public encounters ghost stories is in the form of a movie or a trade paperback book; these modes of presentation frequently emphasize the entertainment value of the supernatural. Along with the prevalence of science as a means to explain away ghost stories, the packaging of the supernatural as entertainment has helped perpetuate the notion that ghost stories are trivial—that is, all they're primarily good for is generating a few goose bumps. This idea is so ubiquitous that it overshadows ghost stories' other significant functions and uses. However, one of the useful things that ghost stories do is communicate to us about culture. Like any form of folklore, supernatural narratives directly or indirectly tell us about culture. However, one of the characteristics that distinguishes supernatural narratives is that they emphasize mystery and the indeterminate, which overtly invites interpretation of various kinds. Unlike other folk narrative forms—such as a folktale that is recognized as a fiction—ghost narratives are more slippery. For instance, one person hears a ghost story as truth, and a different person hears the same narrative as fiction. Ghost stories reveal how culture manifests itself in a twilight world that makes copious room for uncertainty and possibility. Thus, supernatural narratives often encourage debate about issues such as reality, fiction, and perception, which are often assumed to be a given in other forms of narrative folklore. That is, the claims to truth or fiction in other types of folk narrative are seemingly clearer.

The veracity of a ghost story is not a prerequisite in order for cultural meaning to be apparent in the narrative. Scholars, including Gillian Bennett (1999) and Jean-Claude Schmitt (1998), have provided historical views of ghost stories, which also illuminate the culture of particular eras. Believers and nonbelievers alike tell ghost stories because the narratives contain cultural issues relevant to their audience. If the content of a narrative ceases to be interesting to its audiences, it ceases to be told. What ghost stories indicate about the culture of the living can be discerned through attention to narrative detail and storytelling context. When seeking the cultural "truths" revealed by a ghost story, the following are useful questions with which to start:

1. *Cultural Values:* What cultures does the story reflect? What cultural values or "truths" (historical or contemporary) can be discerned in the narrative? Does it reveal or reinforce cultural values?

2. *Cultural Stresses and Conflicts:* Does the story present issues about which there is fear, stress, or conflict in the culture? How are these issues handled in the narrative? What views of trauma, death, and the body emerge from the story?

To demonstrate what can be learned about culture from spectral narratives, this section discusses two types of ghost stories: narratives about haunted bathrooms and stories about ghosts and unpaid debts. Haunted bathroom narratives are ubiquitous, although there is little scholarly discussion of this type of story. That this kind of ghost story is common indicates that even a ghost story that seems especially trivial and easy to dismiss still functions for people, and therefore can yield cultural insight.

Many of my students relate accounts of haunted bathrooms; some of them focus specifically on a haunted toilet. These stories, like other ghost stories from the oral tradition, are deceptively simple albeit memorable. Sometimes told as a memorate, the stories focus on either the bathroom hosting a supernatural presence or on a toilet that is haunted. Narrators of the latter stories describe anomalous toilet-flushing sounds. The home's occupants go to the source of the nocturnal noise only to find that no one is in the bathroom and that it would have been impossible for any of the occupants to flush and leave without detection. In short, an unseen hand seems to have flushed the toilet. A discussion of such narratives with my college students in Indiana prompted one male, Scott, to describe an anomalous experience he had while trying to use the toilet at a party he was attending in an older home. His account was a bit more unusual than the run-of-the-mill metaphysical flushing experience: this time the haunting appeared to be located specifically in the toilet paper itself. Apparently, the roll of toilet paper took it upon itself to unroll without assistance, which startled Scott.

Scott's toilet paper memorate led to a lively, classwide discussion on the physics of toilet paper (How many squares of tissue hanging down will generate the momentum needed for the roll to start to unroll?); toilet paper holders (Was the holder level? Was it mounted in a way that could prompt its unrolling?); and the veracity of the narrator (Was drinking involved?). Scott said that he'd been drinking at the party but was not impaired. He speculated on the role of gravity in the situation, but he concluded by maintaining that nothing fully explained what he had seen in that bathroom. His narrative again follows the pattern that I outlined in response to Gina's story: the account acknowledges the importance of rational or scientific explanations while simultaneously finding such approaches inadequate in fully accounting for the events experienced by the narrator.

Looking at Scott's story from a cultural perspective is suggestive in a variety of ways. For example, stories like Scott's detail unseen forces at work in the bathroom, a room where we confront unseen forces at work on our bodies. Some bathroom ghost stories may dramatize this human reality. Another cultural issue that is closely associated with the human body as the subject of unseen forces is the feeling of vulnerability that being in this room can generate. In bathrooms, people are literally caught with their pants down. Some stories about haunted bathrooms suggest this vulnerability.

Haunted bathroom stories are widespread enough that it is easy to find them in other narrative venues. For example, the book and movie versions of the successful Harry Potter children's stories draw on this motif from the oral tradition in the form of

Moaning Mrytle, a ghost who is described as unhappily inhabiting the girls' restroom at Hogwarts School of Magic (Rowling 1999a, 155). Other films and books with haunted toilet motifs are successfully marketed to teen and adult audiences. For example, the book *The Amityville Horror* depicts dodgy, spooky toilets. Supposedly based on a "true story," the toilets in the house of an Amityville, New York, family ooze black goo of indeterminate origin (Anson 1977, 36–38). The story of the Amityville horror is worth considering because it is exemplary of how Hollywood depicts hauntings in horror movies.

In 1975, the Lutz family moved into a house in Amityville, New York, with their three children. The family purchased the house for a modest price because twenty-four-old Ronnie DeFeo murdered six members of his family in the home in 1974 (see chapter 6 for a discussion of haunted real estate and chapter 5 for a cultural history of the haunted house). After living in the house for twenty-eight days, the family alleged that troublesome toilets and a variety of supernatural manifestations terrorized them, including

> ghostly apparitions of demonic hooded figures
> clouds of flies in the sewing room
> windowpanes that broke simultaneously
> cloven hoofprints in the snow outside the house
> extreme cold alternating with suffocating heat
> spirit marching bands playing music
> strange phone difficulties, especially when talking to the
>   priest
> levitations
> green slime appearing in the rooms
> putrid smells
> objects moving of their own accord
> communication with a devilish pig spirit named Jodie
> the family dog becoming unusually sleepy
> a spectral voice that ordered a priest out of the house.
>   (Anson 1977; Morris 1981)

Although it contains motifs recognizable from the oral tradition, such as cold places and apparitions, this story is strikingly

different from most oral accounts. It includes a great number of
varied supernatural manifestations and is so overly dramatic that
it's as if it were intended to be a best-selling book or movie—
which, in fact, it was. It turns out that the Lutzes and William
Weber, Ronnie DeFeo's attorney, dreamed the whole thing up
to make money. They concocted the hoax over several bottles
of wine shared in the Lutz kitchen (Guiley 1992, 8). However,
the Lutzes embarked on the plan without involving the lawyer,
so he sued for a share of their profits from the book and movie
(which appeared in 1977 and 1979, respectively). The Lutzes
countersued.

The Lutzes moved out of the house, and the next occupants
were not troubled by supernatural occurrences, but they did experience disturbances of the tourist kind (some of the locals called
the sightseers "Amityville horribles"). They sued the Lutzes; the
publisher of the book, Prentice-Hall; and its author, Jay Anson.
Anson had worked on the screenplay for *The Exorcist* (1973), an
experience he drew heavily on when he cranked out the book
version of *The Amityville Horror* (Anson 1977) in less than four
months (Morris 1981, 172). *The Amityville Horror* turned out to
be a case of litigious horror rather than supernatural terror.

Litigation aside, the Amityville haunting is instructive regarding how the mass media presents the supernatural as opposed to
how folk tradition narrates it. Hollywood's supernatural is often
hyperbolic; the folk supernatural is understated in comparison.
Simply hearing the number and dramatic nature of incidents at
the Amityville haunted house should raise questions of veracity
for anyone familiar with the more muted accounts of haunted
houses from everyday life.

Other less sensational bathroom ghosts with both oral and
literary connections include the specter that loiters in the restrooms at the House of the Seven Gables. Nathaniel Hawthorne's
The House of the Seven Gables drew its inspiration from the Turner
house in Salem, Massachusetts (figure 1). Both the historical and
contemporary oral tradition maintain that the house is haunted.
William O. Thompson says, "Nathaniel Hawthorne, who made
the house famous, thought the property was haunted and so

FIGURE 1: The august House of Seven Gables, which also boasts a bathroom ghost. Salem, Massachusetts. (Photo by Jeannie Banks Thomas)

do many of the guides who work there today. . . . The house not only sends out strange sounds, but guides have reported strange events. *Toilets flush when no one has been near a bathroom.* Door latches have been lifted up, (not down). . . . Faucets have been known to go on when again no one was near a sink" (n.d.; emphasis mine). During a visit to the house, a guide I talked with confirmed that such experiences and stories are part of the site's ongoing oral tradition.

Bathroom ghosts are a common part of haunted house narratives, such as the House of the Seven Gables or the Amityville hoax. Bathroom ghost stories may be the most marginalized type of narrative in a genre that is already trivialized. We tend to overlook haunted bathroom stories because we don't see them in the iconography associated with the haunted house, which tends to focus on attics and basements (see chapter 5). Also, bathrooms and what is done in them are not for discussion in polite conversation. This room and its associations may also evoke a sense of shame for some. We also can't escape confronting bodily processes and issues of health in the bathroom. A child who hasn't yet mastered basic bodily functions can find being in the bathroom frightening and surprising. Adults confront illness, aging, and mortality in bathrooms, which may generate fear, sadness, or despair. Given the vulnerability, shame, and fear that are experienced in the bathroom, it makes cultural sense that such an emotionally charged space could become a common locale for hauntings.[3]

Stories from Asia also reflect both adults' and children's fears of anomalous or threatening experiences in the bathroom. In Hong Kong, the staff of the *South China Morning Post*, an English-language daily newspaper, brought in two Buddhist monks to exorcise a ghost from the women's bathroom (Hendricks 2001). In Japan Hanako, the toilet ghost, is a feared ghost among elementary-age children, according to Linda Spetter (2004). Hanako wears red clothes, and kids can contact her by knocking a specified number of times on her stall. She murders children, and her hands reach up from the toilet to grab her vulnerable victims. At other times, she appears when a kid runs out of toilet paper and says, "Which do you want—red paper or blue paper?" If the hapless victim chooses red, that person will bleed; blue calls for Hanako to suck the victim's blood until the person turns blue. Hanako's boyfriend, Taro, inhabits the boy's bathroom but socializes with Hanako at night (Spetter 2004).

Such ghost stories about haunted bathrooms cause bathrooms to become a common site of legend tripping. For example, teens and preteens tell legends about a spectral woman known as Bloody Mary who inhabits the bathroom mirror.[4] The legend trip involves going into a darkened bathroom, reciting "Bloody Mary" the appropriate (and variable) number of times into the mirror, sometimes flushing the toilet, and then running out of the room in terror at the apparition in the mirror—or at the thought of it (see chapter 3; Dégh 2001; Dundes 2002; Langlois 1980; Tucker 2005b). Scholars such as Elizabeth Kenny (quoted in Spetter 2004) with *Hanako* and Alan Dundes with Bloody Mary (2002, 84, 54) argue that these supernatural legends express a specific fear for girls: their concerns about menstruation. Marc Armitage says that the stories are widespread in the Midlands and the north of England. He hypothesizes that the stories are about dealing with irrational fears that come from within the child (2002).

Perhaps all of this lore is a contemporary updating of the common supernatural motif of hauntings occurring near water—in this case it's plumbing instead of a stream or lake. However, culturally speaking, considering the importance of the developmental task of mastering bodily functions and the proper use of toilets in the lives of children, it's not surprising that these kinds of legends exist. Given the toilet's manner of operation and attendant loud noises, it's easy to see why children worry that something frightening might emerge from toilets (Doyle 1998). In light of the toilet's main function—to dispose of what is unwanted (flushing dead goldfish, for example)—these stories present a frustrating twist: one can't get rid of an unwanted toilet ghost by flushing; instead, flushing signals the spectral presence. Also, public restrooms constitute a liminal space where people do private things in public places. Ghost stories are frequently set in liminal spaces, spaces that are "betwixt and between," such as bridges, so it makes sense that a public restroom, which is not quite private or public, is a site for hauntings. In a private home, the bathroom also maintains some of this liminal status. It's part of the house, yet it's the part where we perform some of our most ritually impure acts. It is simultaneously the unclean room and the room where we clean our bodies. As such, it is a place we feel ambivalent about, and it is associated with significant cultural issues: body functions that are seen as unclean, disease, sexuality, dirt, health, and intimacy.[5] For example, health issues—the body bleeding while on the toilet—can be seen in the Hanako stories. Health, the body, maintaining private physical boundaries, and intimate contact with the body can generate tension and are often beyond easy control. Given the nature of the site, the bathroom seems a likely haunt for a ghost, since spectral narratives are ultimately stories about ambiguities and that which escapes surety, control, and the known.

Sometimes my students think the cause of these toilet anomalies is paranormal, and sometimes they think it's cantankerous plumbing. Regardless of issues of belief—or whether the story is a memorate (such as Scott's account), a hoax (such as *The Amityville Horror*), or literary fiction (such as the story of Moaning Myrtle)—the stories address, obliquely or directly, significant cultural issues. The anomalous is a part of everyday life; people commonly have experiences that they cannot readily explain—and some of them happen in the bathroom. Because of the issues that the haunted bathroom stories address and the lowly venue in which the hauntings take place, these stories can also be humorous. However, even though haunted toilet stories are sometimes funny, looking at such tales analytically reveals the reality of common cultural concerns about our own embodiment.

Ghost stories often reflect specific cultural orientations that differ from culture to culture and also change over time. For example, a ghost returning to complete unfinished business is a common and widespread motif. Such stories have been told in the United States, although I rarely hear them currently in the United States. Ghost stories emphasizing an unpaid debt are still told in Cape Breton, Canada. For instance, Father John Angus Rankin, a respected Cape Bretoner well-known for his role in stimulating the resurgence of the Cape Breton fiddling tradition in the 1970s, tells the following story about a visit from his father's ghost. Rankin describes how, shortly after his father's death, he carefully pays his father's taxes and all his unpaid bills at the local stores. Then, a few months later, Father Rankin sees a ghost:

> I snapped on the light, and my father was standing on the other side of the bed. I could see him from the knees up. And the only difference was, when he was in the casket, the undertaker, who knew him, combed his hair the way he used to comb it when he was younger, parted on the side here and all pulled over. As my father got older, the hair got thinner here, so he used to part it down the center and put it this way. That's the way his hair was combed when I saw him standing at the bed. So I got a shock.
>
> And I said, "What do you want? What's the matter?" And then before he would have said anything, I said, "Are you saved?"
>
> He said, "Yes, you know I'd be saved."
>
> And then I said again, "What do you want?"
>
> He said, "A bill."
>
> "Oh," I said, "no, there isn't."
>
> He said, "Yes, there is."
>
> I said, "Where?"
>
> He said, "Malcolm Dan MacLellan's. $16.25. And," he said, "the bill is 25 years old."
>
> By this time, I had lost my fear. And I turned my eyes off him because I was getting ready to ask questions about the other world. I put the book down on the table and turned. There was nothing there. . . . As soon as he got the message across, he disappeared.
>
> Well, I didn't sleep all night. I just sat there and smoked cigarettes. Dawn came, I went out and said Mass. So then I went to see MacLellan, and I told MacLellan. And I said,

"I had an awful experience last night." I said, "I don't believe in this." I said . . . "I'm going to go to Inverness and," I said, "if there's a bill in Inverness, then I've got to believe it. If not," I said, "I'm going to Halifax to see a psychiatrist". . . .

"Well," I said, "if I don't get that bill, I'm going to go to Halifax. Because you told me the bills were paid, and I have no way of knowing."

So we were arguing back and forth, and going through bills, and the son came along. And he said, "What's going on?"

So his father [said], "Well, Father John here . . . is looking for an old bill. And he figures his father owes some money to the stores. And there's no—"

"Oh, Dad," he says, "remember the boxes you gave me the other day?" He said, "There were old bills in there—you told me to burn them." He said, "I didn't get a chance to burn them. There's old bills in there—they go back a long time." (Caplan 2002, 31–35)

The son quickly finds an old bill for $16.25 for hay, and Father Rankin pays the money and destroys the bill. Father Rankin also says, "There's an expression in scripture that says you won't get to heaven til the last farthing is paid" (Chisholm 2000, 67). His ghost story about his father's debt is expressive of this religious view. The local culture and economy are also reflected in his account. Some of these stories are indicative of economic stresses. In a history of Inverness, the town where MacLellan's store was located, Malcolm Dan MacLellan and his business practices are described: "Malcolm rarely took a holiday, enjoyed his chew of gum and chatted with everyone who came into the store. He ran his business on a credit basis, and every one of his customers ran a tab. If the mines were working steady, his Saturday payday would be considerable; if the mines were idle, poor Malcolm invariably took a hit. It was reasoned by many that he never turned his back on a customer, and when he turned the business over to son Freddie, tens of thousands of

FIGURE 2: MacLellan's store, where a Cape Breton ghost owed a debt, is typical of the mundane spaces associated with traditional ghosts. Inverness, Nova Scotia. (Photo by Jeannie Banks Thomas)

dollars remained on his books, never to be collected" (Gillis and MacDonald 2004, 232).

Apparently not all the local residents were as conscientious as the ghost, or they lacked the means to pay their debts back. In a poor economy where credit is important, it's not surprising that paying one's debts is a cultural concern, even if, and especially *because*, it's a difficult goal to realize. The story also reinforces the cultural value that debts should be paid. This kind of a story makes particular sense in tightly connected communities where business owners are neighbors and not some large corporate entity located outside of the community. MacLellan's store was in business through 2006 and still owned by the family (figure 2). If a local customer wanted to continue do business in the store and get credit when necessary—and maintain a comfortable relationship with the family who ran the store and lived in the same small town—paying off at least some debt would be an important part of keeping this relationship going. In these ghost stories, paying debts doesn't always involve money. In a poignant story told by Dan Angus Beaton, a woman who died in childbirth comes back from the dead because she cannot rest until the two blankets she had borrowed "for the purpose of the baby's birth" were returned to their owners (Chisholm 2000, 136–39). That the woman had to borrow blankets for childbirth indicates her stark poverty—and the fact that she feels so strongly that the neighbors need them back, after being used for childbirth no less, suggests that the neighbors might also be poor. Thus, this story presents a vivid picture of a life of hardship and extreme deprivation—the woman is so destitute as to have no blankets. The existing blankets are rare and valued enough that they continue to be used even when employed, and presumably marked by, a childbirth that caused the death of a woman. The blankets tell us about something larger than the story itself. They symbolize the extreme poverty and hardship that has often been a part of the real Cape Breton experience in the last two centuries. Conditions in Cape Breton today are not as draconian as in the past, but it remains a poor region, plagued by unemployment and "remarkable" levels of outward migration due to lack of economic opportunity (Terrain Group, Inc., 2004).

The theme of a ghost returning to settle a debt is familiar enough in contemporary Cape Breton that it has entered regional popular culture. Howie MacDonald, a Cape Breton fiddler and comedian, included a humorous version of such a story on *Celtic Brew* (2002), a live recording of traditional music and comedy. In this story, the narrator encounters a ghostly woman in a house he's entered to escape a rainstorm, and he converses with her:

> I asked her, "Are you of this world?"
> She says, "I was once, but I'm not now."
> I said, "What happened to you?'
> She said, "I died. What do you think happened to me?"

I decided to ask her, "What do you want of me?"
. . . Then she beckoned for me to follow her downstairs
and into the kitchen. Now, I walked down; she kind of
floated down the stairs. We arrive into the kitchen, and
she said, "Loooook into the redddddd box."
I said, "The bread box?"
She said, "No, the redddddd box."
I says, "I'm not getting you."
She says, "Geez, are you stoned?"
Well, I looked into the box; in the box there was a pre-
scription, and two dollars and ninety-five cents. I started
to put things together after that.
I said, "Would you like me to take that money down
to the pharmacy and pay that bill so that you can rest in
peace?"
She said, "Well, it's a little late for a refill."
Pretty sarcastic for a dead woman, I thought.

The story is funny because the ghost expects the narrator to know
the ghost-returns-to-pay-debt storyline better, and she mocks the
narrator when he is slow in recognizing the situation. The audience laughter that accompanies the story reflects their recognition of the playful humor and creativity in the creation of a ghost
who is more sardonic than scary. Finally, some of the humor
arises because of the juxtaposition of the contemporary ("Geez,
are you stoned?") with a traditional motif of a ghost returning to
pay a debt. The story exemplifies the manner in which old, traditional motifs meet the new (and even the sarcastic) in today's
supernatural narratives.

While, the stories' content and meanings are different, both
haunted bathrooms and debt-paying ghosts reveal information
about the cultures in which they are told. In addition to these
types of ghost tales being communicated orally, all sorts of media
also disseminate them, literally creating more "ghostly" images
in contemporary venues such as the Internet or in movies,
popular literature, tourist guidebooks, and compact discs. To
return to language from the introduction, these are old spirits

in new bottles. We consume ghosts in these contemporary forms as readily as we continue to tell ghost stories. We like ghosts because they simultaneously transport us to other worlds and possibilities *and* also because they point us back toward issues of interest in our cultures.

GHOSTS AND THE ENVIRONMENT: PIRATES AND SPOOK LIGHTS

I find the study of folklore particularly engaging because it draws my attention to aspects of the world around me that I might otherwise miss. An awareness of folklore makes seeing and taking in the world a more intense and richer experience. Ghost stories, as a form of folklore, can also assist in expanding our knowledge of the landscapes in which we find ourselves. In some ghost stories, the natural world is a crucial element and a central focus. In these cases, the supernatural can be used to contemplate nature and place. One way to do this is by paying attention to the environment in which the story is set. Another is to attempt to discern the attitudes toward the natural world that the ghost story reveals. These questions can be useful for starting this kind of analysis:

1. *Aspects of the environment:* What does the story reveal about the landscape in which the story takes place? What physical realities does the account describe? Of what natural conditions (such as atmospheric) might the narrative make us aware? Does the story describe unusual or little-known natural phenomena?

2. *Attitudes toward the environment:* How does the story describe the landscape in which the events take place? How tied to the landscape are the events? Do any details in the narrative indicate attitudes toward nature and the environment? Does the story change how those who tell and hear it see the physical setting of the story?

For example, during a softly stormy July evening on Cape Breton Island, Alistair MacLeod and his brother John from

Massachusetts told me a story and showed me a version of it in a slim book of Nova Scotia folklore written by Mary Fraser. In the story, ghosts of pirates angrily chase treasure hunters away from buried treasure on a Broad Cove–area beach, not far from where I was staying and near present-day MacLeod family homes and businesses. Nova Scotian stories about buried treasure often include tales of murders committed with the notion that the resultant ghosts would guard the treasure, which could be the case with the narrative the MacLeods told (Creighton 1994, 46–48). In their story, the treasure hunters seek safety by running into a house, and the ghosts surround the house and glare menacingly at them through the windows. The MacLeod brothers told me that the safe haven referred to in the story was in all likelihood their family home.

They narrated the story, told me about their personal connection to it, and loaned me the book because they knew of my interest in ghosts. That evening all of us experienced the satisfaction of a story shared in good company; theirs was the pleasure of telling, mine of listening. Also, for me, the story in the context of the quiet depth of their kindness and interest in all things Cape Breton—John collects all the publications about the island that he can find—transformed my feeling for the place I was visiting. It made that specific part of Cape Breton more known to me. I realized that particular ground meant something significant to thoughtful people. I felt a connection to that generously treed bit of Cape Breton earth that stretched into the ocean within my gaze. I hadn't felt a bond with that particular place until the MacLeods shared the story. The ghosts in this story helped change my attitude toward place; they reminded me of its mystery and power.

These particular ghosts changed how I looked at the landscape; I was more interested in it and more connected to it because of the story. Other forms of folklore, such as the traditional music in Cape Breton, can also tie people to place. However, the bonds to place that come through supernatural narratives can be stronger, more personal, and more powerful because they deal with the metaphysical. For instance, while the traditional music in Cape Breton helps me connect to the place, it links me to a larger place. The ghost story connected me to a very specific home place in a way the music hadn't. Because supernatural narratives flirt with significant ontological and spiritual questions (such as whether life exists after death), they can be felt in an intimate and intensely individual fashion. Therefore, some supernatural tales invite metaphysical linkages to place. As a type of folklore, ghost stories can offer a connection to place that is less discriminating than are some other folklore forms. For example, the pirate ghost stories didn't require that I appreciate traditional music, know how to play an instrument, or be a native in order to feel a significant bond with the place.

The supernatural is democratic; it will take those who want to come to it. It opens the door to the otherworldly and spiritual; it proffers communion, which is often felt and understood in idiosyncratic ways. Because ghost stories deal with profound metaphysical issues and possibilities, they offer—should one choose it—an enticing, personal, and intense experience. Religious narratives and experiences can offer similar experiences, but ghost legends come with fewer strings attached—one does not have to accept religious principles, participate in an organized group, donate tithes, or even believe in order to feel the pleasant rush of possibility offered by a good ghost story. Supernatural legends invite their listeners into metaphysical mystery in a simple, come-as-you-are and do-it-yourself fashion.

Sometimes the actual physical qualities of place come directly into play in supernatural narratives. For example, many legends exist about what are sometimes called "ghost" or "spook lights." These stories have been told in many cultures throughout history. David Hufford's experience-centered hypothesis could be applied to some of these accounts. He argues, "Some significant portion of traditional supernatural belief is associated with accurate observations interpreted rationally. This does not suggest that *all* such belief has this association. Nor is this association taken as proof that the beliefs are true. This point must be stressed because much of the investigation of supernatural belief, especially since the Enlightenment, has been implicitly governed by a desire to show that the beliefs under investigation are false" (1982b, xviii). The latter type of supernatural exploration leads to the dismissal of the story, which forecloses the possibility of using the story to come to a deeper understanding of culture or the natural world. Here I'm following the argument of folklorist Donald Ward (1977, 216) who asserts that the folklorist need not concern herself with the "question of the existence or non-existence of paranormal phenomena." Also, regardless of where one comes down on issues of belief, one can still find much to take seriously—and to learn from—supernatural narratives. In this framework, even disbelief in a story is not cause for its dismissal.

Hufford's groundbreaking, and now classic, work (1982b, xviii) presents a good model for approaching memorates that detail the supernatural. However, it is not this chapter's intent to do the kind of analysis Hufford does (primarily in relation to memorates). This chapter presents narratives that range from literary fiction to legend, and instead of a Huffordian emphasis (1982b) that elucidates the stories' "descriptive accuracy" ("accurate observation") my focus is on *described or revealed attitudes*. So I discuss what these narratives indicate about the environment and the attitudes toward it.

For example, thinking about the environment and the attitudes toward it depicted in "spook light" stories is informative. Light is a naturally occurring phenomenon, but in these stories it works in unusual or paranormal ways. Like other types of ghost stories from the oral tradition, the narratives are often *slightly* dramatic; the spook light is merely a presence—"Look, there's an unusual light there." However, sometimes they're more dramatic; folklorist Lynwood Montell collected one such legend in Kentucky:

> My grandmother's name was Belle Brizendine. When she was a child, they lived in an old house built in 1867 in Muhlenberg County, not far from Greenville. I remember her telling about the Union soldiers that were in the neighborhood when she was eight or nine years old. And she used to tell me a ghost story about that old house.

She said that when she was a little girl, they used to sit on the front porch in the evening. There was a dirt road that passed in front of their old house, and there was a cemetery just a short distance down the road from the house. Grandmother said that one night when she was out on the porch, she saw a very large ball of light rise slowly from the cemetery and come very slowly down the road in the direction of the house. She always told how scared she got when it got closer and closer. One time, when this light was directly in front of their house, the front gate opened and the ball of fire passed through the gate and came up the sidewalk directly toward my grandmother. She said that she was simply paralyzed as she watched it. As it passed by her, the front door of the house opened and the big ball of fire went into the house. It then proceeded to go up the long flight of steps to the upstairs area; then it disappeared. (2000, 178)

The details in this story indicate certain attitudes toward the natural world and its manifestations: wonder, puzzlement, respect, and fear. In the story, the light rises from the cemetery and moves into the human space of the house. It shows the human and the natural intersecting in a surprising fashion—a subtle but nice dramatization of the fact that although humans live surrounded by nature, those moments when it intersects with their lives in unusual ways are stunning, awe-inspiring, frightening, or enrapturing.

In the oral tradition, these anomalous lights are sometimes called jack o' lanterns, will o' the wisps, or ball lightning. There is a vivid and varied story tradition associated with these lights. Shakespeare's character Puck, from *A Midsummer's Night's Dream*, is a will o' wisp, a trickster figure, a light in the woods that leads you astray (Briggs 1976, 336; 1978, 122). Scottish folklore holds that these lights are the souls of unbaptized infants; they're sometimes called "short hoggers," which is a dialect term for baby booties (Eberly 1991, 234). In Cape Breton, the lights are referred to as "forerunners" and are often seen to be a sign of impending death. In a 1956 interview, Ellis Ogle of Pigeon Forge, Tennessee, describes the lights—or "minerals," as he called them: "The old man, Bob, said, 'In rainy weather,' he said, 'that mineral exploded and throwed these here lights.' Some of them looked like moons, and some of them looked like babies, and some of them looked like fish. . . . This one special light that I saw, looked exactly and fine like a baby, tapered off like a fish's tail. It look like it was flying with its tail, and it absolutely shined brighter than the sun or moon either. For I seen my shadow way on the back mountain, and it look brighter and stronger by that than the sun ever give it" (Lindahl 2004, 417).

The stories point to many realities, including the possibility of getting lost in the woods at night. They can serve to remind listeners that nature is not easily mastered and that a person should have her wits about her when in the natural world. The lights are also linked with death, which can be understood metaphorically as the expression of an awareness that death is part of the natural order of things and that nature can mete out death. In addition, these stories manifest an attitude of wonder and a recognition of the mysterious. The light's connection with death and the supernatural also leads to thoughts of other worlds and the afterlife.

Beyond analyzing the stories for indications about attitudes toward the environment, the stories can reveal what people think about the liminal aspects of the physical world. Too often in the past, as Hufford says, this kind of analysis served to dismiss the stories. Here I'm looking at the narratives to show how much they can offer and how they can be used to make us more aware of the world around us. Some ghost stories can also lead us to more knowledge of science and the physical world. They can also direct us to lesser-known natural phenomena or phenomena whose existence is not well understood or debated (Corliss 1994).

Spook lights correlate with several possible natural events. For example, when folklorist Carl Lindahl contextualizes Ellis Ogle's stories, he says, "The old women [Ellis's neighbors] argued about the nature of the ghostly lights . . . that stalked their mountains after dark. Granny Shields always found rational explanations for the hauntings: the lights were caused by 'minerals' (probably methane gas released from the ground in the form of luminous shapes)" (2004, 413). Because ghost stories invite interpretation, such exploration, debate, and discussion are a traditional part of their telling.

In 2004 Rufus S. Morgan, a doctor from Signal Mountain, Tennessee, described a spook light encounter. He was sitting in front of his house, not far from the site where a moonshiner was murdered one hundred years earlier. As he sat in the dark, he noticed that the frogs and the whip-poor-wills suddenly stopped singing, and then he saw a green light. The light moved around for several minutes, stopping at times as if it were "watching" him. He turned on a light and the spook light disappeared. In relation to this experience, he notes that whip-poor-wills eat the larvae of fireflies, which exude a thick, glowing liquid. He speculates this could be an explanation of the light, especially after he later sees the "small, shining face of a raccoon" that had apparently been eating the larvae. His daughter, however, says that she prefers to think of the light as the ghost of the moonshiner (Morgan, 74–75).

As is apparent in this section, some ghost narratives lend themselves to thinking about the properties of the natural world. Whatever the focus of the story, an analytical discussion of the story after its telling is a common part of the tradition of relating supernatural narratives. In addition to thinking about glowworms and methane gas, some people ponder ghost light accounts in relation to known states of matter. Could the spook light be an example of one of the known states of matter (such as solid, liquid, or gas)? Could it be a plasma? Plasma is similar to gas, except that it is a good electrical conductor and reacts to magnetic fields. Plasmas can occur naturally, and high voltages ionizing the air around power lines can create them (George 1995, 226). If the spook light is a plasma, what aspects of the area where the light appeared are conducive to this phenomenon? Why is it in this particular environment?

Other questions that draw attention to the natural world and the environment where the narrative takes place include: Is the light caused by the refractions and reflections of town and car lights? Is it St. Elmo's fire, a slow discharge of electricity from earth into air (Corliss 1982)? Could the light be caused by the combustion of naturally occurring gases such as methane (as in Granny Shields's theory above) or phosphine (emitted by decaying vegetable matter)? Could it be the gleaming of phosphorescent fungi, sometimes known as "foxfire" (George 1995, 107)? Could it be "corpse light" or "cemetery light"? These terms refer to the luminous products of body decay attributed to phosphoretted hydrogen (George 1995, 112). Could it be a manifestation of ball lightning, and does such a phenomenon really exist (Stenhoff 1999)?[6] Beyond being fascinating in its own right, this approach to ghost stories can help us see aspects of the natural world that we previously did not notice. Whether we choose to believe in shining whip-poor-wills or ghostly moonshiners, thinking on such ghost stories *in situ* leaves us with the rich possibilities offered by both the natural and the supernatural.

Paranormal narratives sometimes prompt legend trips to sites in the stories, where the participants directly encounter nature. Being in a more natural environment is part of the pleasure of the trip. Bob Pyle (1995) describes the extended legend trip he took in the Dark Divide region of the Pacific Northwest while researching his book about a legendary creature, *Where Bigfoot Walks: Crossing the Dark Divide.* Pyle frequently details the natural environs he sees while searching for Bigfoot: "After breakfast I hiked to nearby Middle Falls, where the sound was the river's. Water ouzels danced on the rim of the broad water slide. These slate-gray relatives of wrens, also known as dippers, are synonymous with pure mountain waters. As I watched, one dipper repeatedly plunged its head into the oncoming water, making great fountains over its head at metronomic intervals. Another, closest to me at fifty feet, picked up and stabbed more gingerly in shallower water, point downstream as often as up. . . . The lead-pellet birds maintained their individual behaviors for the quarter-hour I watched" (1995, 60–61)

Looking for legends prompts Pyle's close attention to the natural environment, which in turn rewards him with the wonders of the visible world, such as the ouzels' behavior. Wondering whether there is enough habitat to sustain Bigfoot in the region encourages Pyle to focus sharply on its inhabitants and how they survive. While Bigfoot is a central focus of his book, the *where* in his title—*Where Bigfoot Walks*—is equally important. His words remind us how much there is to see in nature when looking for legends. Additionally, his naturalist's careful attention to and accounting of detail is also a good model for a folkloristic approach to the cultural landscape. That is, a folklorist closely chronicles the folk aspects of the cultural landscape just as a naturalist such as Pyle documents the fauna of the forested one.

GHOSTS AND THE INDIVIDUAL: AMANDA'S GRANDMA AND SPECTRAL HANDPRINTS

While specters communicate with us about realms outside of ourselves, such as the natural world, ghosts also get personal. That is, supernatural narratives can be examined in terms of their reflection of and impact on individual lives. Sometimes ghost stories have the ability to transform the individual worlds of those who tell and hear them. The following questions can provide a way of starting to explore the relationships between ghosts and the individual:

1. *Transforming Individual Thought:* In what specific ways does the story work to transform the thinking of the listener or teller? Why? How is this change made manifest? And following the seminal work of David Hufford, does the experiential (what the person actually experienced) form a basis for the response to the numinous?

2. *Transforming Individual Behavior:* What specific parts of the narrative function to transform behavior? What actions does the story call forth? What is the impact of these actions? How lasting is the transformation wrought by the numinous? Here it is also helpful to recall the folkloric literature on ostension, the acting out of some part of a

legend or supernatural narrative, which reminds us that ostensive behavior can be positive, harmless, or negative (Dégh and Vázsonyi 1983; Ellis 1989, 1991).

A memorate collected at home in California from her forty-eight-year-old mother, Jo Ann, by one of my students, Amanda, illustrates how first an experience with the supernatural, and then an account of it, impacts the thinking and lives of Jo Ann and her daughter:

> It was in July 1986. I woke up out of a dead sleep at about 5 a.m. My grandmother was very sick and was dying; my mother and father were back in Pennsylvania with her at the time. Anyway, I woke up and when I looked to the side of my bed, I saw my grandmother. She looked so peaceful and happy to finally be out of pain. Her image wasn't solid, it was white and looked kind of like she was in a fog, and the lower part of her body was swirling. It's hard for me to describe it to you. When I looked at her, she said, "Goodbye, Jo Ann, I love you."
>
> No sooner did she say that and she was gone; she just vanished. I laid in bed and began to cry; I knew that she had died. I didn't wake up your father because I was afraid that he'd think I was nuts. So I laid in bed and about twenty minutes later the phone rang. I knew it was my mother, so when I answered I just said, "I know, Mom; she's gone." After a few days went by, I talked to my mom about what had happened, and she told me that my cousin also had the same experience but that we were the only ones. (USUFA 1995b)

In response to her mother's narrative, Amanda says, "This incident happened when I was about eleven years old. I can remember it because I woke up that morning because I heard my mother crying. I believe that what my mother saw was real. My mother isn't the type of person who believes in the unknown, but when this happened to her, her views on the subject changed. Since then, she has had other experiences with her grandmother like smelling her or just feeling her presence" (emphasis mine). Jo Ann's narrative shares the same theme as Father Rankin's account: a visitation from a deceased family member (see also Bennett 1999). This type of haunting experience is so common historically that the oral tradition recognizes this type of ghost with its own name: the wraith. While frequently used in contemporary parlance as merely a synonym for "ghost," historically "wraith" referred to someone who had just died or was about to do so; it's a term for the apparition of a person seen at the moment of their death (Guiley 1992, 95).

Obviously, this incident changes Jo Ann's views about "the unknown," and Jo Ann's experience and account of it shapes her daughter's views as well. However, generating *belief* in the supernatural is not the only kind of personal impact tales of the supernatural have. My own experience on a legend trip provides another example of the possibilities of personal meaning generated by out-of-the ordinary experiences. This trip changed my personal awareness and behavior without involving belief or disbelief. In the early summer of 2001, I went legend tripping to a railroad crossing with a group of scholars who were attending the meetings of the International Society for Contemporary Legend Research in San Antonio, Texas. Carl Lindahl gave a paper focusing on Latino culture and the importance of children as they are manifest in the stories and legend tripping traditions associated with this particular site (Lindahl 2005). Later he led several folklorists to the actual tracks.

The legend associated with the site maintains that a train crashed into and killed a busload of school children at the railroad crossing. The children haunt the railroad crossing. Specifically, the legend has it that when a car is placed in neutral at the bottom of the embankment before the crossing, it will miraculously roll uphill and onto and over the railroad crossing. The spirits of the children who died in the school bus crash are supposedly pushing the car. They do not want anyone else harmed at the site, so they move the cars to safety. To obtain evidence of this spectral assist, legend trippers dust the trunks of their cars with baby powder before putting their cars in neutral at the crossing.

FIGURE 3: On Todos Santos 2003, as night falls, carloads of adults and children gather on the downhill side of the railroad tracks to compare their experiences. San Antonio, Texas. (Photo by Carl Lindahl)

Once a car has been "pushed" over to the other side (figure 3), the driver pulls off the road and all the occupants get out to inspect the trunk lid to see if the ghostly children left their fingerprints in the powder (figure 4).

Our car, driven by Carl Lindahl, was adorned with a heavy dusting of powder and did appear to move uphill. Barbara Mikkelson (2003) identifies the San Antonio site as a "gravity hill," an optical illusion where one appears to be moving uphill when one is really moving downhill. Still, it was visually convincing and impressive. It occurred to me that the powder could highlight any preexisting prints, but we pulled over, and at first glance there were no fingerprints on the trunk. Later, a little boy came over to look at our car, and we noticed a sole fingerprint not long after he disappeared. The actions of this little boy and several

FIGURE 4: Todos Santos 2003: Seeking palm prints and fingerprints from the ghostly children, five children inspect the dusted trunk of a car that has just gone over the tracks. San Antonio, Texas. (Photo by Carl Lindahl)

others brought me into different kinds of human interactions than I had previously experienced in the San Antonio area.

Everyone who was at the tracks was "testing" the site or looking for evidence in the same way we did. This was also accomplished by interacting with all the other strangers at the tracks. We all got out, looked at each other's cars, and talked to each other. This meant that among others, I talked to (and shared baby powder with) a busload of shy Latino school girls in uniform from Brownsville, Texas; a couple of male African American teenagers, and a family from Texas with two children and a mom who had the tallest and biggest blonde, bouffant hairdo I'd ever seen.

I'd seen people representing these different demographics on the street and in the restaurants and shops of San Antonio, but nothing had caused us to stop and have a real exchange—until we engaged with the legend. This speaks to the power of story. Sometimes, at least for a moment, a story can help us reach across boundaries that we don't normally traverse. The ghost story briefly changed my habitual pattern of social interaction. On the train tracks on that humid San Antonio night, people connected with each other through attention to and enjoyment of an anomalous place and its story. It was a moment of demographic transcendence through legend tripping. Then we drove back to our hotel, and the next day Carl drove out of the parking garage and headed toward Chicago with a ghostly reminder of the small ways in which stories mark the material world: wisps of baby powder occasionally kited off the trunk of the car as he made his way north.

These two examples illustrate some positive ways in which ghost stories affect personal lives; however, it is only fair to acknowledge that their personal impact can also be negative. Unfortunately, charlatans employ the metaphysical to swindle money from people. Sometimes tales of the supernatural generate unnecessary fear in their audiences. For example, both my colleagues and students have commented that movies such as *The Exorcist* (1973), *Poltergeist* (1982), and *The Ring* (2002) traumatized them. Some of this fear is conditioned by Hollywood's frequent presentation of a more highly dramatic, gory, and threatening supernatural than the one depicted in the oral tradition.[7] An awareness of the difference between what is depicted in Hollywood horror films versus the oral tradition can sometimes lessen the fright associated with such films. In other words, if you encounter the anomalous in everyday life, it's not going to be as dramatic (and therefore not as frightening) as the Amityville haunting, for example.

Some people also experience fright when they hear a story from the oral tradition, especially when they are children. One group of students told me that they were the most frightened by paranormal events that were reported to be true. In this case, a large number of them were especially frightened by a television series, *Unsolved Mysteries* (1987–1999), which purported to depict actual events and happenings—several of them based in urban legends—that could not be easily explained. In response to frightening narratives, people develop folk strategies to deal with the fears that the supernatural and inexplicable raise. Along with the folk analysis of ghost stories mentioned earlier in this chapter, folk strategies for defusing fear are another common, but understudied, component of the supernatural tradition. Over the years, my students have related various methods for defanging fear. Strategies that introduce comforting *companionship* are popular. Examples I've heard include sleeping with a loved one—parent, sibling, friend, partner, or dog—when afraid. Other tactics include using a cell phone if companionship is not immediately available. The use of some sort of *magical action or substance* is also frequent, especially with children. These practices range from leaving a light on to giving a child a spray bottle of "monster juice" that she can shoot under the bed to dissipate fears (and monsters). The mass market recognizes this folk process and has actually commodified it through items such as monster-abatement sprays. Other variants of magic action include *isolation* and *neutralization*. For instance, one of my students told me that she found Hufford's *The Terror That Comes in the Night* (1982b) fascinating but also very, very scary. So when she wasn't reading the book, she stored it in her freezer. In order to contain and literally "put on ice" unnerving aspects of the supernatural, she reported that she employed a contemporary appliance, the freezer, in much the same way that Southerners historically used bottle trees.

Distraction is another method people employ to reduce fear. For example, a student told me of having to help a scared friend in college. First, the friend requested that my student read scriptures aloud to distract her. The frightened woman didn't find reading aloud diverting enough until my student switched to reading political satire. The women threw the scriptures over for P. J. O'Rourke, who proved more effective in this case. Other students said they've tried to divest themselves of fear by singing songs.

Finally, *eradication* or *displacement* are two other creative folk strategies used to address fright. One student confessed to me that the notion of Bloody Mary so frightened him as a child that his mother felt she had to do more than just talk to him about it. She rented the musical *South Pacific* (1958) and had him watch the scenes focusing on Bloody Mary to impress on him that Bloody Mary was really just a woman in a musical and not some demonic being who lived in a bathroom mirror.[8] Author Edith Wharton, "a life-long book lover," confessed that she could not sleep if she knew a volume of ghost stories was in the house, and she would even burn such volumes on occasion to eradicate the threat they posed (Crow 2004, 157). Students also report that thinking about supernatural stories in terms of culture, nature, or the personal also helps move their focus and emotional energy away from fear and into analysis. In these ways, supernatural stories in all their various manifestations both generate fear *and* prompt people to develop methods that help them learn how to cope with and, hopefully, overcome their fear.

All of these examples demonstrate that ghost stories and beliefs can be a positive or negative force—and sometimes both—in individual lives. Ghosts can lead us on a merry, and sometimes scary, chase. We try to capture, contain, and understand them; sometimes we're successful. At other times—just like spook lights in wetlands—they elude us, reminding us of how much in life we cannot control. However, ghost stories are useful forms, and we can harness their supernatural energy in a variety of ways. In this chapter, I've discussed three of those ways. And whether they focus on a child's spectral handprint in Texas, a haunted toilet in New York, or an old debt left by a Canadian ghost, ghost stories awaken us to the skin-crawling pleasure and wonder to be found in all the worlds around us.

Two

Scientific Rationalism and Supernatural Experience Narratives

Diane E. Goldstein

We've all been there. You're sitting around with friends sharing a few stories, when the topic turns to the supernatural. Someone tells a ghost story they heard while camping many years earlier. A second person tells a story about a neighbourhood house that is reputed to be haunted. Eventually and almost inevitably, someone tells a story about a ghost that happened *to her*.

This is not, according to some academics, as it should be. The spontaneous telling of a personal supernatural experience runs counter to one of the central principles of academic rationalist traditions—that supernatural belief would decline as education and technology increased. This chapter will address the climate of scholarly opinion that has surrounded academic discussions of modern rationalism and popular belief and will then move on to examine the role and construction of reasoning in narratives of supernatural belief and experience.

Cultural Evolution and Modern Scientific Rationalism

The conventional academic point of view that supernatural beliefs are survivals from a naive past and must decline as scientific thought ascends is itself quite old, steeped in the rationalist perspectives of David Hume and other eighteenth-century European philosophers who attributed religion to primitive thinking processes and declared that as individuals and societies acquired a more rational understanding of the world, religion would be displaced, initially by philosophy but ultimately by science. The philosophers who repeatedly linked religion and "irrational" thought processes of "primitive" peoples shared a thinly veiled agenda, responding to what they perceived as religious superstitiousness and the oppressive structures of Europe's Roman Catholic Church (Hayden 1987, 590). Nevertheless, this rationalist context heavily influenced the evolutionary perspectives of early antiquarian folklore collectors.

In the context of this evolutionary philosophy, nineteenth- and early twentieth-century antiquarians pursued the collecting of popular belief with a sense of urgency, convinced that failure to collect and preserve belief traditions would mean that they would disappear without documentation. These "survivals" were understood by antiquarian scholars as remnants of ideas that would no longer have currency in academic or "educated" portions of society. Nineteenth-century writings on folklore were full of references to evolutionary ideas, if not explicitly to evolutionary theory. Fletcher Bassett, for example, writing in 1885 about ghost ships[1] noted:

> The old type of sailor, who believed in the mermaid, the sea-snake, and the phantom ship, is fast disappearing, and with the gradual substitution of the steamship for the sailing vessel, he is replaced by the mechanical sea-man, who sees no spectre in the fog, nor sign of disaster in the air, or beneath the wave. ([1885] reprint 1971, 8)

Bassett assumed, as did his contemporaries, an image of the noble but naive fisherman intent on explaining the sights and sounds of the elements by leaping to supernatural conclusions. His son Wilber Bassett, also a maritime folklorist, was even more explicit thirty years later, although somewhat more sympathetic in writing about the tendency of seafaring men to turn to supernatural explanations. He wrote that

> sight and sound alow and aloft are to the sailor as trail and track to the woodsman, eloquent of meaning. His

perception in times of calm or storm is open wide to
the slightest sound or sight that might foretell coming
change. To this consciousness cloud and mist shapes,
mirages, and the thousand sights and sounds of the ever
shifting panorama brings many extraordinary and inexplicable things, which are stored away in memory, and
their expression in the tenacity with which sailors cling to
their belief in the "supernatural." ([1917] 1974, 81)

Both Fletcher and Wilbur Bassett understood the phantom
ship phenomenon as the product of an unequivocal acceptance
of the supernatural combined with the interpretation of standard
sea hallucinations by an unscientific and uncritical mind. This
characterization of the delusional fisherman who sees skeletons
of the dead in flowing shrouds wandering around or chained to
the decks of flaming ghostly vessels predominates even in the
modern literature on ghost ship traditions. Margaret Baker in
1979 wrote that

usually ship-phantoms rise from storm and wreck and,
glowing with light, decks rotted, crews skeletal, helms
untended, they approach, silently on collision courses
from which with diabolical cunning they swing away, leaving shaken crews to marvel that they lived. (53)

Baker's resort to literary clichés is the contemporary and more
respectful (but no less infused with evolutionary theory) version
of the delusional uncritical fisherman. This image of the fisherman who sees ghouls and ghosts of horror films and jumps to
supernatural conclusions at the drop of a hat naturally forces the
prediction that education will quiet the overimaginative mind
and untrained eye of these primitive men of the sea.

While it is not just the fisherman who was associated with
irrational supernatural thought, the occupation and seafaring
context fit nicely with other central perspectives of evolutionary
theory—that cultural survivals would "trickle down" from elite to
lower levels of society; to the undereducated and underemployed,
the poor, the ethnic or cultural "other," and the geographically

isolated (Mullen 2000, 122). Indicative of that point of view, Newbell Niles Puckett wrote in 1931 that folk beliefs "are found mainly with the uncultured and backward classes of society, white or coloured; and it is to such retarded classes rather than to either racial group as a whole that reference is made . . . " (9).

Baker's references to the delusional fisherman is a group-specific manifestation of wider evolutionary thought found even more subtly in the writings of many of the most prominent belief scholars of the twenty-first century. Anthropologist Anthony Wallace argued in 1966, for example, that "belief in supernatural beings and in supernatural forces that affect nature without obeying nature's laws will erode and become only an interesting historical memory . . . " (264), and similarly, historian Keith Thomas noted in 1991 that in contrast to the past, belief in ghosts is now "rightly distained by intelligent persons" (ix).

The legacy of evolutionary theory in the field of belief studies has been significant and continues to reify stereotypical views of both supernatural traditions and those who hold folk beliefs. Bonnie O'Connor argues that

> cultural evolutionism as a theory of culture is now generally academically discredited on grounds of oversimplification and worse of parentalism and ethnocentric bias. Nevertheless this intellectual history has left a pervasive and often damaging legacy. Folk belief has continued to be implicitly or explicitly defined as that body of belief and knowledge which is contradicted or superseded by modern or scientific knowledge. This presumption in turn has conditioned approaches taken to the subject, as would be expected of any subject defined at the outset by its investigators as "incorrect." Evolutionist and survivalist assumptions about culture, cultural processes, and belief and knowledge have until very recently focussed the attention of scholars of folk belief almost exclusively on non-dominant groups, defined by virtue of their social position and different from the dominant culture as "the folk." (1995, 38)

Also tracing the more subtle consequences of cultural evolutionism and scientific rationalism on the study of belief, Gillian Bennett notes that

> of all types of folklore this is the one that seems least respectable and least believable in the so-called scientific age. The main trouble for folklorists is that we have got ourselves into not one, but no less than three vicious circles. Firstly no one will tackle the subject because it is disreputable, and it remains disreputable because no one will tackle it. Secondly, because no one does any research into present day supernatural beliefs, occult traditions are generally represented by old legends about fairies, bogeys and grey ladies. Furthermore, because published collections of supernatural folklore are thus stuck forever in a time warp, folklorists are rightly wary of printing the modern beliefs they do come across for fear of offending their informants by appearing to put deeply felt beliefs on a par with chain-rattling skeletons and other such absurdities. Thirdly, because no one will talk about their experiences of the supernatural there is no evidence for it and because there is no evidence for it no one talks about their experiences of it. (1987, 13)

Bennett's comments point out clearly the materialistic or rationalistic approach in the social sciences that has created a notion of supernatural belief as antithetical to modern thought and therefore destined for imminent demise. The usual expectation among North American intellectuals is that anyone who believes in "science" will not believe in such phenomena as ghosts, spirits, or witches. In fact the first paragraph of Garvin McCain and Erwin Segal's *The Game of Science* begins with the claim that we no longer believe in witches precisely because we believe in science:

> Why don't you believe in witches? That question may seem ridiculous but our ancestors, who were probably as bright as we are, did believe in them, and acted accordingly. Why

are we so different and superior? The evidence for or against witches is no better than it was 400 years ago. For us, it is almost impossible to believe in witches; for our ancestors, it was equally difficult to deny their existence. Our new beliefs exist, in part, due to the development of "scientific attitudes." (1969, 3)

What do we make then, of the friend described earlier who tells the ghost narrative as if it were her own personal experience?

A Dying Tradition, or Is It?

Since the 1970s, a few social scientists have administered surveys to assess the actual state of contemporary belief in the supernatural. Sociologist, author, and priest Andrew Greeley surveyed claims of communication with the dead, clairvoyance, and mystical experience in 1973 and found that almost one-fifth of the American population reported frequent supernatural experiences (Greeley 1975). A few years later, a study by a team from the sociology department at Leeds University in England found that 14 percent of their sizable sample from the United Kingdom believed in astrology, 35 percent in fortune telling, 36 percent in ghosts, 54 percent in clairvoyance, and 61 percent in telepathy (Kakrup 1982).

Public opinion polls reflect similar results. In 2003, the Harris Interactive Poll (which surveys American adults online) found that 89 percent of their sample believe in miracles, 68 percent believe in the devil, 69 percent believe in hell, 51 percent in ghosts, 31 percent in astrology, and 27 percent in reincarnation (Taylor 2003). Most recently, a poll by the Gallup Organization administered in 2005 showed that three in four Americans hold some belief in at least one of the paranormal areas surveyed by Gallup, which included extra-sensory perception (ESP), haunted houses, ghosts, mental telepathy, clairvoyance, astrology, communication with the dead, witches, reincarnation, and channelling. According to the Gallup Organization, who update their audits of these issues every couple of years, continual surveys have demonstrated slight increases in paranormal belief over the last fifteen years with decline in belief in only one area since 1990, that of devil possession. According to the 2005 audit, over half of Americans believe in psychic or spiritual healing and ESP and more than a third believe in haunted houses, possession by the devil, ghosts, telepathy, extraterrestrial beings having visited the earth, and clairvoyance (Gallup Organization 2005).

The Canadian Leger Marketing Survey also found in 2005 that a majority of Canadians surveyed believed in angels and life after death while roughly one third reported a belief that aliens and ghosts existed. The polling firm also indicated that 6.3 percent of respondents reported that they had seen a ghost and 5.8 percent reported seeing an angel (FarShores ParaNews 2005b).

Not only is supernatural belief widespread in North America and the United Kingdom, but so much so that it might even be considered the norm. But what is even more significant in terms of rationalist and evolutionary theories is that supernatural belief was reported by a substantial part of the population *from all classes and educational backgrounds.* The findings of Greeley, the Leeds team, and the public opinion surveys indicate clearly that the extent of belief in the supernatural has for some time been seriously underestimated. Each of these studies includes remarks of astonishment on the part of the investigators, all pointing to one crucial question: "Why have we for so long overlooked the extent of contemporary belief in the supernatural?" So our friend who tells the ghost story is in good company, but is she (and her fellow believers) rational?

THE RATIONAL BELIEVER

The materialistic or rationalistic approach in the social sciences has not only forced a notion of supernatural belief as antithetical to modern thought and therefore destined for imminent demise, but has also meant that we found only that for which we were looking: a world that had forsaken popular belief and replaced it with "rational thought." While the formula itself (supernatural belief ≠ rational, therefore modern/educated = no supernatural belief) was apparently wrong and misleading, the central fallacy on which it is based—that supernatural belief and rational[2] thought are dichotomous—was perhaps the most problematic premise.

When folklorists, sociologists, anthropologists, and other social scientists have looked seriously at the area of contemporary belief, it has largely been through several variations on a single perspective. Central to this perspective is the question, "How can beliefs that are so clearly false still be held to be true?" (Hufford 1982a). Traditionally this question has led to explanation in terms of the historical origins of belief traditions or in terms of social utility. As O'Connor notes, "Such theoretical orientations imply that the beliefs to whose analysis they are applied are false, and the actions those beliefs inform 'really' accomplish something other than what the actor intends and believes them to do" (1995, 44).

Recent phenomenological approaches to belief (Hufford 1982a, 1982b; Virtanen 1990; Bennett 1987, 1999; O'Connor 1995) have, however, opposed traditional academic assumptions that supernatural belief traditions necessarily arise from various kinds of error. These studies demonstrate that careful analysis of belief traditions reveal reasoned consideration and the testing of alternatives on the part of percipients and narrators. As David Hufford has noted, "We should be collecting not only supernatural beliefs and narratives . . . but also people's reasons for holding those beliefs so that we may inductively describe their empirical and logical components" (Hufford 1982b, 54). Though the collection of explicit reasons for holding beliefs is indeed an important task, a close look at the structure of personal supernatural experience narratives suggests that many of those reasons are built into the narratives themselves and are a regular part of the narrating process.

Staying with our earlier theme of the scholar's *imagined* delusional fisherman who sees flaming ships and skeletons of the dead chained to rotting decks, consider (for example) the following *actual* narrative told by a Newfoundland man who believes he encountered a phantom ship while out fishing in the family schooner.

On the night of October second (year about 1930) we left Seldom Come by about four o'clock in the morning and came on up around Cape Freels. It was a nice fine day but when we were half way across Bonavista Bay the wind died out completely. We waited about two hours and then Father decided to get the motor boat cut off the deck and tow the schooner. We towed then until about seven p.m. from two in the afternoon and by seven o'clock in the night the wind was up enough to put some sail on and get underway again. We were across the bay and heading around Cape Bonavista and toward Catalina by nine o'clock. Then we noticed a ship about a mile astern. I was on watch at the wheel. She kept gaining on us and when she got up about broadside and off a couple of gunshots she turned and started to head in towards Catalina. We could see the lights of Catalina by this time. Father thought it must be the "Prospero." She was a coastal vessel. But when he said that, we saw her turn and head away from Catalina and on up the bay again. Father then figured it was a fish steamer headed up to Ryans (a prospering fish plant in Trinity Bay). She kind of faded away and we forgot about it since we were anxious to get home and all. We only did see her lights, mast head light, running lights, port and starboard, and a few porthole lights, as she caught up to us and passed us. When I think about it now, I don't know if the lights were very clear or not. Strikes me they were a bit fuzzy or glimmering. Anyhow, we forgot about her when she faded in the distance. I was still at the wheel since my watch went on till midnight and about 11:30 it came on a living gale. Uncle Don took over at twelve o'clock and he stayed lashed to the wheel all night until daylight because we couldn't get a man aft to relieve him cause she was shipping too much water. The skipper started to haul the canvas off of her and in an hour we were down to mainsail and jumbo.

About twelve-thirty someone spotted her (the phantom) again for a few minutes. We could see the lights for a bit and then they turned sideways and disappeared. We figures she had gone round Horse Chops and was beating on in to Trinity. For about six hours, until daylight, there was a terrific storm. Father said after it was the worst one he was ever out in and he had been out in a good many. We had all sails off except the foresail, and just could keep her to the wind. By daylight we had been blown right over on the South side of Trinity Bay down somewhere off Heart's Content near as we could figure. Anyhow come daylight we squared away and eventually got in around Bonavista Head and on in to Trinity. When we got in Uncle Baxter came on board and he said to father, "Where did ye come from Ken?" Father said that we had been out on the bay all night. "Couldn't have," says Uncle Baxter, "cause nothin' could live out there last night." "We were then," said Father, "because we were right off the Bite when that steamer come in here to Ryan's." "Haven't been a steamer into Ryan's in three days," said Uncle Baxter, "and no vessel came in here last night." So we figured that it must have been the phantom ship, and when she headed in toward Catalina about nine o'clock that must have been a sign for us to head in there too. If we had we wouldn't have been out in the storm at all. It sure did blow from the South East too and that's what they say always happens. (MUNFLA 63–DIT, 100–103)

The melodramatic phantom described by Baker is not present in this narrative and neither is the unscientific and uncritical narrator suggested by Fletcher and Wilbur Bassett. Instead, we find a careful and highly detailed narrative that foregrounds the skills and tools of a sailor: navigational aids, wind directions and changes, sail positions, dates, times, landmarks, and nautical distances. There are no skeletal crews here or rotting decks, but instead a series of sophisticated observations noting a vessel that never arrived at its only possible destination. One would indeed be hard pressed to call this narrative irrational. But is the story told by our friend at the beginning of this chapter likely to be as rational?

THE NARRATIVE WITNESS STAND

Narrative tellings are always shaped and reshaped by the narrator's skill, context, audience, topical links, and many other factors and are therefore always varied and emergent. Supernatural experience narratives, on the other hand, tend to share a common highly detailed, cautious, and sometimes even defensive structure. The sea phantom narrative given above is, in this sense, not alone in its cautiousness, but rather reflects a structure that is common to contemporary supernatural experience narratives. These narratives, or memorates as they are called, are typically told as though one were on the witness stand, detailed and careful, incorporating numerous strategies that outline the nature of the observations, the testing of alternative explanations, and often including an indication of reluctance to interpret what occurred as "supernatural." One ghost enthusiast blog published on the Internet made the following similar observation:

> This weekend some friends and I got to talking about ghost stories. I asked if any of the tales being told were real experiences. Some were hearsay from family and friends, some were campfire tales, and others were urban legends. Then I asked if any of the group had personal experiences with ghosts. One brave soul admitted to what seemed like a ghostly encounter. Once that adventure had been recounted, others began to fess up.
>
> Something occurred to me during that session. There is a difference between "ghost stories" and "haunted encounters." Ghost stories are just that—stories. Each tale has a central character and follows the three-act structure. Haunted encounters don't usually have a beginning, middle and end. The personal experience narratives almost always start with a disclaimer and end with the narrator's voice trailing off and another disclaimer. Ghost stories

are told with gusto and glee. Haunted encounters are told
reluctantly and with apology. Ghost stories are thought to
be entertaining and acceptable. Haunted encounters are
often considered to be the delusions of a troubled mind.
(Haunted Encounters Blog 2005)

Although there is of course no actual witness stand, narrators are
conscious of the potential for being judged irrational and therefore assume a stance that anticipates contestation of observations
and conclusions. The resulting narratives stand in opposition to
the traditional academic assumption that supernatural belief traditions arise from various kinds of error, impaired reasoning, or
poor observation on the part of believers or narrators. Instead
each narrative embeds information on the accumulation and
determination of evidential criteria directed at opening up the
interpretation of the narrative events for discussion. The sense
of evidence used here is not dissimilar from legal definitions.
Bauvier's Law Dictionary, for example, defines evidence as

that which tends to prove or disprove any matter in question or to influence the belief respecting it. Belief is produced by the consideration of something presented to
the mind. The matter thus presented, in whatever shape
it may come, and through whatever material organ it is
derived, is evidence. (Bauvier 1914, 69)

A characteristic feature of the memorate is its structured narrative exploration of evidence. In this sense, not only is the narrative reasoned and logical but it appears to be largely about reasoning and logic. Consider, for example, the following narrative
told by Francis, a native of St. John's, Newfoundland, during an
interview. Francis was forty-six when he related this memorate.

Well, the first one, I was on vigil, and if I had been the
only one, well, I never knew it at the time. During Holy
Week in the Catholic church somebody has to be on vigil.
Vigil is watch, you see, all the time. It's a re-enactment of
the watching of the tomb for Christ. The night shift was
from twelve o'clock to six. We didn't mind. Then ah, it

was in St. Patrick's Church, which is an old church. And
this marvellous, beautiful nun came this way out, and
was coming around the altar. And the only thing that
was confusing me, was that everybody during Lent, especially during Holy Week, were around. And she didn't
speak to me, when I said "hello" to her. Now you kneel
down on this, it's sort of a kneeling chair with velvet pad-
ding for your knees and an armrest. And you don't sit
down, you kneel down. And then, she went around the
altar, down the middle aisle, and came back again. And
she walked around the area of the altar, which is quite
large, to a big statue. She did the Stations of the Cross,
and she came up, passed by me, just passed. And the
church was, uh, there was a different odor. It was nice
and uh, not any odor that I'm familiar with. I guess it
would be sort of an odor like, if you lived in the jungles
of Africa and you smelled a lilac. It would be a different
odor. Well, it was something I never smelled before, and
never smelled after. When she got about five feet in front
of me, she disappeared. And I got a bit of a shock, but
then it went away again immediately. I was about eleven.
But afterwards, I found out that this nun had been seen
for years and years. And if I hadn't known that up to this
time, I probably would have said that it was my imagination. But I never knew it, that other people had seen
her. And I mentioned it to the priest and he said, "Yes,
you're not the first one, we know who it is, and it's probably something she was supposed to do, and did not do."
"Because," he said, "you said she did the Stations of the
Cross." "She must not have done something. She was
supposed to do the Stations of the Cross, probably. For
some old lady or something and didn't. Forgot to do it.
[Didn't have] . . . time to do it and is atoning for it." And
there are many people who can back that story up.

Like the phantom ship narrative recounted earlier, Francis's
account is full of descriptive information. The extraordinary

amount of detail characteristic of supernatural experience narratives has been noted over the years by several scholars, but most notably by Lauri Honko. In his article on the memorate written in 1964, Honko noted that "there are memorates in which there are ample individual, unique features, and in certain respects, unnecessary details" (Honko 1964, 11). Clearly, at many levels, Francis's narrative recounts details that do not seem to advance the narrative action. Yet if we for a moment posit the notion that what appears "unnecessary" to the analyst may be central to the narrator and shift our notion of "where the action is," we may begin to see a different picture. If we allow Francis to include in his narrative not only what took place, but his feelings and decisions, reactions, associations, and conclusions, we begin to see a narrative that can carry us through Francis's thinking and reasoning processes.

By selecting and foregrounding relevant information, contexts, and scenes, Francis shows us how he began to form a meaningful whole from each of the events imparted in his narrative. He tells us that everyone was around for Holy Week and that he did not recognize this nun—a first clue that there was something unusual taking place. Then he spoke to her and she didn't respond—another sign of unusual behavior. Francis begins to define the event by the absence of the expected. He follows the nun's motions, mentions her odor, and then suddenly we find ourselves in the jungles of Africa smelling lilacs. It is not that Africa or the smell of lilacs has anything to do with the narrative events, but rather that the parallel situation explicates the newness of the experience. By analogic reasoning Francis clarifies not simply the events at hand, but his experience of those events. By bringing elements of his experience to bear on the case, Francis reveals for us what Peter Berger and Thomas Luckmann have called his "relevance structures" (Berger and Luckmann 1966, 45). In other words, he presents the manner in which he constructed his interpretation.

What might to some seem "unnecessary" in this narrative are the lengthy descriptions of the church, particularly of the kneeling chair. These aspects of the narrative are unchanging; they remain a part of the everyday, unaffected by the narrative events. Yet the fact that these elements remain the same may be the very reason for their presence in the narrative. By contrasting the simple and the supernatural, Francis demonstrates his ability to distinguish one class from another. He is able to describe the familiar and thus define the characteristics of the unfamiliar. The reasoning is dialectical; the supernatural is seen in contrast to the natural. In this attempt at contrast and differentiation, the key is to separate the changing features. Thus, by carefully following the motions of the nun, Francis is able to investigate and demonstrate the relationship of the actor to her actions. It is not what she does that is unusual but rather her way of doing it.

Hufford has noted that the standard accusation of inadequate observation and reality-testing on the part of percipients is often countered in interview responses by references to specific testing strategies (Hufford 1982b, xviii). These strategies range beyond the proverbial "pinch to see if I was dreaming" to references to actual experimentation. Such references appear often in Francis's narratives and are indicative of his desire to scientifically explain his experiences. In a different memorate, Francis related another experience he once had.

> I'll tell you something, my first real fright. We had a summer home around the bay, but we lived here in St. John's. And I was fourteen, and I was the only one at home, and I had a set of encyclopaedias. Now you have to remember, all the doors are closed. And I'm asleep, very sound asleep. I wake up. And from the bedroom all the way out the hallway, and on each step going downstairs, for about eight feet, there, the books had run out. And my total set of encyclopaedias is open, to page 39, 40, 40, and 41. You know, I tried it after. Just to place a book, a hardcover book on the floor, and open it to any particular page, and let it stay there. It's impossible. But these things, they're all about a foot apart, systematically laid out. So I immediately, when I saw that, I just got out. For some strange reason, I just got a fright. Then I waited till my aunt, who

was out shopping down the street, came home. I went back in, and collected all the books. And, and she, she figured I did it for a joke, which I did not. But I wouldn't tell her too much. I just said that I got a bit of a start. I never read anything out of them either. Thinking back, maybe I should have. What it meant, I don't know.

In this narrative Francis recognizes duplication and replicability as standard scientific criteria. One third of the narrative is concerned with his attempt to replicate even a part of the event. He recognizes the implications for interpretation of the whole by explaining a part. Here the concern focuses on approximating the least sensational of the events, in the hope of illuminating what transpired.

Francis's narratives are full of references to other witnesses and to himself and his own credibility. He begins and ends the first narrative with direct reference to others who have had the same experience. In so doing, he acknowledges the importance of precedent as evidence for his case. Rather than using the common narrative strategy of embedding several narratives into one story, he embeds narrators; that is, he fills his stories with others who have reported the same or similar events.

Francis recognizes the trustworthiness of numbers of witnesses, as well as specific characteristics of reliability. Among these, the sceptic appears to be the most credible. His narratives are filled with references to witnesses who were nonbelievers and, of particular importance, the priest. Although Francis's narrative recounts his own experience of the events, he still classifies himself as less credible than other witnesses as is evidenced in his comment, "And if I hadn't known that up to this time, I would have said it was probably my imagination." Francis always gives full information concerning his age and mental state at the time of the narrative events. Further, he discriminates between full witnesses and circumstantial witnesses. In the second account, he notes that his aunt only saw the result of the events, and determines that this is not sufficient evidence to prove what transpired to an unsympathetic audience. Thus, the aunt is not given prominence as a witness.

Characteristic of much of the work done on memorates is the assumption that these narratives are heavily laden with the experiencer's interpretation of the content and significance of, and reasons for, the experience (Cartwright 1982, 58). Francis's ability to bracket these beliefs and interpretations is demonstrated in all of his supernatural experience narratives. In the first account given here, the notion that a ghost returns to resolve something that remained undone is only brought into the narrative as reported speech, thus setting it off as one interpretation. In the second narrative, Francis notes that the page numbers might have meant something, but suggests this only in his evaluation (Labov and Waletsky 1967, 12). Throughout the body of the narratives themselves, there are very few (if any) interpretive statements. This is true, to the extent that Francis never actually says what he thinks either phenomenon actually was. His tendency to discriminate between his beliefs and his accounts of experience can be seen in the conclusion to another of his narratives. In this story Francis has an unusual discussion on the street with an elderly man. He ended the narrative by saying

> The man said, "I've got to go now," and he walked into the graveyard on Waterford Bridge Road. He said, "Good night," and vanished. And the night was moonlit, clear as a bell. And I was neither scared, oddly enough. Yet, if I go through a graveyard, I will whistle and cross both my fingers, to make sure I get across. Now, that's a contradiction, isn't it?

In this account Francis distinguishes between what he would call his "superstitions" and the actual personal experience.

Francis provides a useful case study here, but, as a retrospective look back at ghost ship narrative or a careful focus on other memorates will demonstrate,[3] he is not alone in the way he structures his narratives. Consider, for example, the following randomly chosen ghost narrative from one of the many online ghost story archives:

Our room's window and the mirror were haunted. It so happened that one day as I stood in front of it brushing my hair (long and straight) I experienced a strange thing. Half of the image was mine; the other half seemed to belong to somebody else. The mirror is rather distorted, so I thought it was an optical illusion. But as I noticed, the other image had short curly hair, white pupil-less slightly red eyes (mine are dark brown) and a beard. I was slightly confused and turned to look at the window right behind it; no one there. As I looked closely, I moved my head from side to side. On one side was my own image, but on the other side was something truly terrible. I screamed and ran out of the room to my mom. She comforted me and told me to come with her. I was afraid but went inside; as I peered in the mirror, there was no one in there. I dismissed the idea from my mind considering I was having hallucinations. The next day however, as I stood in front of the mirror, my whole image changed and that strange man leered at me. Again I ran out, convinced that it was not my imagination. At first mom was reluctant to believe, but after a few days our sweeper complained of a man following him around. He said, I can't do my work properly with him around me; although he was alone speaking to my mom with no one around him. I began to see that man in every mirror or glass, even the ones on the cupboard. I was scared. In an attempt to end it we removed all the mirrors from the house but that man appeared in the cupboard glass; complete man in every one. I didn't go there alone. (Castle of Spirits.com 2005)

Francis's narrations demonstrate that evidential criteria are central in supernatural experience narratives, demonstrated through continual reference to relevance structures, detailing, case differentiation, the relationship of actor to action, duplication and replicability, and the assessment of credibility. The ghost in the mirror narrative uses the same strategies; the narrator provides the ordinary/extraordinary contrast and case differentiation, tries experimentation to test replicability, explores the possibility of optical illusion, and cites other witnesses. Further, the embedding of evidence in Francis's supernatural experience narratives, the incredibly careful detail in the phantom ship narrative, and the emphasis on replicability in the mirror narrative all appear rhetorically to be less about convincing an audience that the events took place and more about the narrator explaining how it was that he or she came to understand what happened, how it happened, and why it happened.

This exploration of embedded use of evidence is not intended to suggest the ontological reality of supernatural experience but rather to illustrate that these narratives are generally well-reasoned and more to the point, *concerned* with reason. In the narrative emphasis on evidence and rational belief, we can see that the personal supernatural experience narrative doesn't exist *in the face of* modern scientific knowledge, but in content and structure it exists *because* of modern scientific knowledge.[4]

Part II:

Narrating Socialization and Gender

THREE

GENDER AND GHOSTS

JEANNIE BANKS THOMAS

In the mid-nineteenth century, Coventry Patmore published the well-known poem "The Angel in the House," which defines the Victorian model of the ideal, submissive woman and wife: "Man must be pleased; but him to please / Is woman's pleasure." Well into the twentieth century, the Angel in the House was still haunting women and urging them to sacrifice their own happiness and "fling" themselves down "the gulf" of their husbands' "necessities" (Melani 2005; Patmore 2003). Virginia Woolf famously wrote that she had to eradicate the Angel in order to write truthfully: "Thus, whenever I felt the shadow of her wing or the radiance of her halo upon my page, I took up the inkpot and flung it at her. She died hard. Her fictitious nature was of great assistance to her. It is far harder to kill a phantom than a reality. She was always creeping back when I thought I had dispatched her" (2004).

The literary tradition gives us an ethereal angel in the house, but the oral tradition gives us the phantom crazy woman haunting the house. In this manner, folklore provides the Angel in the House with an evil twin. I argue that supernatural manifestations of this deviant woman are a common pattern in ghost stories and that she has an excessively aggressive male counterpart. However, wronged parties of either gender are among the most common types of ghosts. Typically in these ghost stories, a murder victim or the victim of a tragic accident draws attention to his or her plight by haunting a particular site (e.g., Lindahl 2004, 451).

Despite some popular arguments that galactic-sized differences exist between men and woman (Gray 1992), sociologists maintain that men and women are actually more alike than different (Kimmel 2000, xi). The large number of supernatural legends that focus on wronged parties who could just as easily be gendered male or female provides narrative illustration of this argument. In these cases, gender makes little difference to the storyline. However, gender does play a larger role in some supernatural legends. It is to these stories that I turn my attention. The focus of this chapter is on supernatural legends that in some way raise, emphasize, or rework gender and the cultural ideas associated with it. I look closely at two types of gendered figures that are apparent in such ghost legends, referring to them as the Extreme Guy and the Deviant Femme. The Extreme Guy closely mirrors a kind of exaggerated masculinity that is found in everyday life. Often the Extreme Guy actually appears in human form in supernatural legends; sometimes he assumes spectral form as well.

The Extreme Guy exaggerates many of the characteristics most stereotypically associated with masculinity, such as toughness and violence. The Deviant Femme is the antithesis of the traits traditionally associated with femininity; for example, she is a murdering mother. In short, she's the Angel in the House gone horribly wrong. As such, she's also more interesting and dramatic than the Angel in the House. She is a manifestation of all that the Angel represses: rage, violence, mental illness, and eccentricity. Neither the Angel nor the Femme tradition presents an adult, female figure who is both strong and well-balanced.

This chapter identifies the Extreme Guy and the Deviant Femme as gendered patterns in ghost stories—but, as I said earlier, not as the *only* patterns in ghost stories. Along with the ghosts of wronged parties, nurturing ghosts of both sexes also exist in the supernatural tradition (especially in memorates) as does another type of ghost that has no apparent spectral embodiment or gender of any sort. I refer to this ghost type as the Genderless Presence; some poltergeists exemplify this category.

Compared to the Genderless Presence, the Extreme Guy and the Deviant Femme are conservative in that they replicate ideas about gender and gendered behavior that exist in contemporary culture. The Genderless Presence is a much greater departure from human and material reality. In the course of everyday life, how often are we in the presence of a being whose gender remains an unaddressed mystery? In the figure of the Genderless Presence, the supernatural gives us its most radical take on gender: it eliminates it entirely.

THE EXTREME GUY: THE WILLOW HOLLOW MURDERER AND BLOODY MARY'S BOYFRIEND

Patmore's poem overlooks the cultural reality that too many of those flesh-and-blood, self-sacrificing Angels in the House were married to Extreme Guys. However, the oral tradition does not ignore this fact. Ghost legends commonly depict Extreme Guys and domestic violence. Also, ghost stories in which gender is a significant factor often mirror cultural notions about gender and gendered behaviors. For example, a ghost story set in Oaktown, Indiana, told by a twenty-nine-year-old woman focuses on a house that is haunted by the ghost of a man who was killed in the house (ISUFA 1996a). The residents of the house reported seeing a male ghost, and they also said that he often haunted the bathroom. Women in the household noticed that he frequently left the toilet seat up after they had just put it down. This story contains the haunted toilet motif discussed in chapter 1 and raises a spectral parallel to human conflict: the battle of the sexes that sometimes erupts concerning whether the toilet seat should be left up or put down. Although the ghost is not corporeal and therefore not subject to the physical demands of a human body, it engages in activities—such as leaving the toilet seat up (and presumably using the toilet)—that are very human and also very masculine.

Ghost stories present the masculine and the feminine in culturally familiar ways, regardless of whether the characters in the story are human or spectral. Consider the following three supernatural narratives linking men to violence. The first legend, from the Indiana State University Folklore Archives (ISUFA), is told by

Jerry, a forty-eight-year-old white male coal miner. He talks about a place he knows near Bruceville, Indiana[1]:

> There's a stump down in Willow Hollow that has been there for years. On that stump, a man cut his wife's head off, and you can still see the cut in the stump from the ax. If you go through Willow Hollow at night on the night of the murder, you can see the woman looking for her head. But don't try to chase her because now she has the ax! (ISUFA 1996c)

Michelle, a nineteen-year-old white woman from Selma, Indiana, tells the second legend. She heard this ghost story at slumber parties; it is associated with the well-known childhood ritual, often simply referred to as "Bloody Mary," which is discussed in chapter 1:

> There once was this girl named Mary, and she had a slumber party and invited her girlfriends to come over. She also had a boyfriend, so she invited him over, too. Well, legend has it that when Mary's boyfriend came over, both of them went in this room and started messing around. As they were messing around, Mary's boyfriend took out a knife and stabbed Mary to death. Legend says if you are at a slumber party and at the strike of midnight with the lights out say "Bloody Mary" twelve times, Mary's ghost will appear. (ISUFA 1993a)

The Bloody Mary legend was popular with many African American teenagers, both male and female, whom I taught in folklore workshops in Indiana. For example, Lamar, an African American teenager, told this version of Bloody Mary:

> The story began because this lady named Mary was really pretty. In a way you can say that she was conceited. Nobody liked her because she kept to herself. She didn't love anyone but herself and her baby. She loved her baby dearly and didn't want anything to happen to it, so she rarely left the house except for when she needed to go to

the market. When she went to the market, no one ever said anything to her. All of the men liked her, but she wouldn't give them a chance.

So one day she was going to the market and some guys dragged her down an alley and raped her. She tried to get away, but they killed her as her baby laid crying. Then they killed the baby. The guys ran off and were never caught. They eventually got what they deserved.

Remember, Mary always looked in the mirror, and that's where she rests now. She tries to get revenge on everyone who dares to look in a mirror and say her name. That's how her killers got what they deserved: she killed them all because they killed her, but they didn't kill her soul.

Ollie, an African American male teenager, related a simpler version of the story, omitting how Bloody Mary got into the mirror but maintaining that if someone puts his or her hands on the mirror, "She will pull you into the mirror; she will kill you by decapitation." Rashonda, an African American female teenager, knew a version similar to Lamar's. She said, "For her vanity she was kind of punished because her soul is trapped in the mirror. . . . If you are in a completely dark room with a mirror and call her name three to five times, she will appear and cut you. But if you do the same and tell her you have her baby, she will kill you. . . . I have different feelings about this legend. . . . I myself do not have an explanation for how this story got started. It could be easy to say that someone made it up, but why would they go through all that trouble?"

All three stories present men and women in situations of violence, with men as the aggressors and women as the victims. These gender roles and behaviors generally reflect what we see in everyday life, with the exception of what the female character does after she's victimized: she becomes a Deviant Femme, which is discussed in more detail in the next section. However, this section focuses on masculine violence. Both the first Bloody Mary legend and the ax story are about domestic violence; the decapitation in the first story is more dramatic than many violent acts in the home, but it encapsulates, with symbolic economy, the pain and destruction of domestic violence and makes the story memorable enough to be told and retold. Both legends dovetail with the reality that the American home is one of the most dangerous places for women and children. Sociologists say that it may be the most violent American institution, with the exception of the military in time of war (Kimmel 2000, 258). In these two supernatural legends, human men initiate violence and direct it at women with whom they are intimate.

In the other two Bloody Mary stories, the woman is "punished" for characteristics that are frequently gendered "female": being too vain or too focused on or protective of her child. She is not interested in men, who then engage in extreme violence, rape, and murder to punish her for her rejection of them. Rashonda raises the question about why people go through all the trouble of narrating these stories. Often we do so because they are meaningful to us. They work differently for us at various stages in life (e.g., chapter 4 on children and ghost stories), but as chapter 1 argues, they reflect cultural and personal issues. Bloody Mary legends express significant issues, including gender-role pressures along with fears of violence and sexuality. The last two Bloody Mary versions can be understood as cautionary tales about what happens to women who deviate from the norm, reject men (heterosexuality), or who get too caught up in themselves or their children. Not only is the woman victimized by the men but she, like the men, also goes on to hurt others in extreme and dramatic ways: stabbing, decapitation, murder.

These ghostly depictions mirror a too-common social pattern of male violence and domestic violence. Some research indicates that women also use violence in intimate relationships, but at nowhere near the same rates or severity. Statistics from the U.S. Department of Justice reveal that women undergo more than ten times as many incidents of violence by intimates than do men: "On average, women experienced about 575,000 violent victimizations, compared with about 49,000 for men. Perhaps it's a bit higher—perhaps as much as 3 percent to 4 percent of all spousal violence is committed by women according to criminologist

Martin Schwartz. . . . And when women are violent, they use the least violent tactics and the most violent ones. Women shove, slap and kick . . . but they also use guns almost as often as men do" (Kimmel 2000, 261).

In both the Willow Hollow and Bloody Mary legends, the female apparitions, though they are victims themselves, also become villains as well. They engage in threatening and violent acts: the first woman chases people with an ax, and the second haunts mirrors, stabs, decapitates, and murders those who disturb her. Interestingly, the female ghost's use of violence parallels what criminologists say about women and violence. In the first Bloody Mary version, the woman uses the least violent route—intimidation. In the Willow Hollow story she uses the most violent tactic—the weapon her husband used to murder her. The spectral woman in the other Bloody Mary versions also resorts to violent acts. At any rate, woman as victim, villain, or both are common roles in these supernatural legends. These roles may be reflective of the negative associations and low status historically accorded the female gender.

Research indicates that domestic situations in which power is concentrated in the hands of a man leads to a greater likelihood of any type of violence, whether against women or men. Kersti Yllö (2004) found that men are more likely to use domestic violence instrumentally: for terrorizing women to obtain compliance and passive acceptance of the male's rule in the domestic situation. Women's violence tends to be less routine and systematic; women are more apt to use violence expressively (to express frustration or anger) or defensively. The female violence in all these stories is expressive and responsive. The narratives show the female ghosts acting threateningly or violently in response to the brutality that they experience. Female violence is statistically unusual, but some ghost stories tend to focus on and play up dramatic female violence—just like the mass media does with its sensational replaying of accounts of female violence in everyday life.

In Bloody Mary legends, men are not only violent abusers but also sexual predators. A common assumption in contemporary

Western culture is that men find it more difficult to control their sex drives than women. History reveals that in earlier eras, such as the fifteenth century, women—not men—were thought to have this problem. For example, *The Malleus Mallificarum* (a handbook of witchcraft persecution) posits that women are the chief doers of evil; the reason is "carnal lust, which is in women insatiable" (Summers 1971, 47). Now the view is reversed; the stereotype is that men can't control their sexual urges. However, as Peggy Reeves Sanday says in her classic cross-cultural study of rape, "It is not that men are necessarily prone to rape; rather, where interpersonal violence is a way of life, violence frequently achieves sexual expression" (2000, 65; see also Scully 1990). These historical shifts (along with actual cultural studies such as Sanday's) remind us that many notions about gender are rooted in custom and stereotypes—and not in biology.

The Bloody Mary legends not only link sexuality and violence but one version also points directly to the fact that adolescent girls too often face violence at the hands of their boyfriends, a danger that schools and sociological literature are recently giving significant attention (Wiseman 2002, 269–75).[2] The traditional notion that sexual expression is dangerous for women and should be feared is apparent in the story. Also, the woman is punished for sexual behavior, which is a theme that shows up commonly in other legends (Brunvand 1989). These themes may be a reflection of the cultural double standard about sex: the stud-slut syndrome in which men are seen as "studs" when they engage in sex, whereas women run the risk of being seen as "sluts" for engaging in sex with the same men.

The point here is *not* that all men are violent; most are not. However, American culture commonly links masculinity with toughness or violence. According to sociologists, males learn early in their lives that violence is an acceptable form of conflict resolution and one that is often admired (Kimmel 2000, 10–11). Overly adhering to notions of masculinity that include violence as a solution is a type of exaggerated masculinity. The two stories about the ax and knife murders evince this type of extreme masculinity.[3] Ghost narratives evince the same tendencies associated with gender, such as violence as a kind of extreme masculinity, which can be found to some degree in everyday life and especially in crime stories in the mass media. Emphasis on extreme masculinity is a cultural *and* a narrative commonplace in the oral tradition and mass media.

Ghost legends mirror conflict and cultural stresses, and some are quite similar to mainstream news stories because they grow out of tragedy. Both ghost stories and news stories frequently focus on wronged parties, and sometimes both do so in ways that are revealing of cultural notions about gender. For example, the following supernatural legend reminds me of the Matthew Shepard murder in Wyoming in 1998, which was widely covered by news organizations. Shepard was an openly gay student who was abducted, beaten, tied to a fence, and left for dead by two young men he had met at a bar. He later died in a hospital. Candy, a twenty-three-year-old white factory worker in Indiana, tells about a cemetery that is haunted, and she says the story is based in real-life violence:

> Shiloh is haunted. I'm serious. A guy was murdered there, and he chases people away from the cemetery. I have heard several stories, but I will tell you the one I heard from my dad.
>
> Two guys in a truck were out cruising one night, and they picked up a hitchhiker. Well, this guy turned out to be gay, and these two guys really hated gays. Anyway, this guy started making passes at them, and they got mad. They took him over to Shiloh and made him take off his clothes. They killed him and dumped the body off an overpass on 74.
>
> The police found the bloody clothes in the attic of one of the guy's house. He was arrested and taken to court, but the court set him free. The police had failed to get a search warrant before going to the house. Ever since then, no one has been able to get into Shiloh. They say it is because the ghost came back to protect the cemetery from any other violence. (ISUFA 1993b)

This legend again reflects the American association of masculinity and violence, but the ghost story also gives us a gay image of masculinity. In a sense, the story feminizes the gay man when he was alive. Just like women who are deemed to be "asking" for rape, his behavior (he is depicted as making a pass at the murderers) is presented as a sort of excuse for the crime. Just like the she-was-asking-for-it defense, this kind of argument has no real credibility, but the use of this "excuse" is not exclusive to the story; it comes from the world of the living. The gay ghost is an interesting male figure because he complicates the picture of masculinity that supernatural legends commonly present. He is frightening, protective, admirable, and heroic—the last three are characteristics of a positive type of masculinity—in his purported wish to protect the cemetery from further violence. This story also reflects an old "wronged party" motif: the ghost who cannot rest until his killers are brought to justice. With its focus on a gay man denied justice, this legend is also topically timely; it appears during the conflict generated as gays and lesbians seek civil and legal rights, such as marriage.

Just as most men are not murderers, abusers, or rapists, ghost stories such as the aforementioned also present alternatives to violent masculinity. Spectral narratives sometimes depict men who are kind and loving. A loving (but powerless) male can be discerned in a legend told by Tracy, a twenty-seven-year-old white female teacher:

> Near Odon, Indiana, is a graveyard that has partially sunken into the ground. The story behind this goes that a young man was just married to a young woman. The day after the wedding, he was feeding his cattle when the herd stampeded and killed him. So they buried him in this graveyard. After a time his widow remarried. She got married to an abusive husband. This caused the spirit of her [first] husband, who had been so happy in life to be with the woman he loved, to collapse, which in turn caused the graveyard to sink. (ISUFA 1995c)

Men of violence and men of compassion exist in the world of the corporeal; they also inhabit the world presented in ghost stories. This narrative presents the abusive male, but this vision of exaggerated masculinity is tempered with the spirit of the loving husband, who represents a nurturing masculinity. Ghost stories reflect male roles that can be found in life. Both good guys and bad guys exist in the corporeal realm, so both visions of masculinity exist in the spectral realm as well. However, the nurturing male is less dramatic—and therefore perhaps less memorable—than the Extreme Guy.

THE DEVIANT FEMME: LA LLORONA AND SCARY MARY

Given the long history of violence against women, it's not surprising that women appear as victims in ghost stories. What is perhaps more interesting is the propensity for women to appear as villainous or deviant in ghost stories. These are women who flagrantly failed basic Angel-in-the-House training. Their house may have also been a dangerous place for them, or they may have mental illnesses or criminal tendencies. The Willow Hollow story in the previous section shows what happens when you give this type of Angel in the House an ax: you get a woman with Lizzie Borden tendencies. This is a kind of deviance that can be found in the human world on a small scale, but the level of interest in it is high, as the media attention it garners attests. The very anomalousness of women in this role fascinates us. The appearance of the deviant woman in supernatural narratives reflects the fascination with these same women in life. Just as an unsavory, violent masculine extreme is depicted in ghost stories, a frightening female extreme is manifest in them as well.

Of course, not all the women in supernatural narratives are deviant. For example, many memorates exist about family members, such as mothers who return from the dead in a positive and comforting fashion (see Jo Ann's account in chapter 1). The role of mother as caregiver is one of the most common roles ascribed to women, so perhaps, culturally, few things shock us more than when a mother harms instead of nurtures. Just as the news media produces a plethora of stories about murderous mothers, such as Susan Smith who drowned her two sons in 1994 in a South Carolina lake or Andrea Yates in Texas who drowned her five children in the bathtub of the family home in 2001, so too does the oral supernatural tradition. For example, in her study of Appalachian singer and storyteller Bessie Eldreth, Patricia Sawin notes that the female ghosts in Eldreth's stories violate "women's specific roles as wives and mothers" (2004, 111), which includes murdering their children.

This type of Deviant Femme is prominent in the La Llorona, or weeping woman, legend cycle. Denise, a Mexican American college student from Idaho, describes how this story is told in her family:

> My mom remembers the stories of La Llorona as if it were part of family history. She comments about how as a child my grandmother would never let them leave the house after dark because La Llorona would come to get them. She doesn't really remember understanding this as a child, but she remembers everyone knew this. As she got older, she too would have her time to teach this tradition to her children. As my mom recalls she is called "La Llorona," which translates in English to "the weeping woman," because of her cries at night.
>
> The general legend is that there was a beautiful Native American girl. A handsome man came riding into town and ended up marrying her. She had a child or maybe two or three; no one is really quite sure. When her husband left her, she threw her children into the river out of madness. When she realized what she had done, she ran after her children. The next day she was found dead on the river bank. They buried her, but that night they heard a shrieking cry of "*AIIIEEE mis hijos*," which means, "Oh, my children!" Legend has it that she wanders the river at night looking for her children. Parents warned their children that if they were out late at the

river at night La Llorona might mistake them for her own children and take them.

Denise says that her mother would always tell her children this story as they were growing up: "She would tell my younger brother and me this story when we were not behaving and wanted to go out late at night to play. She would tell it to us more as younger kids because we always believed things that my mother would say." Ironically, Denise's mother tells the story to her children to remind them to obey her and also to draw their attention to the dangers existing in the world *outside* of—instead of inside of—the family. Denise's mother, Florentina, uses this ghost story about a deviant woman to get her children to change their desires and actions; she employs it to encourage good behavior. The story's message is *don't be out late* and *don't go down by the river.* Also, both in the way the story functions for Denise and in the rendering of La Llorona in the legend, the story serves to underline the power women have over their children.

Denise continues with a story about La Llorona from her father, whom she describes in the following fashion: "My father's persona is one that when he talks, you listen. You never really doubt the words that come from his mouth, especially those relating to personal experience. He is an honest man." Denise's father, Gustavo, is Mexican American, a mechanic, and a restaurateur with his wife in Franklin, Idaho. This is Denise's account of his story:

> Everyone hears different sides to the legends. Even at my home where both of my parents grew up in the same hometown, they have a different legend to tell about La Llorona. If you ask my father about the legend that comes with the name La Llorona, he will give you a completely different version than my mother; you would think that they were speaking about different legends. My father remembers my grandfather warning them to never sneak out at night for La Llorona would take custody of them. La Llorona appeared to young men who roamed about at night. The young men believed that she was a young, beautiful woman, but when they approached her with

sexual intent in mind, she would appear to them as a hag or a terrible image of death personified.

My father was always very rebellious and would wait until my grandparents were asleep to sneak out to neighboring towns and go to parties and such. He remembers that to get to the town of Totolmajach [Mexico] you would have to cross this bridge, and he would always think about the legend of La Llorona and how it wasn't true. There was this one night that he had gone out partying and was coming home. . . . It was around 4 a.m., and he was crossing the bridge, remembering the supposed idiotic tale of La Llorona, when he says he heard this [high] pitched scream. He says it almost sounded like a banshee shrieking. He remembers looking and not seeing anything. He started running, but the scream kept getting louder as if they were getting closer to him. . . . As soon as he got across the bridge, the screams seemed as if they weren't getting any closer until they finally just stopped. He says he never looked back, just kept running until he was steps from home, "I know I was drunk, but the scare was enough to sober me up. I ran faster than I have ever run before in my life. To this day, I refuse to go on that bridge alone. I know that if I would have turned around, I would have seen that devil or La Llorona chasing after me." My father swears by this night and that it was La Llorona coming for him, and so to this day he accepts the tale of La Llorona.

As Denise points out, these two narratives demonstrate that legends about well-known supernatural figures, such as La Llorona, exist in multiple versions. Both stories told in her family work as cautionary tales about the dangers in the world. Even though some ghost stories depict dangerous family members, they often relocate that danger outside the home (for example, down by the river or out in Willow Hollow).[4]

Florentina uses the story to shape her children's behaviors, and Gustavo's parents also used the story as a means to affect the behavior of their son. In a fashion similar to the first Bloody Mary version in this chapter, Gustavo's story about La Llorona functions as a sexual cautionary tale. However, in this case it warns men about female sexuality and the dangers of women, which is indicated metaphorically by the beautiful woman turning into a hag or "death personified." Also it suggests that a sexual encounter with a young and beautiful woman could end up in a confrontation with an aging woman, a hag, which may be a symbolic comment about youth, beauty, and sex leading one into a marriage that ends in aging and death. This is also a manifestation of the old linkage between woman, sexuality, and death (Thomas 2003, 55).[5]

Another deviant image of women in ghost stories, which is drawn from real-life events and demonstrates common cultural views about women, is exemplified by another story from Jerry, the Indiana coal miner, about a woman named "Scary Mary":

> Mary was an elderly widow that lived on the outskirts of Bicknell, Indiana. She lived in an old, brick, beaten-down, one-story house that was engulfed in a mass of trees, bushes, and weeds. Mary would seldom leave the house, but when she did, it was always at night. She would carry an oil lantern to light her way through the brush. They say she would look for her cat that had disappeared some time before. Now that she is dead, they say you can still see the lantern light floating through the brush even though her house is torn down. Many people frequent this site trying to see the lantern.
>
> One night about a year after the house was destroyed, a group of teenagers went to Scary Mary's to drink and fool around. One young girl saw the light of Mary's lantern and drifted away from the group to investigate without mentioning what she had seen to the others. The group was startled when the girl tore through the brush, screaming and yelling, and quickly opened the door of one of the cars and begged the others to leave Mary's. The others searched through the brush, but nothing was found. The girl, crying hysterically, said that she had

seen Mary wandering through the brush wearing a black veil and carrying a lantern. That girl never went back to Scary Mary's again. (ISUFA 1996b)

This account mentions a legend trip; the teens in this story go to Scary Mary's house "to drink and fool around." The story depicts an anomalous place where the usual rules of society have been suspended some way. In this case, a Deviant Femme lived in the house. The teens then go to this place to escape some of the rules and control of society; such sites become good places for them to engage in underage drinking and explore sexuality.

While the Extreme Guy is typically violent, the Deviant Femme does not have to engage in violence to be deviant. Scary Mary is a deviant woman primarily because she is a woman alone, without a man. Her behavior is not all that strange, although like witches, she is associated with a cat. There are other legends, some supernatural and some not, about such women, and their behavior is merely eccentric. They keep scores of cats, for example. Some of these stories exist about men, although I have not encountered as many supernatural legends that focus on the *man being alone* as a primary reason he is frightening. Instead, he often engages in threatening behavior. When the lone, eccentric woman becomes the subject of a supernatural legend, in some cases the story behind her strange behaviors does not get told. The oral tradition merely recounts her strange actions.

Sometimes narratives about a real-life, eccentric women are enough to lend the shadow of the supernatural to situations that are simply more weird than paranormal. The Winchester Mystery House in San Jose, California, is a case in point. Members of the mass media sometimes refer to it as "America's most haunted house." Situated in Silicon Valley, it seems kitschily out of place in that high-tech land of the sleek and smart. Yet, like Silicon Valley itself, the house is a monument to what capitalism and technology can build. A group of private investors renovated the house in the 1970s, and today an admission fee buys a visitor a guided tour of the mansion. Basic tours typically focus more on stories of Sarah Winchester's eccentricities than accounts of contemporary paranormal activities in the house.

FIGURE 1: Spider web window panes, Winchester Mystery House. San Jose, California. (Photo by Jeannie Banks Thomas)

Winchester was heiress to the fortune her husband's family made from Winchester gun sales. She began round-the-clock construction on the house in 1884, which finally stopped after thirty-eight years, when she died. The story goes that, traumatized by the early death of her only child and the later death of her husband, she consulted a medium who informed her that she was cursed because of all the deaths caused by the guns that made her husband wealthy. To appease the spirits, the medium told her to embark on the construction of a house that would never be finished. Perhaps, at least to some degree, the house embodies the old folk notion that one way to keep a ghost from returning to and haunting a house is to confuse it by changing things around in the household. Winchester's house may be the epitome of this idea; she created a house that could confuse anyone, living or dead. Architecturally, the Winchester Mystery House also moves easily from the somewhat spooky to the blatantly quirky with its unfinished ballrooms, spider web window panes (figure 1), room for nightly séances, and its obsession with both the number thirteen and daisies.

I embarked on the guided tour of the Winchester Mystery House in the summer of 2005. I wondered if the experience would be similar to a ghost tour (see chapter 6), but it was not. I wondered if the tour would present the mansion as a haunted house (see chapter 5), but it did not. The tour guide did not relate the kind of supernatural legends commonly told on ghost tours and also associated with haunted houses.Instead the house is actually somewhere in between a haunted house and something one might see on a ghost tour. Its official title, "Winchester Mystery House," alludes accurately to its in-between status. However, specifically, it's the house of a Deviant Femme.

Joining me on the Winchester Mystery House tour were my six-year-old son (who was a little nervous that we might encounter ghosts on the way), my ten-year-old daughter (who was disappointed that we didn't), and my game but sardonic sister (who jokingly muttered that the real mystery of the Winchester Mystery House was why we paid so much to see it). What was striking to me was that during the sixty-five-minute tour of 110 of the 160 rooms in "America's most haunted house," the tour guide did not mention *a single* ghost story. The Winchester ghosts remain not only invisible but also anonymous. The tour narrative instead focused on the curious facts of the house and on Sarah Winchester, who was a veritable diva of deviance.

The tour emphasized stories relating Winchester's penchant for peculiar architecture. The gift shop also focuses on the house, with lots of cute refrigerator magnets of the Victorian-mansion-gone-wild and much less attention accorded the supernatural. However, in an oblique nod to the nineteenth-century spiritualism that held Winchester so in its thrall, the gift shop also houses an out-of-context row of mostly new machines of the sort that used to be found carnivals, which commodify and simplify spiritualism and mediums. These gift shop machines took our money and told us how romantic we were and what kind of personalities we had. Our quarters also activated the unseen forces in a cemetery scene, and brought to life the fortune-teller in a glass case who spit out proverbial fortunes on sturdy cards (figure 2). Just as we were reaching for our fortune,

FiGURE 2: Mechanical fortune teller, Winchester
Mystery House. San Jose, California. (Photo by
Jeannie Banks Thomas)

a Hispanic family passed behind us. The father, noticing that we
were getting a fortune, humorously supplied the voice-over for
the silent fortune teller: "Build another room! My brother is the
contractor!" This blend of goofiness, kitsch, and eccentricity—
with a just dash of the supernatural thrown in—is what makes
the mansion what it is.

My experience of the Winchester Mystery House was typical;
when I ask others who've taken the tour what its focus was, they

often simply say "a crazy lady." The mansion is to the classic, haunted Victorian house (as described in chapter 5) as a group of Las Vegas Elvis impersonators is to Elvis himself: not quite the real thing, though managing to capture some of the essence of the real—while going way over the top in the process. The aptly named "mystery" (instead of "haunted") house generates its small bit of spooky capital these days by playing up Sarah Winchester as a Deviant Femme. Because the Deviant Femme is a common figure in ghost stories, emphasizing her in the Winchester story generates more uncanny feelings than does architecture alone. The supernatural has marketing cachet, so the Winchester Mystery House attracts some of its paying customers by relying not only on its appeal as a roadside attraction (an architectural oddity) but also through its emphasis on Winchester as a deviant woman who believed in ghosts. The latter allows for a kind of supernatural slippage; the Deviant Femme lends herself to generating an eerie (and hence even more marketable) aura around the Winchester Mystery House.

Winchester made the house in her own odd image. She was not the Angel in the House, but she was the Eccentric in the House. Her radical variance from the feminine norm of the era was expressed in her highly visible and deviant architectural flair. She created a house that was literally dysfunctional—that is, its parts did not function as they should. For example, the house has doors and staircases that lead nowhere (figure 3).

Winchester's séances and worries about ghosts, along with her personal eccentricities, are enough today to bolster the claims that this strange house is haunted. The common linkage of female deviance to the supernatural in ghost stories helps make Winchester's real-life deviance that much more spooky. While it's possible to find some paranormal tales associated with it (Moran and Sceurman 2004, 165), in general the reality is that the mansion is not much of a haunted house—it's an eccentric's house. However, in 2002, popular culture finally turned the Winchester Mystery House into a bona fide haunted house. Stephen King gave the mansion a full supernatural makeover, turning it into a fictional entity known as "Rose Red" which is

FIGURE 3: The oft-photographed staircase leading to nowhere demonstrates the mansion's dysfunctional qualities,
Winchester Mystery House. San Jose, California. (Photo
by Jeannie Banks Thomas)

crammed with ghosts (see chapter 5 for more on the televised
miniseries *Rose Red*).

Narratives about Deviant Femmes, such as La Llorona and
Scary Mary—along with the marketing uses to which stories
about eccentric women such as Sarah Winchester are put—all
indicate our fascination with odd women. We often populate
our supernatural narratives with women who represent a deviant

kind of femininity and men who embody an extreme masculinity with some stories depicting less extreme, more normal, and more nurturing human behaviors. In other words, in predictable ways we project the everyday—especially those parts of it that are dramatic—onto the numinous. The mass media both feeds off of and feeds into this legend process and the images of gender that accompany it. Today, Coventry Patmore's "Angel in the House" lacks currency as a trope in contemporary literature. However, the oral tradition's Deviant Femme is harder to kill. Not only is she a current figure in ghost stories but she is also engaging enough that she generates profit for moneymaking groups, such as the one that owns the Winchester Mystery House. From a marketing standpoint, the Deviant Femme has put the Angel right out of house, home, and business.

The Genderless Presence: Poltergeists and Ghost Cars

When a child costumes as a ghost for Halloween, the outfit is often simple: a white sheet with eyeholes. This image of the ghost eradicates gender, just as do some types of ghost stories. As the previous section indicates, clear gender patterns can be discerned when one examines ghost stories from the oral tradition. However, another pattern also emerges: ghosts have less to say about gender than humans do. That is, if we look at the larger body of ghost narratives, gender is less an issue in the ghostly world than it is in ours. In some ghost stories, gender either doesn't matter much to the story line or the ghost is not gendered at all. Gender matters to the living because it proscribes and affects behaviors. Kimmel says, "Gender, we now know, is one of the axes around which social life is organized and through which we understand our own experiences" (2000, 5). The Genderless Presence is the most radical take on gender that ghost stories give us.

Historically, people recognized many different types of ghosts and had terms for them—fetches, doppelgangers, bogeys, and poltergeists. Today, if I ask my students to define these terms, the majority of them recognize only one of the terms: poltergeist. "A poltergeist is literally a 'noisy spirit.' The term is used to describe an outbreak of unexplained events that is commonly ascribed to the actions of occult beings" (George 1995, 223). My students may be more familiar with this type of ghost because of its ubiquity in both the oral tradition and popular culture, particularly the *Poltergeist* movies. Also, in some ways, poltergeists are a more frightening type of ghost because they are active and also disembodied. They are not visible; rather, their presence is manifest by their impact on other things.

Archie Neil Chisholm collected several poltergeist stories in Cape Breton, Canada. The story that follows provides a good illustration of how gender appears in poltergeist accounts. In the story, a powerful, older "gentleman" and soldier desires the wife of his younger neighbor. The younger neighbor also has a small child and a handsome pair of boots. The older gentleman is heard to say, "It will not be too long before I will have those boots, and they'll be under the widow's bed while I am in the widow's bed." Unfortunately, the young husband gets in a "pinkie," an early kind of coastal boat, with the older man. The older man returns to shore alone, saying that the younger man drowned and left his boots behind in the boat. Several months pass, and the older man marries his neighbor's widow. He also wears the younger man's boots, which he places under the widow's bed each night. Strange kicking noises begin to be heard in the house, and every day, the boots are moved from underneath the bed.

> Mabou [on Cape Breton Island] was just in the process of being opened up for settlement so, about 1792, the couple moved to the village of Mabou. . . . For the first six months things went pretty well, but after that things really began to happen. Boots again began to move around the house, noises were heard upstairs and downstairs, and the first child born to the young woman and the veteran had a very curious birthmark, in the middle of his chest in the shape of a boot.
>
> So the couple decided that perhaps they should no longer live in this spot, and they moved from there to a

place further out, away from what came to be known as
Mabou Village.

Things did not go well with them. A number of sudden deaths of young children in their family occurred.
They were able, however, to give their crown lease to a
land speculator who came from Halifax. He lived on the
property for about six months and decided he had heard
enough knocks and bumps and groans in the night, and
seen enough strange lights. He decided to sell the property, but before he was able to do so, he drowned, very near
to the present entrance of Mabou Harbor [figure 4].

The property remained mostly vacant for some years
with various people living there off and on. There never
seemed to be much success for anybody who lived there.

The next family to acquire the property settled some
distance away from the "noisy" spot where no crops would
grow, but that family too has had its share of misfortunes:
a number of very sudden deaths including a drowning.

There seems somehow to have been a continuing
curse on the particular piece of property that may go all
the way back to a young man with a new pair of boots and
a very beautiful wife. (Chisholm 2000, 102–4)

Instead of a spectral figure, the story makes the young husband's
presence known though the activities of the boots and then the
knocks, groans, and strange lights. The story progresses from the
corporeal and material to the ethereal. It moves from man to
boots to strange noises and lights, thus progressively eliminating
the ghost's more human attributes, such as form and gender.

Poltergeists are an old type of ghost story: the Roman historian Livy speaks of them, and Martin Luther tells of a poltergeist
encounter that involved a noisy sack of nuts. John Wesley, the
founder of Methodism, credulously "endured two months of knock-
ings and groanings of no known origin; although a small animal
like a badger or rabbit, 'which seems likely to be some witch,' was
spotted in the house" (George 1995, 223). Alan Gauld and A. D.
Cornell (1979) surveyed 500 poltergeist cases reported since 1800.

FIGURE 4: Mabou Harbor, another everyday space which figures in a poltergeist story. Cape Breton, Nova Scotia. (Photo by Jeannie Banks Thomas)

They found that most outbreaks last between two weeks and two months. The most frequently reported feature is the movement of small objects, such as the boots in the Cape Breton story. The mysterious disappearance or reappearance of small objects is common, as well as sounds of unknown origins. However, gendered, humanlike apparitions are not prominent in poltergeist stories.

Some poltergeist stories eliminate the link to the human world altogether and do not detail the origins of the poltergeist. My own family history contains one such poltergeist story, which happened several generations back. Unlike the Mabou account, this story does not explain the origins of the haunting or link it to a human form, so gender is entirely eliminated in this story. This poltergeist briefly haunted a tavern (figure 5); today the building is a museum in Georgetown, Massachusetts. The poltergeist activity centered on a chest:

Upon entering the old Tavern Room, one encounters a restored "walk-in" fireplace which is said to be one of the largest in New England. The "Haunted Meal Chest" sits against one wall of the same room. Local legend holds that a young servant girl found that the large meal chest moved mysteriously whenever her skirt brushed up against it. The phenomenon lasted only a few weeks but made a lasting impression on all who witnessed it. The chest, which had passed hands to the House of Seven Gables in Salem was returned to its original hometown in the 1970s. (Georgetown Historical Society 2005)

Many poltergeist outbreaks occur in the presence of a particular person, as is the case with the "Haunted Meal Chest." Occasionally the poltergeist leaves pinch marks, bruises, or scratches on the person. Theories abound for poltergeist activity that centers around a person, ranging from assertions that the focal person (or perhaps really the person who proposes the hypothesis!) is "seething with unexpressed sexuality (not an atypical condition for an adolescent)"; to "psi fields," energy purported to radiate from a person; to hoaxes, which are notoriously easy conjure up in association with poltergeists (George 1995, 224).

Whatever their origins, poltergeists are particularly frightening because of their formlessness and unpredictability. Even more amorphous than other types of ghosts, they can be especially aggressive. It's not surprising that we often try to add some order or logic to poltergeist stories by linking them to a human body in some sort of backstory, which explains the haunting. For instance, the first story linked the poltergeist to the drowned young neighbor; the haunted meal chest legend links the poltergeist to a servant. Also, other forms (the boots, the meal chest) associated with poltergeists assume prominence in the narratives. The poltergeist is formless, but materiality of some sort is often important to the story. So, in narratives, we often link the poltergeist to some material manifestation, which is somewhat less troubling than a being that is not tethered to form. Although the supernatural is an ethereal realm, we continually tie it to the

FIGURE 5: Brocklebank House, home to a haunted meal chest and a poltergeist. Georgetown, Massachusetts. (Photo by Jeannie Banks Thomas)

real and the material. The earlier stories' use of gendered bodies (the legends with Extreme Guys and Deviant Femmes) is part of this impulse. In poltergeist stories, we can't see these disembodied ghosts, so we focus on the forms we can see.

Along with poltergeists, other types of genderless ghosts exist in the oral tradition.

A friend of mine, Allison, once told me a memorate about another kind of disembodied being. Allison is of Kiowa, Northern Cheyenne, and Creek descent, and she has ties through family members to the Pine Ridge Reservation in South Dakota. She and her husband at the time were there, driving on a deserted reservation road, and they encountered a ghost car:

> Let me see, yes, the ghost car was in South Dakota, and we were driving at night from a powwow. It was late and the full moon was out, which made it easy to see the road. As

we were driving, we went over a rise and noticed a set of headlights way behind us; this was unusual but we ignored it. We drove on and in no time those same headlights were right on our tail, and they followed us a good ways.

My husband at the time, who was white, freaked out and said, "Who the hell is that, and what are they trying to do?" He began to panic because the faster we went, the faster the car went behind us.

I told him not to panic and to keep his eyes on the road, as I figured it was the ghost car that one hears about on all the reservation roads. At any rate, the ghost car now rode alongside with us; my husband wanted to look into the car window, and I told him not to because I knew he would run off the road.

I, however, turned my head slowly, and there was no one in the car, not a soul. As we went through all the winding roads of the reservation, out of the blue it disappeared. Needless to say my husband was never the same after that; he was petrified and talked for months about what happened. My son was with us at the time and was a little boy, five or six years old. He witnessed the whole event and was in the back seat on his knees looking right at the ghost car and saying, "What are they doing, Mom?"

I told my ex-sister-in-law who lived in Pine Ridge [on the reservation] about the incident, and she said it was in fact a ghost car and that they had intended to run us off the road because it was a white man driving, but they probably decided not to run us off the road because they saw the *wakanyeja* (Indian child) in the backseat and so disappeared.

This narrative is rich in the kind of cultural meaning discussed in chapter 1. First, it takes place in Indian country after a cultural event, a powwow, a pan-tribal social dance gathering. The locale of the incident is near historically significant sites of ethnic conflict and tragedy; the Wounded Knee massacre took place in 1890 not far from where Allison encounters the ghost car.[6] Wounded Knee and the Pine Ridge area are also famous as a staging ground for clashes between members of the American Indian Movement (AIM) and the FBI during the 1970s. The assertion that the ghost car wants to run a white driver off the road reflects Native-white tensions, which have been particularly pronounced in this region.

The story also indicates the traditional value and power of children in Lakota culture: the ex-sister-in-law talks about the presence of Allison's young son as a saving grace. In the word *wakanyeja,* the root *wakan* means "sacred," which is an indication of how important children are.[7] The existence of the ghost car in the oral tradition also points to both the tragic number of highway deaths in the area and the importance of the car in contemporary life. This story is an example of the mingling of the technological and supernatural that is part of today's ghost stories. Because Allison is familiar with the ghost-car tradition, she keeps calm and helps her then-husband avoid the siren appeal of gazing too long at the faceless unknown, which could lead to disaster.

In addition to the rich cultural context and meanings, however, is the fact that one of the most eerie elements of this story is the manner in which it depicts the impact of a disembodied presence on the physical world of the living. Ghosts don't unsettle us by wreaking havoc with and mixing up our gender constructions but instead by playing with our notions of corporeality. So we give even these most evasive of ghosts form through words and stories. Like Allison and her family, we turn these events over in our minds, wondering what they have to tell us.

The Genderless Presence is a common, if amorphous, part of the corpus of supernatural narratives. Other examples of it include accounts of people feeling some sort of a presence or a cold spot in a room, for example. Sometimes the Genderless Presence is merely felt and sometimes it is described as feeling comforting or threatening. Its meaning is variable and elusive. The Genderless Presence repudiates culture by offering the possibilities of a realm were gender does not matter. Such a world exists only in our stories and not in our lived experience.

The Extreme Guy and the Deviant Femme replicate cultural notions about gender that we see in the media and in daily life.

The Genderless Presence does not mirror daily life as readily. These beings without bodies present us with a world without gender—something that is not easily found outside the realm of the supernatural. Perhaps the Genderless Presence, depending upon the story, indicates some reaching toward, horror of, or recognition of states of being other than gendered ones.

In this chapter, I trace the workings of gender in supernatural narratives and argue that common patterns emerge. Some of these patterns mirror realities found in the world around us; however, the pattern of the Genderless Presence does not. Pondering *why* this notable split between reflecting and *not* reflecting everyday life exists in ghost stories reminds me of experiences I had at the house of a childhood friend. All her bathroom walls were lined with mirrors. When I was in her bathroom, I could see my individual image. I could also see repeated images (and parts) of myself that were seemingly without end. Additionally, depending upon where I stood and what I did, I could see bits and pieces of myself doing impossible things. For example, if I stood a certain way and kicked my leg upwards, the mirrors doubled my leg and reflected it back to me as a two human legs connected to each other, an odd shape that defied both gravity and physiology.

Ghost stories are like this room of mirrors. They reflect clear images of us, and they also show us intriguing glimpses of other seemingly impossible states of being. So in supernatural narratives, reality—with its varying emphases on gender, wronged parties, Extreme Guys, or Deviant Femmes—can be reflected directly back to us. However, perhaps most interestingly of all, ghost stories also offer us a view into a radically reconfigured world in which gender does not matter. Whether that's a hell or a utopia or something else entirely is a question that specters leave for humans to answer.

FOUR

CHILDREN'S
GHOST STORIES

SYLVIA ANN GRIDER

Children's ghost stories are among the most popular and most durable traditional narratives in the United States. The formulaic and often silly ghost stories that children tell one another—not necessarily those that they learn from storybooks or adult story-tellers—are essentially different from the more threatening and psychologically disturbing tales appropriated by the mass media as plots for movies, TV exposés, and best-selling novels. Typical children's ghost stories are usually quite short, monoepisodic, and conclude with an incongruous and jokelike punch line.

The rollicking ghost stories in which most American children take delight at Halloween, slumber parties, and campouts are grounded in imagery of rotting corpses, dancing skeletons, and wandering souls which stretches back at least as far as medieval times. Early European literature and history are filled with tales of the unknown and the supernatural, including a threatening and macabre *dramatis personae* of evil spirits and wandering souls of the dead who menace the living.

Some of these narratives apparently filtered down from the adult level of society into the realm of childhood, the so-called "children's underground," resulting in a wide variety of traditional and highly formulaic stories about ghosts and other aspects of death and the supernatural that still circulate widely in the

United States. As this body of knowledge lodged in the worldview
of modern childhood, supernatural beings—especially ghosts,
vampires, and witches—lost many of their horrifying aspects and
instead became benign figures of amusement and derision. That
such ghoulish images have become entertainment for modern
children may seem perplexing at first glance, but is not really
surprising to those who have studied children's traditions. For
example, according to the most eminent chroniclers of modern
childhood, Iona and Peter Opie, "When children are about ten
years old they enter a period in which the outward material facts
about death seem extraordinarily funny. . . . Death, which when
they were younger they may have regarded as a frightening and
private subject, has now come out into the open. They have
found that it is still a long way off, and these songs are a sign
of their emancipation" (Opie 1959, 32–35). To "songs" I would
add "and stories." Today, most children tell ghost stories for their
own entertainment, which often paradoxically includes frightening one another. This chapter will survey the various types of
traditional ghost stories typically told by American children, as
well as their possible historical antecedents and the settings in
which children acquire and perform them.

DEFINITIONS AND BACKGROUND

The best way to determine what is and what is not a ghost story
is to get comfortable with the fuzzy, circular definition that children most often use, "A ghost story is about ghosts." To this emic
definition we can add "and witches, and haunted houses, and
monsters, and Frankenstein, and Dracula" almost ad infinitum.
In other words, in common usage today among children a ghost
story is any narrative which deals with the scary world of the
supernatural dead/undead.

Although they are not strictly categorized as being supernatural, monsters nevertheless occupy a key role among many children's "ghost stories." According to Marina Warner, "Monsters
have become children's best friends, alter egos, inner selves.
While the monster mania of the last few years has obviously

been fostered by commercial interests, it has also diagnosed an identification that children themselves willingly and enthusiastically accept" (1998, 15). The monsters are never described in children's oral ghost stories, which is one way that children can control their fear of these nightmarish creatures that lurk in their closets or under their beds. "And then there was this big old monster," is a typical reference in children's oral stories. The media, on the other hand, provide ample cartoonish and nonthreatening portrayals of monsters, ranging from the "wild things" of best-selling author and artist Maurice Sendak to Sully and his friends in the animated movie *Monsters, Inc.* (2001). The pre-verbal toddler in *Monsters, Inc.* is terrified of the monster who haunts her closet, but she refers to the cuddly Sully as "Kitty" and does not regard him as frightening at all.

Defining "ghost" (and its many synonyms—"specter," "phantom," "wraith," "revenant," "apparition," "shade," "spirit," and so on) is a bit more problematic. The metaphoric imagery of idiomatic spoken English further complicates the definition because we speak of having "a ghost of a chance," "ghostwriting" a manuscript, or "ghosts" on TV or computer screens. Amputees suffer from "phantom pain" and people are "haunted" by unpleasant memories. Traditional ghosts are frightening figures, the unwanted and wandering spirits or souls of the dead which come back to interact with, or haunt, the living. For most children, however, these supernatural beings simply *are*, invoking a Zen-like acceptance of them. Children frequently solve the problem of definition by drawing a picture of a ghost as a sheet-shrouded figure with two eye holes (and sometimes a mouth) floating in the air and saying, "Boo!"[1] These childish drawings, which appear regularly on Halloween greeting cards, party decorations, and such may represent vestiges of a venerable bit of cultural baggage that we have carried in our collective memories since the Black Death of the fourteenth century.

The bubonic plague which swept Europe and Asia was the most devastating catastrophe within human memory, and so many deaths changed the course of modern history. During the plague, hundreds of thousands of people died so quickly that the corpses stacked up faster than they could be buried, and the living were surrounded by the unburied and decaying dead. At the height of the plague, with the deaths of so many clergy, victims often were buried without receiving last rites and thus provided an undercurrent of fear of their wandering, malevolent souls among the terrified survivors. Bodies wrapped in burial shrouds were carried to burial grounds in individual caskets whenever possible, but the caskets were not buried with the corpses because they were reused over and over for the transport of plague victims. Art of the period is filled with images of burials of corpses wrapped in winding sheets (figure 1) as well as dancing skeletons cavorting with enshrouded, rotting corpses (figure 2). We can only assume that the images on which such art was based were familiar to the children who survived the plague.

The emotional core of a persistent plague that has lodged among contemporary children appears to be the ubiquitous winding sheet or shroud. This shroud memory may very well be the source for the contemporary image of the sheeted ghost of children's drawings and Halloween decorations. This possible connection between children's ghost stories and the plague is a reminder that even the seemingly most trivial of traditions may, in fact, preserve vestiges of our venerable shared human past.

Memories of the plague endure at many levels, so children's maintenance of burial shroud images as sheeted ghosts would not be inconsistent with other levels of cultural memory. There are first-person literary descriptions of the ravages of the plague, such as the writings of the Italian master Giovanni Boccaccio (1313–75) in the *Decameron*. In English literature, Thomas Dekker (1570?–1632), Samuel Pepys (1633–1703), and Daniel Defoe (1660–1731) all provided reliable descriptions of the plagues that swept across England, especially London. In architecture, the Duomo of Siena stands as a monument to the plague because so many artisans died in that city that the building was never finished. And according to local legend, the famous Oberammergau Passion Play originated as an attempt to assuage the epidemic.

FiGURE 1: Sixteenth-century painting of burials of shrouded plague victims. San Sebastian pierced by arrows that represent the plague is typical of the iconography that developed during this period. The tilted position of the head of the foreground figure with upraised arms indicates that he has just been stricken by plague. The bubo is visible on his neck. Note that corpses were buried in their shrouds; caskets were too valuable to bury. (Photo by permission of Walters Art Museum, 37.1995. *Saint Sebastian Interceding for the Plague Stricken.* Josse Lieferinxe, ca. 1500.)

FIGURE 2: Woodcut from a fifteenth-century book depicting skeletons dancing on the grave of a shrouded, rotten corpse. The iconography of this image may have influenced contemporary depictions on Halloween cards and other decorations. (Photo by permission of Wellcome Trust, Medical Photographic Library, L0006816. *Dance of Death*. Hartmann Schedel, 1493.)

Popular culture, too, perpetuates memories of the plague. For example, a persistent metatradition alleges that "Ring Around the Rosie" was originally a charm to ward off the plague. Popular articles by authors who are not historians or social scientists frequently appear in the press, online, and elsewhere which describe the pat but totally unsupported explanation of the children's rhyme along the lines that the ring stands for beads of the rosary or the markings on plague victims' bodies; posies represent the garlands of flowers that people wore to mask the smell of rotting corpses; ashes refer to the custom of burning the bodies of victims; and "all fall down" means everybody died. Such fanciful explanations have been categorically refuted by scholars from the online Urban Legends Reference Pages (2005) to folklorists Iona and Peter Opie, who lament, "This story has obtained such circulation in recent years it can itself be said to be epidemic" (1985, 221). They go on to point out that "those infected with the belief seem unperturbed" that there are no references to this rhyme in any of the contemporary accounts of the plague. The game and the rhyme may not have *originated* during an outbreak of the plague, but the metatradition explaining its content persists and with every telling reinforces for modern audiences, including children, the imagery of plague infection and death. Children throughout the world turn catastrophe and devastation into mimetic play: children play at being terrorists and drive-by shooters as well as "cops and robbers." With "Ring Around the Rosie," they turn the plague itself into play.

CHILDREN'S ORAL GHOST STORIES

The sense of awe and mystery that characterizes the renditions of so many adult and adolescent narratives about the supernatural is absent from the highly structured, artistic, and whimsical narrative performances of childhood. During my many years of research on the topic of children's ghost stories, I have observed that elementary school youngsters are sophisticated in the ways of Halloween and horror movies, but in their own storytelling sessions they attempt to keep the terror of the supernatural and the perverse under control by humor and parody.[2] Their favorite ghost stories involve liberal doses of fantasy and imagination rather than direct confrontation with the horrible, unknown, and unknowable. Other types of serious, genuinely frightening narratives—such as urban legends about ax murderers and escaped lunatics—are acquired later, after children have more command of basic literary narrative technique (including plot sequence and development as well as dramatic timing) and after they have begun to understand more of the fundamentals of the overall supernatural belief network and an awareness of some of the truly terrifying and threatening aspects of the everyday world. Telling urban legends about killers in the backseat and escaped mass murderers requires sophisticated dramatic technique and timing, as well as the ability to gauge and manipulate audience reaction. Learning to tell ghost stories is, for many children, the precursor to telling urban legends later. The formulaic, non-threatening content of traditional children's ghost stories makes them good beginning narratives for novice storytellers.

In their storytelling sessions, children maintain control of the level of fright generated by their frequently formulaic stories. Their stories can be frightening, but not too frightening. In *No Go the Bogeyman: Scaring, Lulling, and Making Mock*, Marina Warner proposes, "Being scared by a story or an image—scared witless, scared to death—can deliver ecstatic relief from the terror that the thing itself would inspire if it were to appear for real. The children's word 'scary' covers responses ranging from pure terror to sheer delight, and the condition of being scared is becoming increasingly sought after not only as a source of pleasure but as a means of strengthening the sense of being alive, of having a command over self" (1998, 6).

Although, as discussed above, young children depict ghosts graphically as disembodied sheeted figures saying "boo," not all children's oral ghost stories contain these stereotypical sheeted ghosts. The concept and image of the ghost are so universal among children that a mere reference is sufficient in a storytelling session to establish the character during a story performance, as for example, "And then you hear this big old ghost." Some ghost stories don't even require a direct reference to a ghost at all; the audience knows the story genre so well that no character definition is necessary. For example, in this typical children's ghost story told by a sixth-grade boy, the ghostly antagonist is merely "a voice":

> This boy's mom told him to go to the store and get him some, get her some liver. But by the time he got to the store the store was closed. So there was a graveyard beside the store and so he went over there and dug up a person

and got the liver out of him and took it home and they ate it that night. And that night he heard something. He heard a voice: "Johnny, I'm on the first step. Johnny, I'm at the second step. Johnny, I'm at the third step. Johnny, I'm in the hall. Johnny, I'm by your door. Johnny, I'm opening your door. Johnny, I'm in your room. Johnny, I'm by your dresser. Johnny, I'm by your posters. Johnny, I'm by your bed. Johnny, I GOTCHA!" (Grider 1976, 198–99)

A literary analysis of this seemingly simple but silly story, in which the narrator delights the audience by lunging at and grabbing one of them at the end, reveals a tightly structured narrative. This little cautionary tale encompasses a wide range of taboos: grave robbing, cannibalism, lying to mother. In the telling, however, these topics are merely implied or only superficially mentioned ("dug up a person and got the liver out of him and took it home and they ate it that night"). The lack of elaboration and description helps children maintain emotional distance from the genuine horrors that this story encompasses.

Opening in medias res, in the style of the traditional ballad, the story provides no context or explanation for the action, and gives no recognizable setting. The nuclear family provides the two main characters: the mother and the disobedient son. Nouns are clear and unadorned: liver, store, graveyard, bed, stairs, posters, dresser. The liver is always the purloined body part in these stories. This may be because the liver is one of the few human body parts that people might unwittingly eat without recognizing it; arms, legs, and so forth would be difficult to disguise. On the other hand, there are also widespread jokes about how much children dislike eating liver.

The poetic cadence of the corpse's progress up the stairs as well as the delicious suspense of waiting for the screaming and grabbing at the end all create verbal art on a level that children never seem to tire of. The story likewise enables children to control and deal with fears of the unknown. A child who is really afraid of monsters lurking in the dark after he has gone to bed may cope with his fear a little better if he can control the unknown monster by trapping him in the story matrix and making the monster methodically climb the stairs. This story gives children a way to verbalize their fears in a controlled, predictable manner.

The chant as the ghost stalks up the stairs approaches the *cante fable* in form, especially when the audience joins in. The metronomic, formulaic repetition pushes the tension of the impending disaster to its very limits. The punishment visited upon the terrified and guilty young protagonist is too terrible to articulate. In aesthetic desperation to achieve a sense of absolute climax, the story literally reaches out and yanks the audience into its spell. For a split second, the fantasy becomes reality. The screaming and grabbing of a member of the audience by the narrator unleashes a rowdy catharsis as the audience suddenly shares the punishment of the fictional thief for his triple crime of grave robbing, disobedience, and cannibalism. Such ghoulish and bizarre imagery seems out of place in the entertainment repertoire of contemporary children and, therefore, deserves closer analysis.

The grabbing and subsequent screaming of this traditional tale are reminiscent of the play action in "Bloody Mary" discussed in chapter 1, in which children deliberately try to invoke the creature in the mirror to attack them by uttering a formulaic incantation. Using ghost stories to test the limits of reality was researched by anthropologist Gregory Bateson in the 1960s, when he "developed a theory of play, according to which testing the limits of safety and entertaining the terror of murder and torment help confirm the child's sense of security with the parent or caregiver." Furthermore, "Games of thrills and spills, stirring phantoms of bogeymen, snatchers and watchers, then become part of the process of learning the norms of social languages, and of differentiating oneself within them" (Warner 1998, 144).

Versions of this traditional tale of grave robbing and punishment have been collected by folklorists for decades, primarily from the American South but also throughout western Europe from England to Spain, with a heavy concentration in Denmark (Thompson 1946, 42). Today it is perhaps the most common ghost story told by American children; versions of it can be heard at practically any slumber party or Halloween gathering.

Its inclusion in a wide range of children's storybooks may help reinforce its circulation in oral tradition.[3]

Folklorists know the tale as Aarne/Thompson Tale Type 366, "The Man from the Gallows." The theft of a corpse from a gibbet provides the first clue to the antiquity of the tale.

> A man steals the heart (liver, stomach, clothing) of one who has been hanged. He gives it to his wife to eat. The ghost comes to claim his property and carries the man off. (NB: The English and American forms are always used as scaring stories; the teller at the end impersonates the ghost or the victim and shouts directly at a member of the audience.)

Variants of this tale also have separate motif numbers in Stith Thompson's *Motif Index of Folk Literature*: E230, "Return from the dead to inflict punishment"; E235.4.1, "Return from dead to punish theft of golden arm from grave"; and F235.4.4, "Return from dead to punish theft of liver from man on gallows."

Ernest Baughman, in *Type and Motif Index of the Folktales of England and North America* (1966), elaborates upon the distinctive punch line of Tale Type 366:

> The English and American form, except for the theft of a golden or silver arm from a corpse, usually involves the finding of a part of the body by a man who uses it in soup. The owner returns at night and takes the man away. All forms cited are used as scaring stories; the teller at the end impersonates the ghost or the victim and shouts at a member of the audience, "Thou hast it!" or "Take it!"

The dramatic punch line is so characteristic of this particular tale that Baughman catalogued it with a separate pair of motif numbers: Z13.1, "Tale-teller frightens listener: yells 'Boo' at exciting point"; and Z13.1(a), "Man coming to get girl calls out from each step of the stairs that he is coming. Final line: 'Sally I have hold of thee!' (Here the teller grabs the listener.)"

Corpses left hanging on the gibbet were common in medieval Europe. A gruesome, chilling pre-plague image tells of "people eating their own children, of the poor in Poland feeding on hanged bodies taken down from the gibbet" during a period of famine in the early fourteenth century (Tuchman 1978, 24). No record exists of whether these Polish peasants feared that the ghosts of their ghoulish meals would haunt them, but the innocuous children's story cited above provides such revenge for cannibalism, in an incongruous, jocular setting. The ravaged corpse of the children's ghost story also punishes the young protagonist for disobedience to his mother, a crime that would be more familiar to contemporary children than cannibalizing the corpse of a criminal. A final point of interest regarding the content of the story is that in all known collected versions, the protagonist is always a boy. Oral tradition apparently has no tolerance for a girl who would steal a corpse and then lie to her mother.

A fairly stable repertoire of traditional ghost story plots has circulated among American children for decades and probably much longer. All of these stories follow a rather distinct and predictable structural pattern, which has enhanced the stability of this story cycle. In general the pattern consists of:

1) A child is the protagonist, often the same age as the narrator, but usually a boy

2) A disembodied ghost is the antagonist

3) Adults are flat, ineffectual background characters

4) A haunted house is the most common setting

5) The stories are clearly presented by the narrator and recognized by the audience as "not true" or "not real"

6) The stories are short and frequently formulaic

7) The ending is generally a comic or surprise punch line

More than any other feature, this distinctive comic or surprise punch line is an essential structural feature of children's traditional ghost stories that sets them apart from the more serious narratives of adults and older adolescents. The ubiquitous "Boo!" of cartoons and practical jokes reinforces children's awareness of the dramatic function of surprise endings, especially when the children play at grabbing and scaring one another. The ending helps keep these stories from ever being truly frightening because the grabbing and screaming usually dissolves into giggles and laughter.

THE GOLDEN ARM

The story about Johnny and the stolen liver is only one common variant of Tale Type 366: "The Man from the Gallows." Most of the children's variants of this traditional tale type are so deeply embedded in the child-to-child conduit of the childhood underground that they are unfamiliar to American adults. However, adults do know and tell the version of the story entitled "The Golden Arm," which may be how many children first hear and then learn the story (Hudson 1953). The following version was collected from a sixth-grade girl:

> Once upon a time, there was this lady that had a golden arm. She was in a wreck, and her arm got cut off, so she had, they took her to the hospital, and they decided that they would put a golden arm on her, so they did. And, the next night when they went to sleep, someone came in and killed the lady, and so, a week after that they had buried her and, with the golden arm. And so it started snowing that night when they buried her, and then someone thought, decided that they would go dig up the woman and get her golden arm. So they, he went and dug her up, dug the woman up, and got her golden arm . . . and so he took it home, and he always kept it under the bed, and every time that he would hear a creepy noise, he would always go up, get up and see about it because he was afraid that someone would get her golden arm. And so, one night he heard someone coming up the stairs and heard someone say, "Who's got my golden arm? Who's got my golden arm? Who's got my golden arm? HAVE YOU GOT MY GOLDEN ARM?" (Burrison 1968, 31)

British storybooks for children picked up versions of this and similar tales as early as the 1860s. In the United States, attention was first focused on it by two distinguished nineteenth-century authors, Mark Twain and Joel Chandler Harris (Burrison 1968). Twain sent a summary of the tale to Harris, suggesting that the latter use it in some of his Uncle Remus material. Twain mentioned that he had first heard the tale when he was a child from a family slave. Harris responded that he had not heard the story before and requested more information about it. Not long afterward, Harris published a version of the tale (1881), substituting silver coins for the golden arm. Twain frequently told a version of "The Golden Arm" during his public lecture tours and readings and also published the tale (1897).

Although Twain and Harris both credited oral sources for their versions of the tale, many contemporary tellers trace their knowledge of it directly to these two widely read and still popular authors. Many children's storybook anthologies include at least synopses of Twain's version of the tale. This tale is an outstanding example of the interplay between print and oral performance. It has also been interpreted as a parody of adult literary horror stories (Stewart 1982, 45).

The main question that this branch of the tale raises is why a golden arm is the object of the theft. One possible explanation involves the general aesthetic of the traditional fairytale, or *Märchen*, which focuses on primary colors, fantasy, and hard glittering surfaces. Since the story is told for entertainment and not as a memorate of a real ghostly encounter, the audience must simply exercise a "willing suspension of disbelief" and accept the golden arm as part of the story. The incongruity of using gold for a prosthetic arm provides a clue to the audience that this story is fantasy and is not really "real." On the other hand, greed for gold also helps make the heinous crime of grave robbing more plausible for a modern audience.

The other branches of Tale Type 366 in the United States are most commonly told by adults to children. The first of these, "The Big Toe," is the form best known in the South and emphasizes local foodways and customs. In this story cycle, a human toe is accidentally dug up in the garden or potato patch. The poor, hungry hero cooks the windfall meat in a pot of beans or greens, a staple of the Southern diet, and then unexpectedly encounters the wrath of the rampaging ghost in search of its missing digit. The other category, "Tailypo," is another Southern, regional adaptation told to children by adults. The creature seeking revenge is not supernatural, but rather is an infuriated animal in search of its tail, which has been chopped off by accident. In oral tradition, this form of the story can function as a kind of cautionary tale advising children not to abuse animals. Many versions of this story as commonly told by professional storytellers and librarians play down or eliminate the dramatic ending and emphasize instead the righteous fury of the mutilated animal. Both "The Big Toe" and "Tailypo" have been published as illustrated children's books (Galdone 1977; Rockwell 1981).

Tag, You're It!

A popular children's narrative with structural affinity to Tale Type 366 but with totally different content and ambiance is known as "Tag, You're It" (Brunvand 1961; Paredes 1960). The concluding punch line ironically parodies "The Golden Arm" versions of the tale type by failing to satisfy the frightening expectations that the narrative deliberately creates. Jan Brunvand cataloged this tale as Shaggy Dog #100, "The Encounter with a Horrible Monster." It is also motif Z13.4* (i), "Escaped inmate from insane asylum chases man. They run and run until the pursued falls. The inmate with a long knife approaches, touches victim with free hand and says, 'Tag.'"

In addition to being an entertaining story, it brings the everyday world of other children's traditions into the realm of ghost stories by parodying the almost universal children's game of "Tag." According to William Wells Newell, an early American folklorist who published a book on children's games in 1883, *Games and Songs of American Children*, "As in several other games of chase, the pursuer represents an evil spirit. . . . The chaser, it seems, was conceived as . . . a malignant character. Thus we get a vivid idea of the extent to which such representations once affected the lives even of children, and see that an amusement that is now a mere pleasurable muscular exercise followed the direction imposed by belief" ([1883] 1963, 158–59).

As told by most contemporary children, the story features a generic and undescribed monster instead of a ghost as the antagonist. As long as they are entertained by a good story, children are uncritical about including monsters and other creatures from popular culture in what they regard as ghost stories. The following version, collected from a sixth-grade boy, features a "monster" that for all practical purposes functions the same way a ghost does in a haunted house, and at least in the introduction parodies the plot of the cult movie *Rocky Horror Picture Show* (1975).

> OK, now see, there was this boy and he was delivering papers and it started storming and so he ran up to this one old haunted house and it had a, there was a man living in it still, though. And um he knocked on the door and asked if he could stay until the rain stopped and he goes, "Yeah, but don't go down in the basement." And so he said, "OK." And um, so that night it, it rained all night, you know. He stayed all night, you know. And about the middle of the night he got up and he went down and he was curious, you know, and he wondered, "Now what could be in that basement?" And um, he started to open up the door and that guy ran up to him and he said, "No, don't!" And he slammed the door back shut. And said, "Don't go down there!" So he said, "OK, I won't" and went back to bed. And it got to be about three o'clock and he got back up and that guy didn't know he got back up and went down there and opened the door and he went in and there was the great big monster and it took off after him and chased him all over the house. And it got him cornered in this corner by the refrigerator and it walked up to him and it touched him and it said, "Tag, you're it." (Grider 1976, 162–63)

SPEAKING GHOSTS: "THE GHOST OF THE WHITE EYE"

Another distinct and popular cycle of children's ghost stories with joke or catch endings features a disembodied ghost that identifies itself by calling out its own name, much as Rumpelstiltskin did in the well-known Grimm tale (Vlach 1971). The humorous punch line is the play-on-words retort of the diminutive hero to the vociferous ghost. The punch line puts the emphasis on the successful "man of words" who fights words with words rather than emphasizing the gratuitous violence and mayhem so common in some other narratives and certainly in many movies and video games. Child narrators and listeners differentiate the various stories in this cycle according to the punch line, no matter how the story has developed up to that point. The punch lines are also used as titles for some of the stories. Following is a typical example of "The Ghost of the White Eye" as told by a sixth-grade boy:

> There's this baby and he was going across the floor and he dropped his bottle down the stairs and so he went and told his big brother, "Big Brother, will you go get my bottle?" And so the big brother started down there and the ghost goes, "I'm the Ghost of the White Eye." And so the big brother ran up there and so the baby told his second biggest brother, and he goes, "Second Biggest Brother, will you go get my bottle?" And so he gets down there and the ghost goes, "I'm the Ghost of the White Eye." So he runs back up there and the baby tells his next to the biggest brother, "Will you go get my bottle?" So he goes down there and comes back up because of the ghost saying, "I'm the Ghost of the White Eye." And so the baby goes down there and goes, "You better shut up or you're going to be the Ghost of the Black Eye!" (Grider 1976, 212–13)

In storytelling sessions, children generally howl with delight at the punch line, regardless of how many times they may have heard the story or told it themselves. The image of the baby getting the best of an adversary that frightened away the big brothers is especially satisfactory for younger children. Another entertaining feature of this story is the opportunity it provides for a talented narrator to use different voices to depict the characters: a high-pitched lisp for the baby; a low, menacing snarl for the ghost; and a strong, assertive voice when delivering the punch line. The *Märchen* characteristics of this tale are immediately apparent. There is sophisticated triple incremental repetition as the baby asks others, in descending order, to go downstairs and retrieve his bottle. When all are frightened and run away from the ghostly voice, the baby himself performs the task, thus becoming the "victorious youngest child" so common in folktales. The amorphous, disembodied voice is a neutral character; only the fright of the baby's superiors signifies that the voice is malevolent. But in this tale, the loquacious, precocious, and belligerent baby openly threatens the ghost instead of vice versa. Although it is not carried out, there is potential violence suggested in the baby's threat to blacken the ghost's eye. In some ways, the fearless little baby is an alter ego for all children who wish that they could vanquish the terrors of the night with such assertive but casual aplomb.

The only attribute of the ghost present in the narrative is its voice, making it a Genderless Presence, as described in chapter 3. This lack of description could stem from the assumption that everybody already knows what a ghost looks like. A more plausible explanation is that some children really are afraid of ghosts. One way to rationalize this fear or at least to keep it under control is to keep the data as superficial as possible by avoiding prolonged, gruesome descriptions that conjure up explicit and frightening visual images. Apparently what frightens children most about late-night TV or videos is not the voices but seeing what the creatures look like. In response, children (and some adults) commonly cover up their eyes (but not their ears) during especially graphic or frightening sequences. In the narratives, children achieve essentially the same detachment or emotional distancing by omitting any description of the ghost.

Young children who are just learning the aesthetic and worldview of the typical ghost story sometimes misinterpret or misunderstand what they are hearing, as the following anecdote related by an instructor of clinical psychiatry who researches the supernatural illustrates. The frightening "Black Eye" creature the child fears can only be a fragment of an elliptical, misunderstood version of "Ghost of the White Eye," of which his father, in his search for empirical reality, is unaware:

> I am not aware of any dictionary that defines the term "ghost hunter." However, nearly all of us have at one time or another acted as one. Even my five-year-old son, Damien, is not immune. He has insisted on being present at more than a few "haunted" locations when I have been involved in filming television documentaries on the paranormal. While he has never seriously reported any strange occurrences at these sites, he occasionally claims that a witchlike ghost he calls "Black Eye" is lurking in our home. His tears attest that he is not joking. Does this specter derive from a scary television show, a fleeting glimpse of an unrecognizable shadow, or some inner turmoil that is expressed through the imagery of ghosts? I still do not know despite my repeated attempts to understand the source of his experiences. (Houran 2004, xiii)

Children's ghost stories often garble traditional plots by fusing different tales into one narrative. The following story, told by a first-grade girl, demonstrates the precocity of a six-year-old narrator as she blends together her apparent revulsion toward dirty diapers and the name of an ogre who is common is English and southern American folklore, "Raw Head and Bloody Bones" (Taylor 1956; Wilgus 1960). Appropriately for a girl narrator, she includes a sister and a "mommy" as characters.

> There was this baby and its bottle fell down the stairs and he told his mommy to go down and get it and he said, "Mommy, will you go get my bottle?" And while she was down there getting the bottle, and she said, "OK." And while she was down there getting the bottle she heard this,

"Bloody Bones and Dirty Diapers. Bloody Bones and Dirty Diapers. Bloody Bones." And she went upstairs and said, "Tell your dad to get it." And so they went to the daddy and he said, "Will you go down and get my bottle?" And so he went down the stairs and he started to pick up the bottle, and "Bloody Bones and Dirty Diapers. Bloody Bones and Dirty Diapers." And so he went back up the stairs and said, "Tell your sister to get it." And so he went to his sister and she went down the stairs and as she was picking up the bottle, goes, "Bloody Bones and Dirty Diapers. Bloody Bones." And then she went back up the stairs and said, "Tell your brother to go get it." And he went and got his brother to get it. And his brother went down and started getting it, and "Bloody Bones and Dirty Diapers. Bloody Bones and Dirty Diapers." And then he ran, ran back up the stairs and said, "Why don't you go get it?" And so he went downstairs and he said, and he started to pick up the bottle, and, "Bloody Bones and Dirty Diapers." And then he said, "Um, throw away the bloody bones and clean up the diapers." (Grider 1976, 179–80)

The young narrator has mastered the incremental repetition, the chanting, and the concept of a ghost in the basement, but the white eye/black eye pun has totally escaped her as she resorts to an anticlimactic practical injunction to "throw away the bloody bones and clean up the diapers." It is even possible that the narrator has incorporated her quotidian reality of dirty diapers into the story because she finds them so inherently disgusting and hates being told to "clean up the diapers." Nevertheless, this version gives us insight into how young children learn the basic components of oral storytelling competence, even as they mix up and misinterpret various components of the stories.

Another first grader in the same storytelling session resorted to a stream-of-consciousness version that clearly indicates his lack of understanding of plot development or the significance of an appropriate conclusion. Nevertheless, he had obviously heard several different types of ghost stories and was practicing and trying to learn, much as children do when they struggle with learning knock-knock jokes and what makes them funny. Frankenstein, robots, and violence replace any semblance of ghosts and the narrator's editorial comment, "Now here comes the stupid part," underscores his overall lack of understanding of this traditional story form.

> This little boy dropped his bottle in the trash and when he went to get it Frankenstein appeared. This is true! And Frankenstein got the bottle, no, the baby went to the cliff. And Frankenstein went over to the cliff and Frankenstein fell off the cliff and he wasn't hurt at all. And now he can't move 'cause he's just a robot. And then the baby went back and got his bottle, got a new one from inside the cabinet from the house. And do you know what happened next? A dead man! And he got blood all over the cabinet and his head, and his legs off, his legs cut off! Now here comes the stupid part. Not Frankenstein, the guy was dead. And when he, the baby killed Frankenstein with a knife and when he went, when the baby went down in the basement and when he went down there he said, "I'm the White Eye of Frankenstein." And he said, "Shut up and be quiet and clean up the dirty diapers." (Grider 1976, 188–89)

SPEAKING GHOSTS: "BLOODY FINGERS"

Another less well-known cycle of talking ghosts is generally told by older children who are sophisticated enough to deliberately control the fear levels generated during storytelling sessions by breaking the tension with a story that more closely resembles a joke than a ghost story. Designating the protagonist as a "hippie" may also provide insight into the relatively recent origin of the story, perhaps in the late 1950s or 1960s. By comparison, the morbid cannibalism of "The Man from the Gallows" indicates its possible antiquity. The story of "Bloody Fingers" is a useful tension-breaker in storytelling sessions because even though it follows the structure of the stories described above, it lacks any really frightening elements. In fact, the sixth-grade girl who told this story prefaced her performance with the caveat, "It's in some, in some ways like a ghost story but it's not really scary though."

> Um, there was these, there was this guy and he went to a hotel and he goes, "I want to rent a room." And the guy says, "Well, we only have one room left and it's haunted. There's already been one guy killed in there." But he said, "I'll take it anyway." And he went up there and heard somebody saying, "Bloody fingers!" And, um, and it scared him you know, real bad, so he jumped out the window and killed hisself. And there's this, another guy come and he said, "I want to rent a room." And he said, "We only have one and there's been two people killed in there." And he says, "Oh well, I don't care." And he goes in there and he hears, "Bloody Fingers!" And he jumps out the window and kills hisself. And then the hippie comes in, he says, "I want to rent a room." And he says, "We're all filled up and three men have already been killed in there." "Oh, I don't give a darn." And so he goes up to his room and hears, "Bloody Fingers!" And the hippie replies, "Bandaids in the bathroom." (Grider 1976, 217–18)

HAUNTED BATHROOMS

Just as the hippie in the above story vanquishes the ghostly voice with a bathroom reference, another cycle of whimsical children's stories deal with ghostly voices emanating from the toilet in the bathroom. These moderately scatological tales are apparently parodies of the narrative form and aesthetic of some of the ghost stories with comical punch lines described earlier in this chapter. These stories also foreshadow the "haunted toilet" tales told by adolescents and young adults, discussed in chapter 1. The children's cycle of humorous stories about talking toilets may, in fact, help prepare children for the genuinely frightening legends about haunted bathrooms in which malevolent beings, such as the infamous Bloody Mary, emerge from the mirrors or stalls of the restroom and literally attack the children who summon them through play rituals and formulaic chants (see chapter 3 for a more detailed discussion of this topic).

In this cycle, as the story progresses, listeners realize that the "ghostly" voices are coming from talking insects floating in the toilet. The structure of the stories at first implies that the voices are from supernatural beings (i.e., ghosts) and humor depends in large part on the audience's familiarity with the "Bloody Fingers" prototype, which makes the stories much closer to jokes than traditional folktales or ghost stories. To many adults, if they know about them at all, these jokifications of the ghost story form are offensive, surreal, or nonsensical. But considering the barrage of talking animals and insects to which children are constantly subjected by popular culture and the media, the talking insects in the toilet are not so unusual. Except for the obvious scatology, the insects in these stories are little different from Jiminy Cricket in Walt Disney's *Pinocchio* (1940) or Flik in *A Bug's Life* (1998). The following example told by a sixth-grade boy is typical:

> This man came and he came to this hotel and he asked for a room and the man said, "Yeah." And he went upstairs into the room and he heard some words and it was, "Roll over, roll over." And he came down, he ran down the stairs, tripped over a rock, tripped over a rock and killed himself. Another man came and, and asked for a room and the man just said, "Yeah. I've got a room but it's haunted." And he went up there and he heard some words going, "Roll over, roll over." And he ran down the stairs and ran into a tree and killed himself. And then another man came up, another man came and asked for a room and um, the man said, "It's haunted." And he said, "I don't care. I've got my flashlight with me." And he went upstairs and heard some words, "Roll over, roll over." And he turned his flashlight on and started look-ing around and he went into the bathroom and looked in the bathtub. Nothing there. And then he looked in the sink and nothing there. And then he looked in the toilet

and he seen this turd and these two termites saying, "Roll over, roll over." (Grider, 1976, 595–96)

Locating the floating termites with a flashlight is reminiscent of the *Ghost Hunters* (2004–2007) programs that are so popular on TV—i.e., the use of modern technology exposes the haunting hoax. But the main reason that this story cycle is so popular with children is that it gives them an excuse to say the word "turd" and other scatological terms. This scatology is the main reason that most adults don't know about these stories because most children know better than to tell these stories to adults, who they know will disapprove. The "bathroom humor" of these innocuous and silly stories provides children with yet another opportunity to express cultural taboos in a controlled setting, much as they do when telling stories about grave robbing and cannibalism in stories of "The Golden Arm" type. Other punch lines are popular in stories of this type, including: "Now I gotcha where I wantcha, and I'm gonna eatcha"; "I see your hiney, all black and shiny; if you don't hide it, I think I'll bite it"; and "Going down the river on a little brown log."

ACQUISITION AND PERFORMANCE

Humorous ghost stories with catch endings are among the first traditional narratives that children hear and repeat among themselves without adult assistance or intervention. Most children are well aware that adults and most adolescents regard these stories as silly and childish. In order to avoid possible ridicule or censure, therefore, children are generally cautious about telling these stories when adults are listening. For many children, these are the first stories that they learn to tell themselves. They can practice with one another until they master the structure and sequencing of the formulaic narratives, thus preparing them to learn more complicated stories when they are older. Some children never quite master the telling of these stories, but others become young virtuosos and are much sought out and respected by their peers. Such positive reinforcement in childhood can result in becoming master storytellers later in life.

Most young children recognize some of these stories by the time they are in the first or second grade, whether or not they can tell the stories themselves. Older siblings are the most common sources for learning the stories, but classmates and other peers are also an active source. Most children stop telling these stories at about age ten or twelve, when they enter puberty and have more adolescent concerns. A mastery of these often comical and sometimes superficial childhood tales prepares the way for the extensive story repertoire of adolescence, which includes macabre and gruesome tales which are too frightening and intense for the sensibilities of young children. Many of these more sophisticated and psychologically disturbing tales, commonly referred to as "urban legends," have been widely anthologized in a popular series by folklorist Jan Brunvand and today have almost dropped out of oral tradition because they are circulating so widely on the Internet (Brunvand 2004). Children's humorous ghost stories, on the other hand, have generally remained comfortably ensconced in oral tradition.

The telling of children's ghost stories usually takes place in a very predictable context, which evokes what folklorists term as the "legend climate," which can include darkness, spooky sounds and music, candles, flashlights, and so forth. As Iona and Peter Opie describe these typical settings, "Yet another entertainment is the 'spooky' rhyme or story recited when the lights are low, as when members of a gang gather together in their hut or den, and the wind whistles through the chinks of the door, fluttering the candle flame. One of them tells a story to the new-comers in a slow blood-curdling voice, saying the traditional words very quietly so that the listeners have to crane their heads forward to catch the words . . . " (1959, 35). Children most frequently tell these traditional tales at Halloween parties or late at night, either at camp or during a slumber party after all the lights have been turned off and the supervising adults have told everybody to go to sleep. Then, amid whispers and clandestine flashlights, the storytelling begins. Many children learn new stories in such sessions and then relate them to their peers when they return home, which helps spread the tales. Another type of storytelling

session involves a camp counselor or other benign older authority figure telling a few of these stories around the campfire at
night before bedtime (Ellis 1981; Leary 1973; Mechling 1980).
Often these campfire storytelling sessions are the prelude to
elaborate pranks involving taking the children into the woods
where costumed "monsters" jump out at them and enact other
scary tableaux.

The children who have never heard such stories before are
sometimes frightened so much that they whimper and cry, which
only adds to the overall spooky atmosphere. Ghost stories with
catch endings are frequently interspersed among more serious
and frightening tales and usually function as tension relievers,
especially when very young and impressionable children are
present. Young children quickly learn to recognize the formulaic structure and format of these distinctive humorous ghost
stories and frequently will ask somebody to tell one of these stories which is "not real." This tension-relieving function is essential for keeping some particularly intense storytelling sessions
under control so that the children will not become excessively
frightened or upset, which disrupts and ruins a good storytelling session.

Since telling ghost stories is an integral part of the celebration of Halloween, this holiday is another significant setting in
the perpetuation and popularity of these stories. Each year the
parties and informal get-togethers at Halloween introduce more
children to the wonders of spook houses, trick-or-treat, and
ghost stories; due to the popularity of Halloween, the storytelling repertoire annually is added to, reinforced, and perpetuated.
Because children say that conditions must be "just right" for a
good storytelling session, these stories generally are not told at
school or in the daytime. Storytelling will normally develop at a
slumber party, campout, or Halloween party if the appropriate
mood develops as the evening progresses.

Repeated telling of these ghost stories with catch endings
makes them so familiar that many children can recognize a given
type from the opening lines. The tales have such fixed aesthetic
limits that many performances sound like memorized recitations,

and the linear, predictable texts of most of the stories not only make them easy to learn, but also help make the scary seem safe. Some narrators even introduce their stories by title, much as they would a poem or other formal recitation. The young audiences never seem to mind these stylized conventions. Their interest is usually more in hearing a familiar story told interestingly and well than in hearing a completely new story. This predilection for the familiar is not surprising; small children feel the same way about storybooks which are read to them regularly. They want the storybooks read to them the same way each time, with no adlibs or omissions. Serious narrators are nearly always interested in picking up new variations or twists to make their own renditions more effective, so sometimes several children will deliberately tell their versions of the same story for comparative purposes. Some gifted and popular narrators even take pride in having their style and repertoire copied by apprentices who are trying to master the genre, and they will help along the beginners with prompting or sound effects.

As opposed to adult and adolescent storytelling, children do not seem to mind too much if these tales get garbled or presented in fragmentary form. The tale corpus is so familiar that the listeners can recognize the basic and familiar story type from very scant and garbled cues. Under such favorable conditions, beginning storytellers are comfortable trying to tell these tales for the first time without fear of audience rejection if they "mess up." Truncated or hybrid versions also serve as additional tension relievers or mood breakers during intense sessions. Children will often suspend storytelling temporarily to discuss the effectiveness of a new hybrid or to point out where a performance went awry. They will also argue about which version is right or the best. In fact, such fledgling oral literary criticism or dialectic sometimes becomes more important to the children than the actual storytelling. Since a talented storyteller occupies a position of great prestige among most young peer groups, the standards of what is or is not a good story are very important.

Conclusion

The overall American worldview is complex, but one undeniable component of that worldview is a persistent interest and certain level of belief in the world of the supernatural, especially the undead. Generation after generation, children actively participate in this supernatural worldview by learning and telling the same basic corpus of ghost stories to one another. These stories have three basic functions: enculturation, cognitive skill development, and entertainment.

General knowledge of the supernatural is reinforced by the barrage of images and information from the mass media and advertising. The enculturation of young children into a worldview that encompasses ghosts, haunted houses, and other supernatural entities reinforces a sincere belief in the reality of these beings in later life, or at least reduces skepticism. Adolescents and adults who grew up hearing and telling ghost stories may very well be more likely to believe in ghosts and such than those who were not enculturated into this supernatural worldview at an early age.

Another clear function of telling ghost stories is to enhance the development of cognitive skills, especially literary and dramatic competence, among young narrators. Good storytellers are highly regarded by their young peers. In order for ghost (or traditional) stories to make sense the narrator has to understand the importance of episode sequence and plot development in addition to character development and dramatic timing. Good listening skills are also important to enable children to learn these stories so that they can tell them themselves. By listening to and telling ghost stories, children broaden their overall aesthetic awareness.

Perhaps the most significant function of children telling ghost stories is entertainment. Because children enjoy the stories so much and have such fun telling and listening to them, they keep the story corpus alive generation after generation. In spite of their sometimes grotesque subject matter, such as cannibalizing the corpse of an executed criminal, children regard the content of most ghost stories as funny. Of course the incongruous, joke-like punch line further enhances the overall entertainment value of the stories. They also enjoy the camaraderie of snuggling together around a candle or a campfire or a flashlight and sharing the mood of suspense and suppressed tension created by a good storytelling session. They know that as soon as the lights are turned on, they will be back in the safety of everyday reality.

The so-called "triviality barrier" still constitutes the greatest obstacle to the documentation and understanding of this small but distinctive group of traditional folktales (Sutton-Smith 1970). Research with children and investigation of their traditions, including narratives, still does not have the credibility and prestige of some other types of folkloric research. Few scholars are working in this field, and their work is not always well received. Professional storytellers and performers with no theoretical folklore training, as well as authors of simplified popular children's storybooks, have practically co-opted the field of children's storytelling. Whether this adult participation has inhibited or changed the way children tell stories to one another when adults aren't present is another field of inquiry that needs to be undertaken.

One result of the limited research in this field is that accurate texts of narratives told by children and contextual data about when children tell these stories to each other are rare in folklore publications, which causes a lack of reliable comparative data for research purposes. The bulk of research on children's narratives is found in dissertations by folklore graduate students. There seems to have been little cross-fertilization of ideas among the various academic disciplines, and this lack of interchange further inhibits serious and ongoing research into the phenomenon of children's storytelling.

In addition to the need for more in-depth fieldwork and collecting, including accurate textual documentation as well as contextual and ethnographic data, a number of theoretical questions still need to be addressed. The classification by genre of children's ghost stories with catch endings presents some basic problems, even though the texts *per se* are clearly folktales. For example, we need a better understanding of the relationship between these distinctive stories and the more pervasive narrative genre of the joke. The brevity and distinctive ending ally these tales structurally almost as much to the joke as the *Märchen*. Their relationship to the subcategory or subgenre that Jan Brunvand classified as the "Shaggy Dog Story" is also open to investigation (1963). To further complicate the issue of genre classification, in performance the stories also take on many characteristics of the legend. For example, the stories are frequently elliptical, communally performed, and highly localized.

Although children's ghost stories may not be widely known and respected by adults, they nevertheless constitute an incredibly stable and widespread oral tradition that has resisted being overwhelmed by the media and popular culture. These formulaic, jokelike tales are one of the cornerstones of contemporary ghost lore.

Part III:

Old Spirits in New Contexts

FiVE

HAUNTED HOUSES

SYLVIA ANN GRIDER

The quintessential "haunting experience" is entering a haunted house, either literally while legend tripping or figuratively while telling or listening to a ghost story (see chapter 1 for a full discussion of legend tripping). Ghosts and their haunted domains are inseparable in ghost stories because the presence of the ghost is what changes an otherwise mundane place into a portal through which the living encounter the realm of the supernatural. This chapter is not concerned with considering the empirical reality of either ghosts or haunted houses, but rather with trying to describe and understand the metaphysical landscape in which the stories about these supernatural entities are set. Highly stylized haunted houses are especially important in children's ghost stories. Children explore the limits of reality through imaginative play in various kinds of metahouses—dollhouses, playhouses, tree houses, carnival fun houses, etc.—and haunted houses function much the same way for them.

Houses are the primary domains that ghosts inhabit or "haunt," although ghosts do lurk in various other sites—castles, forests, caves, and so on. We humans have an incredibly powerful psychological attachment to our houses—our sanctuaries—and the intrusion of a threatening, otherworldly force in that otherwise safe setting is terrifying to consider. As one researcher pointed out, "As long as houses remain a central symbol in American culture, our writers are likely to inhabit them with the anxieties that haunt our day-to-day lives" (Bailey 1999, 109). In oral tradition and popular fiction, humans either unwittingly stumble into haunted houses or, paradoxically, seek out the haunted house and confront it as a way of testing their courage. The result is nearly always the same: the person entering the haunted house comes away profoundly changed by the experience.

In many ghost stories, the haunted house functions as both setting and character, with the sentient and self-aware house taking precedence over the beings that haunt it. Haunted houses are active participants in the development of the narrative plot, especially in popular fiction, and exhibit malevolent intentions toward the humans who dare to enter them. Staircases twist and turn and trip human visitors, doors mysteriously appear and disappear or lock and unlock. The house and the ghosts that haunt it are partners in the supernatural assault upon humans who invade their domain. This chapter will examine how the shared image of the iconic haunted house and its narrative function have developed over time and now are remarkably consistent throughout all the genres and media in which it is represented, ranging from literature to oral tradition.

LOOKING BACKWARD: LITERARY GOTHIC PREDECESSORS

The haunted house stories that are so popular today, primarily in the English-speaking world, have a distinguished literary lineage. At first, the haunted house was a rather passive setting for ghostly activity. For example, among the earliest written ghost stories set in haunted houses are those of the Romans, specifically Plautus, Pliny the Younger, and Lucian. These ancient literary ghost stories deal with the familiar formula of restless ghosts who haunt the houses where they lived until their deaths are discovered and avenged (Felton 1999). The houses themselves are of little importance beyond providing a setting for the interactions between the ghosts and humans. Haunted houses were not a significant literary setting again until the Romantic period.

FiGURE 1: A deserted house with the reputation of being haunted. Shortly after this photograph was taken, the house mysteriously burned. St. John's, Newfoundland. (Photo by Diane Goldstein)

The concept of the haunted house as the focus of a distinctive type of Romantic literature originated in the gothic novels of eighteenth and early nineteenth-century England, and was influenced somewhat by French and other continental literature of the period. The first true English-language gothic was *The Castle of Otranto* by Horace Walpole, published in 1764 and—like Mary Shelley's *Frankenstein, or, the Modern Prometheus* ([1818] 1983)—it was allegedly inspired by the author's dream. Over time, according to one literary critic, "gothic novelists employed their gloomy settings as a shorthand for the hierarchies of aristocracy and theocracy which they detested and which their revolutionary age fatally undermined" (Bailey 1999, 5).

The decrepit, gloomy castles and mansions that became the stock settings of these early English novels were based on the real landscape of England and other parts of Europe that were filled with crumbling castles and other ancient ruins and monuments. Lacking ruined castles on the landscape, the American literary imagination instead focused on the dowager Victorian and Second Empire mansions that were popular with wealthy aristocrats throughout the country during the Gilded Age of the nineteenth century. With their distinctive mansard roofs, towers and turrets, multiple stories, and ornate architectural embellishments, these buildings became symbols of opulence and decadence (figure 1). What went on inside these mansions was the subject of much speculation by the general public. Since these were the dwellings of the super-rich, most Americans never set foot inside these mansions, which gave the buildings a sort of other-worldliness, anonymity, and mystery analogous to that of ruined European castles. After the financial busts following the turn of the century, many of these American buildings were abandoned and began to fall into disrepair. Darkened and boarded up, they attracted the attention and imagination of passersby in a way that they never had when they were glittering and new. Local legends of hauntings and other strange goings-on began to accrue to these decrepit, abandoned buildings. Over time, these local legends generalized into what we today call ghost stories.

Literary critic and author Dale Bailey, in *American Nightmares: The Haunted House Formula in American Popular Fiction* (1999), focuses specifically on literary haunted houses rather than those in which the ghost stories of oral tradition are set. He agrees that the haunted houses of contemporary popular fiction are indebted to the gothic tradition, but he goes on to conclude that the houses of popular fiction are a metaphor for the despairs and fault lines of contemporary society—moral, psychological, and economic. According to Bailey, the haunted house formula is "a profoundly versatile tool for examining the anxieties and tensions inherent in our national experiment, the haunted house finally seems like nothing less than a symbol of America and the American mind, of all the ghosts that haunt us, from the dark legacy of slavery to the failed war in Vietnam" (114).

The haunted houses in which ghost stories from oral tradition are set have a slightly different function, especially in the formulaic stories children tell. These spooky and stylized settings allow children to examine the limits of reality during storytelling sessions, and then return to the safety and security of the schoolroom, party, or bedroom. The haunted house settings of most adult traditional oral ghost stories, on the other hand, are rather benign. In fact, the traditional ghost story overall is not nearly as dramatic as the tales presented in contemporary popular fiction.

What Does a Haunted House Look Like?

Ask any group of children, or even adults, to draw a picture of a haunted house and they will all draw essentially the same picture of the outside facade of the house. Depictions of an archetypal haunted house contain some combination of the following distinctive motifs: multistoried, mansard or gambrel roof, turrets or towers, and broken or boarded-up windows with "spooky" inhabitants peeking out (figure 2). Furthermore, the darkened house is generally on an isolated hilltop, surrounded by a high broken fence, with leafless dead trees and/or a witch on a broomstick silhouetted against a full moon. Black cats and bats lurk in the background of typical drawings and occasionally a ghost peeks out of an upstairs window, saying "Boo!"

As pointed out in the examples in chapter 3, oral tradition (especially stories told by adults) encompasses many other types of haunted houses—ranging from suburban, split-level ranch houses to fraternity houses to businesses and so on. This variety of setting is appropriate because oral tradition holds that any structure in which a ghost appears is thereby haunted. Nevertheless, the most common depiction of the haunted house, especially in children's narratives and popular culture, is the stereotypical multistoried mansion discussed above.

One way to conceptualize the exterior of the traditional haunted house is to compare it to the enchanted castle, a common folktale setting. The traditional folktale or magic tale is an ancient and elegant narrative genre best known to contemporary audiences through the printed redactions of the Grimm Brothers,

FIGURE 2: A typical Halloween party decoration depicting a haunted house, complete with full moon, bats in the belfry, lurking ghosts and skeletons, and broken windows. (Image courtesy of The Beistle Company, Shippensburg, Pennsylvania, Design 01370.)

Jakob and Wilhelm, in the early nineteenth century (Grimm [1812–14] 1944). The genre is characterized by one-dimensional characters, especially princes and princesses, who live in or yearn for enchanted castles and who must overcome seemingly insurmountable odds through the assistance of benign supernatural helpers. The luminous and enchanted castle, especially its exterior facade, is so deeply embedded within the narrative structure of the folktale that the ancient, oral genre cannot exist without it. Both the enchanted castle and the haunted house of literature and oral tradition are generally set apart from mundane, quotidian reality by being isolated high up on a hill, but there the similarity ends. The enchanted castle is bright and shining; the haunted house is dark and brooding. The enchanted castle is filled with music and laughter; the haunted house contains evil and frightening, mysterious noises. The lines of the enchanted castle are geometrically precise and the perspective is reliable; the haunted house is skewed and out of focus. The inhabitants of the enchanted castle are radiant, shining, and joyful. Dark, vague, ephemeral creatures and apparitions drift through haunted houses. The two settings are diametric opposites or, to use folktale imagery, the haunted house is the evil mirror image of the enchanted castle.

Interestingly, even with the overall agreement regarding what the exterior of a haunted house looks like, little of the action of a good ghost story takes place outside of a haunted house. Characters may be terrified as they approach the house, but nothing happens to them until they enter it, passing from the reality of the outside world to the supernatural domain inside the house. Thus in ghost stories the distinctive exterior is subordinated to the dramatic action which takes place *inside* the haunted house—usually in the upper stories, the basement, or on the staircase.

Actual houses on the American landscape—both lived in and vacant—gain the reputation for being haunted simply on the basis of how closely they resemble the iconic haunted house of oral tradition and literature (figure 3). People take one look at these houses, especially if they are a bit run-down or surrounded

FIGURE 3: A house in Las Vegas, New Mexico, with the reputation of being haunted. (Photo by Joan Alessi)

by dense foliage and a broken fence, and decide immediately that they are haunted. The negative reputation of these buildings is enhanced if the inhabitants are elderly or reclusive. Owners of these houses report frequent vandalism and harassment, especially around Halloween.

One house which has become a lucrative tourist attraction because it looks like a haunted house is the famous Winchester Mystery House, discussed at some length in chapter 3. Although there is no resident ghost or other reason to designate this eccentric, never-finished mansion as haunted, when tourists go inside of the Winchester Mystery House it speaks to them through disembodied voices emanating from interpretive loudspeakers hidden in its walls and grounds. There's just enough that's oddly creepy about the Winchester Mystery House that one can see why

Stephen King took the idea to Hollywood horror heights in his TV miniseries *Rose Red* (2002). According to one Web site, "The house itself actually becomes a character in the film, taking on a monstrous life of its own. And like Sarah Winchester's mansion, it is never quite finished and at one point, the characters hear the sounds of otherworldly hammering and sawing" (Taylor 2002). In the movie, Rose Red is in Seattle, but despite the change of address and heightened drama, the parallels between Rose Red and the Winchester mansion are clear, as the movie's official Web site indicates: "[Rose Red] was built in 1907 by Seattle oil magnate John P. Rimbauer. His wife, Ellen, had spent her life adding on to the house—bizarre rooms like a mirror-floored library and stairs leading nowhere—until she mysteriously disappeared into it. Yet in the decades since Mrs. Rimbauer vanished and the construction stopped, the house has gotten even bigger, seemingly all by itself" (The Tale 2002). An even more creative twist on the theme of a self-creating house is an innovative novel by Anne Rivers Siddons, *The House Next Door* (1979). In this "utterly familiar and strikingly innovative" novel, the house destroys every family that inhabits it because the house literally personifies the evil that underlies the unfortunate life history of the architect (Bailey 1999, 79). Popular culture haunted houses that have a life of their own and draw energy from their human inhabitants or intruders are rarely found in oral tradition.

Interior of a Haunted House

To better understand how the haunted house functions as the setting for ghost stories, conceptually one must cross the threshold and be enveloped by the supernatural domain within. Oral tradition and its ability to tap into our psychological collective unconscious presents the interior of the iconic haunted house as a setting in which to verbalize our deepest fear and loathing. For example, with the lyrical imagery of innocence, a child reacting to the sight of the bombed-out shell of the Alfred P. Murrah Federal Building in Oklahoma City remarked, "It looked like a haunted house without walls." Familiarity with the iconic architecture of the haunted house provided a way for this child to conceptualize an otherwise inconceivable sight (Ross and Myers 1996, 13).

Although the exterior of the iconic haunted house is ideal for visual representation in popular culture to set a receptive and creepy, chill-bumpy mood, the interior of the house takes on special significance in the narrative development of ghost stories. Contemporary ghost stories about haunted houses told by American children generally dismiss the exterior of the house with a simple reference such as "and there was this big old haunted house." No description is necessary because the image is so well fixed through literature and popular culture. A mere reference is sufficient to evoke the image in the minds of the listeners. Likewise, in oral tales the interior of the house is not described in any detail. There is no need to specify the type or arrangement of furniture or the color of the wall hangings or drapes. When listening to or telling a ghost story, the internal imagination of the listener or teller furnishes the interior of the house. The only necessary cue is the realization that once the door slams shut after the protagonist has crossed the threshold, whatever takes place inside the house will be other-worldly and surreal, and the laws of logic and physics no longer apply.

Once inside the haunted house, the action of the ghost story usually takes place in the attic or the basement or on the connecting staircase, locations rich with psychological symbolism of isolation and evil (Grider 1976; Tucker 1980; Felton 1999). According to folklorist Gillian Bennett, "Haunted places are thus seen to be no-go areas such as cellars and attics, or betwixt-and-between places such as stairs and doorways. . . . All these expressions and assumptions may be found time and again in accounts of hauntings from medieval sermon stories to popular ghost gazetteers" (1999, 44). By crossing the threshold from the safe natural world outside into the interior of the haunted house, the human characters have moved horizontally from one reality into another. The liminal staircase, which is neither up nor down, enables the human characters to move vertically between the levels of horror within the haunted house. The attic and the basement are the extreme or most remote locations within the house and, therefore, the farthest away from reality. The attic or garret is at the top of the house, closest to the roof and the safety of the reality outside. But that roof or vaulted ceiling is still an impenetrable barrier that traps the human in the supernatural realm. The basement is organically at the bottom of the house; it is below the ground, in contact with the forces of the underworld. Whereas the roof or windows of the attic provide tantalizing hopes for escape and reunion with the outside world and reality, escape from an earth-dug cellar is hopeless and impossible, psychologically analogous to being buried alive.

These locations within the haunted house are spatially unambiguous and favor tight, well-defined, enclosed spaces. To a viewer outside of a house, the general floor plan of the building may be ambiguous, but the top/attic and bottom/basement are unmistakable. The relative position of horizontal bedrooms, sitting rooms, parlors, and so forth follows no logical pattern and cannot be discerned from observing the outside facade of the house. Neither do these rooms figure in most narrative ghost stories, unless there is a secret staircase or passageway connected to one of these rooms. But it is obvious to one viewing the outside of a multistoried house that it must have an attic and a basement connected by a staircase and that those areas delineate the top and bottom of the house. This dynamic focus of activity on the staircase and its upper and lower termini explains why the haunted house of tradition and popular culture is nearly always multistoried. The interior action of a ghost story dictates the exterior configuration of the limits of a haunted house.

The liminal staircase, of course, joins the two terminal loci of the attic and the basement; being on the staircase means that one is neither up nor down. In oral ghost stories, the general pattern is for the helpless human victim to hide or take refuge in an upstairs bedroom or the attic when the ghost is first heard or appears on the stairs. The ghost and not the human controls the action on the staircase (figure 4).

FIGURE 4: A contemporary child's drawing of a haunted house depicting a ghost moving up the stairs from the basement to the top story bedroom. The ghost on the staircase may depict the antagonist of the popular children's ghost story, "The Ghost of One Black Eye." (Drawing courtesy of Jeannie Banks Thomas)

The most dramatic example of a ghost story that fits this pattern is the common children's adaptation of Mark Twain's "The Golden Arm" discussed in chapter 4 in which the ghost methodically ascends the staircase, announcing his progress step-by-step by intoning, "I want my golden arm." The story concludes with a dramatic scream from the narrator, who grabs a listener and shouts, "Now I've got it!" In this popular story, the ghost rises from the grave to reclaim whatever the human protagonist has stolen from it. As the story unfolds, it becomes a drama that breaches the "fourth wall" and makes both storyteller and audience active members of the cast. The house to which the protagonist retreats after robbing the corpse is not haunted until the vengeful ghost enters and stalks the guilty human. As told by children, part of what makes this story so popular is the terrifying concept of the invasion of a safe haven by an evil, supernatural force intent on justified revenge. The story becomes a cautionary tale that implies that no place is really safe for one who breaks society's rules, in this case by stealing from a corpse.

The subliminal association of house basements with castle dungeons and torture chambers makes the basement infinitely more threatening than the attic, which frequently serves as a last refuge. Humans generally hide in attics to escape ghosts, but they still do not escape unscathed. A common ghost story motif is the human protagonist who survives the encounter with a ghost in a haunted house, but is later found catatonic—with their hair turned white—in an attic or closet (motif F1041.7). The popular culture stereotype features ghostly sounds coming from the attic, and the most common sound is rattling chains. Ghosts frequently pursue their human prey to the absolute upper limits of the house—namely, the attic. But ghosts and monsters do hide in basements and cellars, where they lure unsuspecting humans to suffer unspeakable terrors. In reality, murder victims are sometimes buried in cellars or basements, thus adding to the general perception that these lower reaches of domesticity are dangerous and frightening. Perhaps one reason the murder of child beauty queen JonBenet Ramsey in the basement of the elegant family home in Boulder, Colorado, during the Christmas holidays in 1996 created such intense popular interest is the juxtaposition of potent but conflicting cultural symbols: basement, murder, beautiful child, Christmas (e.g., Douglas and Olshaker 2000; Schiller 1999; Wecht 1998).

As folklorist William Nicholaisen points out, the juxtaposition of upper and lower is a dominant feature of folktale settings and the lower realms are always associated with evil and other-worldliness: "the vertical descent always remains just that—a going down through a hole, a crack, a passage into a dark and unfamiliar and therefore exotically threatening world below" (1990, 17). Perhaps as a way of defusing some of the intrinsic terror of going into a real basement in a real house, many children's ghost stories have a jokelike structure that ends with a punch line rather than the murder or torture of the child protagonist. One cycle of these ghost stories parodies childish fears of basements by having the child protagonist beat up or otherwise subdue the invisible entity in the dark basement. In these stories, the unseen ghostly voice keeps chanting, "One black eye, one black eye." The ingenuous or otherwise innocent child protagonist turns the world of the ghost story upside down by finally replying, "Shut up or you'll be the Ghost of Two Black Eyes." Children readily understand the not-so-subtle pun on who's going to get black eyes in a fight between the ghost and the protagonist (Vlach 1971; Grider 1976, 1980a, 1980b; Tucker 1980). This story is discussed in more detail in chapter 4.

In this jocular tale, the young hero demonstrates that the enclosed spaces of the basement in children's ghost stories are, according to Nicholaisen, "worlds of magic and otherness, of evil intentions and deserving rewards for kindness shown, which the adventurous, the bold, the fortunate, and the sweet-tempered can reach without damage—though not without risk—and from which one can return better, richer, and more favored than ever" (17). As chapter 4 explains, children's ghost stories enable children to explore the world of the supernatural and at the same time maintain emotional distance from the truly frightening concepts.

POPULAR LITERATURE

Consistent with the ghost stories of oral tradition, the aesthetic of contemporary literary supernatural terror is introspective. Within the walls of the haunted house of popular fiction lurk all manner of supernatural and sadistic terrors, expected and unexpected. Readers know that any human foolish enough to enter one of these haunted houses will be the victim of supernatural or demented, evil-possessed villains.

Popular literature ghost stories and haunted houses do, however, differ from oral tradition in one main aspect. For one thing, the literary haunted house puts the entire nuclear family at risk. In children's ghost stories, on the other hand, only the young protagonist actually enters the haunted house; no adults are around to provide assistance or rescue. Popular literature also exploits the haunted house formula in order to achieve unusual or dramatic variations on the theme of supernatural encounters. This formula is clearly outlined in Dale Bailey's *American Nightmares: The Haunted House Formula in American Popular Fiction.* According to this formula, the plot employs a sequential structure in which "an escalating series of supernatural events...isolates the family physically and psychologically" followed by "the discovery of provenance of those events." The climax of this discovery is either "the escape of the family and the destruction of the house" or "the escape of the family and the continued existence of the house" and "a twist ending which establishes the recurring nature of evil" (1999, 56).

Oral tradition, as is appropriate to tradition's innate conservatism, adheres rather consistently to a few basic themes which differ significantly from those of popular fiction; for example, ghosts go away when they are avenged, humans who encounter ghosts frequently come off badly or at least are changed by the encounter, and traditional ghost narratives are generally low-key and nondramatic.

Following a trend utilized earlier by Edgar Allen Poe in *Fall of the House of Usher* ([1839] 1979) and Nathaniel Hawthorne's *The House of the Seven Gables* ([1851] 1933), popular literature has brought the literary innovation of the haunted house as character to unexpected heights of psychological terror. The unseen supernatural inhabitants of these haunted houses assume the role of supporting characters who are seemingly controlled by the house itself. Instead of functioning as a deus ex machina, the haunted house *is* the machina, completely outside of human control. As pointed out by E. J. Clery in *The Rise of Supernatural Fiction, 1762–1800* (1995), this particular role of the haunted house is at least as old as the gothic novel itself. According to Clery,

Montague Summers was one of the first, though not the last, to remark that it is the haunted castle, rather than any of the assorted heroes or villains, that takes the role of protagonist in the majority of Gothic fictions, embodying the influence of the past over the present, the dead over the living. From *The Castle of Otranto* onwards this priority is reflected in their titles. . . . Formally speaking, inanimate property takes on independent life; the existence of its inhabitants is subordinate to the unfolding of its fate. (1995,73)

Almost two hundred years after Walpole wrote *The Castle of Otranto*, Shirley Jackson, an undisputed master of the genre, created one of the most chilling descriptions in all of literature of a haunted house:

No human eye can isolate the unhappy coincidence of line and place which suggests evil in the face of a house, and yet somehow a maniac juxtaposition, a badly turned angle, some chance meeting of roof and sky, turned Hill House into a place of despair, more frightening because the face of Hill House seemed awake, with a watchfulness from the blank windows and a touch of glee in the eyebrow of a cornice. Almost any house, caught unexpectedly or at an odd angle, can turn a deeply humorous look on a watching person; even a mischievous little chimney, or a dormer like a dimple, can catch up a beholder with a sense of fellowship; but a house arrogant and hating, never off guard, can only be evil. This house, which seemed somehow to have formed itself, flying together into its own powerful pattern under the hands of its builders, fitting itself into its own construction of lines and angles, reared its great head back against the sky without concession to humanity. It was a house without kindness, never meant to be lived in, not a fit place for people or for love or for hope. Exorcism cannot alter the countenance of a house; Hill House would stay as it was until it was destroyed. (1959, 34–35)

In contrast to the female Monster House discussed later in this chapter, Hill House, "with its tower erect against the sky is 'unmistakably male' . . . and it doesn't treat its women kindly" (Bailey 1999, 14). Shirley Jackson's description of Hill House echoes Poe's introduction to *Fall of the House of Usher*:

> During the whole of a dull, dark, and soundless day in the autumn of the year, when the clouds hung oppressively low in the heavens, I had been passing alone, on horseback, through a singularly dreary tract of country; and at length found myself, as the shades of the evening drew on, within view of the melancholy House of Usher. I know not how it was—but, with the first glimpse of the building, a sense of insufferable gloom pervaded my spirit. . . . I looked upon the scene before me—upon the mere house, and the simple landscape features of the domain—upon the bleak walls—upon the vacant eye-like windows—upon a few rank sedges—and upon a few white trunks of decayed trees—with an utter depression of soul which I can compare to no earthly sensation more properly than to the after-dream of the reveller upon opium—the bitter lapse into common life—the hideous dropping off of the veil. . . . (Poe [1839] 1979, 1237–38)

Recognition of these famous literary haunted houses is so widespread in American culture that these images synergistically reinforce the haunted houses of tradition, which are minimally, even elliptically, described in ghost stories. No external description of them is necessary for a reader or listener to know exactly in what setting the action of a good ghost story unfolds.

POPULAR CULTURE SPIN-OFFS THAT REINFORCE TRADITION

Haunted houses are a staple of popular fiction, and images of haunted houses in a wide range of other contexts have become a staple of American popular culture in general. The famous New Yorker cartoonist Charles Addams (1912–88) probably has done more than any other individual to standardize the stereotypical image of the haunted house in America discussed earlier in this chapter. Hired in the 1940s as a full time cartoonist for the *New Yorker,* he drew over 1,300 cartoons before his death in 1988. He also published numerous anthologies and collections of his cartoons (e.g., Addams 1991). Through the years he created, expanded, and refined his famous "Addams Family" who lived in what has become the quintessential haunted house image of popular culture. Addams drew his haunted house with the familiar motifs: dilapidated, multistoried, broken windows, mansard roof, turrets, and leafless trees surrounded by a broken fence, and with a dark and stormy background. He drew scores of similar images during his career, culminating with the so-called Addams House in which his menagerie of creepy ghouls and monsters live. According to Ron MacCloskey, founder of the Charles Addams Art Scholarship Fund, Addams's famous cartoon haunted house is modeled on a Second Empire house in Westfield, New Jersey, his hometown (Charles Addams n.d.).

The appeal of Addams's haunted creation was spread even wider when *The Addams Family* became a popular TV sitcom which ran from 1964 to 1966 and still appears in reruns. In 1977 a made-for-TV movie, *Halloween with the New Addams Family,* was telecast. In 1991 *The Addams Family* was released in theaters as a movie, followed in 1993 by *Addams Family Values.* Although these movies and television episodes featured live actors, an animated version based on the Addams characters ran on TV from 1973–75. The animated characters also made a guest appearance on *Scooby Doo,* resulting in the "haunted" castle or mansion set that is now a standard feature of this animated children's comedy about a talking dog and his mystery-solving human companions (1969–72). The perennially popular characters moved from cartoons to live action movies in *Scooby Doo* (2002) and *Scooby Doo 2: Monsters Unleashed* (2004). Although considerably less popular than *The Addams Family, The Munsters,* another live-character TV sitcom, which ran from 1964 to 1966, also featured a family of eccentrics and supernaturals living in a haunted mansion. These characters all live on and on in TV reruns, introducing successive generations of American children to the primary motifs of the quirky popular culture haunted house and its many supernatural and sometimes zany denizens. In the past forty years or so, other movies have featured or parodied a haunted house remarkably similar to Charles Addams's creepy mansion, including *Rocky Horror Picture Show* (1975), *Psycho* (1960), and *Texas Chainsaw Massacre* (1974), all of which have developed devoted cult followings that keep them in circulation decade after decade.

There have been innumerable movies featuring haunted houses in the thirty or so years since the Addams Family TV sitcom and movies. The most recent of these is the animated, PG-rated *Monster House*, released in the summer of 2006. This eponymous house is perhaps the best example of a haunted house that exhibits virtually every literary conceit and traditional motif associated with the theme. Similar to *Rose Red* and *The House Next Door*, this house is alive because it has absorbed the spirit of its angry and eccentric builder. A much-maligned fat lady in a circus, this woman hates children because they were her primary tormenters in the circus. She died during the construction of her dream house when she was chasing a gang of hooligans away from the site. She slipped and fell, with the cement mixer, into the unfinished basement and her corpse was entombed there in the concrete. This episode resonates with folklorists as a variation on the well-known ballad "The Walled-Up Wife," with its echoes of foundation sacrifice (Dundes 1996). Her bereft husband finished the house, which erupts in fury years later when some neighborhood children go inside and are trapped in the basement and then escape.

In an action-filled, suspenseful sequence several minutes long *Monster House* tears itself from its foundation and chases the terrified children into a construction site. In the process, the house totally deconstructs and is finally dynamited out of existence by one of the children. And of course this walking haunted house is reminiscent of the hut on dancing chicken legs of the Russian fairy tale witch, Baba Yaga. The self-deconstruction of *Monster House* also resembles the more lyrical and surrealistic mechanical castle in *Howl's Moving Castle* (2004), a classic animated film by the Japanese master of the medium, Hayao Miyazaki. The force that drives Howl's castle is not human hatred but rather a benign fire spirit who is the custodian of the hero's heart or life force. All of these various media creations combined—from magazine cartoons to TV sitcoms to animated movies to online video games—have helped etch the multistoried, turreted mansion into American popular culture as the prototypical haunted house.

THE MATERIAL CULTURE OF POPULAR CULTURE HAUNTED HOUSES

Haunted houses have become a kind of metaphysical category of material culture through their representation in a variety of popular culture media. Stylized images of haunted houses are especially prevalent at Halloween, when graphics of haunted houses are featured on greeting cards, book covers, and other seasonal decorations (Belk 1994). Miniature haunted houses, complete with lights and spooky sound effects, are popular decorations during the Halloween season. Advertising for everything from candy to new cars exploits the pop culture repertoire of Halloween in every context imaginable, and haunted houses are part of nearly every advertisement. Knowledge of this shared cultural archetype is thus taught to each new generation and renewed annually by Halloween marketing (figure 5).

Halloween marketing has made Halloween the second most lucrative holiday for merchants, closely following Christmas for consumer expenditures (Belk 1994). Although early in the twentieth century Halloween was largely a vernacular holiday celebrated by children wearing homemade costumes, today the holiday is big business targeting adults perhaps even more than children. Children's Halloween activities in many communities have been relegated to carefully regulated costume parades in shopping malls and local neighborhoods before dark, after which parents take the children to local hospitals to have their candy treats X-rayed for "razor blades in apples," an apparent popular response to the murder in 1974 of a child in Texas with trick-or-treat candy (Ellis 1994). Although the Texas

FiGURE 5: Children playing with a haunted house pop-up book that features a staircase. (Photo by Jeannie Banks Thomas)

murderer, the child's father, used packaged Pixi Stix candy laced with cyanide to kill his child, the popular imagination has seized instead on the more threatening and hyperbolic image of razor blades and straight pins allegedly being inserted into the treats by unknown persons (Best and Horiuchi 1985; Grider 1984).

But what of haunted houses at Halloween? As mentioned above, images of fanciful, stereotypical haunted houses are used in all sorts of Halloween advertising, especially to advertise "spooktacular" sales at local department stores and such. Party favors and decorations also feature haunted houses in various combinations with other Halloween motifs, including ghosts, witches, black cats, and bats. Special topical, mass-market picture books are published annually around Halloween, many of which portray visits to cartoonish haunted houses (e.g., Bunting 1994). Halloween greeting cards are perhaps the most common medium in which haunted houses are depicted. Surrounded by this avalanche of holiday-themed popular culture, the connection between haunted houses and Halloween is annually and emphatically reinforced.

As a result of this flood of marketing, the haunted house of current popular culture has lost most of the ominous and numinous quality associated with the literary haunted house and has become instead a benign, stereotyped cartoon or other medium of entertainment. Nevertheless, the constant reinforcement by popular culture of the image of the stereotypical haunted house keeps the darker concept in the forefront of public awareness. Advertisements and other popular culture venues never have to explain what a haunted house is to viewers. Consumers recognize a haunted house when they see one!

The popular appeal of haunted house images extends far beyond Halloween. One of the most popular attractions at Disneyland Anaheim is the venerable Haunted Mansion in New Orleans Square, which opened in 1965 (Grim Ghosts 2004). This elaborate and stereotypical haunted house contains practically every conceit associated with the genre, from both literature and popular culture, including a vast cast of animatronic ghosts as well as architectural features inside and out designed to both fascinate and shock visitors (Baham 2002). The designers of the attraction readily admit their debt to popular literature, including Shirley Jackson's *The Haunting of Hill House* (1959), during the planning of the Haunted Mansion attraction.

Disneyland's Pirates of the Caribbean ride opened in 1967, and in many ways is an extension of the Haunted Mansion attraction. The ghostly pirates and their ghost ship, the *Black Pearl*, were the inspiration for the 2003 movie blockbuster *Pirates of the Caribbean: The Curse of the Black Pearl* and its sequel *Pirates of the Caribbean: Dead Man's Chest* (2006). The final movie in the trilogy, *Pirates of the Caribbean: At World's End*, was released in the spring of 2007. Disneyland's animatronic ghosts were the apparent inspiration for Johnny Depp's Academy Award–nominated portrayal of pirate Jack Sparrow, which further reinforces the close bond between the Disneyland ride and the movie. In movies such as these, the folk and literary traditions merge into a larger cultural phenomenon of popular culture imitating or quoting other popular culture.

Toy haunted houses and model kits have been marketed since at least the 1960s, when the famed Aurora Plastics Company manufactured a detailed Addams Family Haunted House model kit. Another toy haunted house is the Whipstaff Manor Playset, a marketing tie-in with the haunted house in the movie *Casper* (1995), marketed by Trendmasters, Inc. The most recent example of toy haunted houses is the Goosebumps Terror Tower Playset, marketed by MicroVerse by Kenner, which contains "spring action executions, trap doors, dungeons, and revolving fireplace." Such mass-marketing directed toward children has transformed not only haunted houses but also Dracula, Frankenstein, werewolves, witches, and ghosts into children's cartoons and playthings. The enormously successful Goosebumps children's books owe a tremendous debt to this general acceptance of the supernatural by American children, especially their fondness for haunted houses.

COMMERCIAL AND CONTRIVED HAUNTED HOUSES AT HALLOWEEN

By the 1950s, dramatic mock-ups of various haunted house tableaux became popular throughout the country as fundraising and entertainment venues during the Halloween season. Typically, a respected service organization will transform a local vacant building into a mock interactive haunted house by creating various rooms, each of which is a scary tableau depicting familiar scenes and characters from the world of the supernatural as well as the crazed and demented, including insane butchers and mad scientists. The exterior of the venue is of little consequence; all that matters is the action that takes place inside. Designated members of the organization dress up as various characters who either act out frightening minidramas of torture and ghostly encounters or escort paying customers through the maze (Magliocco 1985). The earlier mock haunted houses were more "kid friendly" than the houses today with their elaborate gory tableaux. For example, in the earlier venues of thirty or forty years ago customers were blindfolded and led through a series of tactile experiences such as plunging their hands into bowls of peeled grapes that they were told were eyeballs, bowls of cooked spaghetti that they were told were brains, and so forth.

The mock haunted house phenomenon at Halloween accentuates the connection between ghost stories and haunted houses. Mimicking the plots of ghost stories, visitors physically enter the staged scenes and are forced to interact in carefully contrived interior tableaux which are designed to shock and frighten visitors, especially when a costumed member of the cast unexpectedly jumps out at the visitors or grabs them. The "ghost tour" phenomenon discussed in chapter 6 utilizes many of these same techniques, especially having costumed characters scream and lunge at customers during especially dark and scary parts of the tour. The popularity of Halloween haunted house concessions is their focus on action in the interior of the venue, instead of allowing customers to merely view the fixed and static exteriors that the greeting cards, party decorations, figurines, and storybook illustrations portray. Literally and psychologically, these commercial haunted houses are intimate and introspective. The whole point of these productions is to lure customers inside.

These haunted house venues have become so profitable that various "how-to" books are on the market explaining business strategies to enhance profits, in addition to detailed instructions on setting up various scary tableaux (Chavez 1997; Morris and Phillips 1985). The general public, however, resists total year-round commercialization of these local events, preferring instead to keep them as annual Halloween fund-raisers for community charities. In many communities in which trick-or-treating has been banned or is closely restricted and monitored, visits to these haunted house fund-raisers have replaced trick-or-treating.

"Hell Houses"

Since the advent in the 1970s of the ultraconservative political movement commonly known as the "Christian Right," a new and different type of Halloween haunted house venue is becoming increasingly popular in some parts of the United States. Called "hell houses," these disturbing productions eschew the conventional supernatural in favor of hyper-realistic depictions of drunken car wrecks, abortions, bad drug trips, gay marriages, and so forth, all of which are intended to create terror and revulsion among audiences. These hell houses conclude with a scene portraying Jesus in heaven and thus, according to one Web site, "proselytize the unsaved public" and also "promote certain conservative Christian beliefs" (Religious Tolerance 2004). After the concluding heavenly tableau, many hell houses then direct visitors to a consultation room where they can pray, fill out visitation forms, or meet with counselors. The goal of hell houses, of course, is to gain converts. These controversial venues have received widespread coverage by both the national and international media, and in 2001 a documentary video was released about the Hell House at Trinity Church of Cedar Hill, Texas (Hell House n.d.; Joseph-Witham 2004).

Hell houses represent the most extreme appropriation and manipulation of the haunted house formula in order to further a religio-political agenda. Nevertheless, these hell houses also can be classified as contemporary variants on the older, more traditional haunted house fund-raising venues. The traditional Halloween haunted houses focus on depictions of the bizarre and the supernatural, but with no agenda other than raising money for charity and entertaining visitors with a good but temporary scare. Special effects at these more conventional venues are usually fairly limited in order to avoid negative publicity that would keep away paying patrons—especially children, the primary audience. The hell houses, on the other hand, definitely do have an outspoken agenda of "in-your-face, high-flyin', death-defyin', Satan-be-cryin', keep-ya-from-fryin', theater with no holds barred, cuttin-edge evangelism" (God Destiny 2006).

In recent years, as hell houses have become more and more extreme, some of them have allegedly bordered on the illegal and pornographic. There have been unconfirmed reports of the use of real human corpses in at least one hell house in 1999 and also reports of reluctant converts being beaten until they repent while church members watch. In order to maintain the intense and focused presentation style and subject matter, the fundamentalist Destiny Church of the Assemblies of God of Broomfield, Colorado, markets the Hell House Outreach Kit for $299 (God Destiny 2006; Pam's House Blend 2005).

In October 2006, the hell house phenomenon emerged in a surprisingly unconventional venue, serious theater. Produced in a Brooklyn theater "usually reserved for edgy bands and performance artists," the script closely followed the walk-through tableaux format of regular amateur church productions, "presenting a grotesque and shocking imagining of contemporary secular culture." Carefully avoiding spoof and parody, the actors' performances were straightforward and serious. As a result, they successfully "gave viewers a peek, albeit extreme, inside an unfamiliar world." The Brooklyn production played to full houses throughout its run and was reviewed by the mainline New York media (Philips and Miller 2006).

Conclusion

The interplay between oral tradition and popular culture invests the haunted house with the power of an almost universally recognized cultural icon. Since each new generation of American children is enculturated annually at Halloween with a whole panoply of supernatural information, including the appearance and significance of the haunted house, mass marketing responds with more and more books, movies, and artifacts each year. The cycle of knowledge is thus perpetuated and strengthened. Oral tradition, however, still clings to its ancient roots.

Although the glittering enchanted castle will always be the quintessential setting for the fairy tale or *Märchen*, the haunted house of the ghost story—with its shadowy darkness, skewed perspectives, and evil countenance—is a negative mirror image that is brooding and introspective, inviting psychological involvement. The haunted house image—both inside and out—has remained consistent for at least the past two hundred years, the result of dynamic sharing and borrowing across genres and across media. The debate regarding the empirical reality of ghosts and the places they allegedly haunt exists on a conceptual plane quite separate from the shared cultural image, or mental template, of the haunted house. Regardless of whether one can point out an actual, literal haunted house on the landscape of one's own neighborhood, the shared image of what such a haunted structure would look like and what could happen inside it is a reality. The stories we tell about haunted houses reinforce this reality. According to the distinguished cultural theorist Yi-Fu Tuan, discussing the medieval church at Glastonbury,

> In those times, certain types of artifacts did appear to glow with numinous presence, but such attention as they attracted depended to a large degree on speech—on the circulation of vivid tales concerning a particular object or place. A sword lost its magic and a house ceased to be haunted if people no longer talked about them. Words are necessary to sustain the potency of a visual symbol. (1980, 467)

The marketing uses to which the haunted house is subjected in our postmodern world demonstrate that good sales don't dilute the potency of a visual symbol but probably enhance it. In the final analysis, the haunted house can be conceptualized in folkloric terms as the ugly stepsister of the enchanted castle, just as the evil fairy who curses Sleeping Beauty is the negative counterpart of her sparkling sisters. Both the enchanted castle and the haunted house have the "rooms . . . sharp borders and horizontal and vertical interior lines" that Swiss folklorist Max Lüthi attributes to the fictional and fanciful folktale (1976). The lines and angles of the haunted house, however, are forever skewed and out of focus. The enchanted castle often floats above the terrestrial world on a cloud or is protected from contact with the "real world" by other means. The basement or cellar of the haunted house, however, is dug into the primordial earth and is thus another manifestation of Lüthi's shadowy and threatening legend cave (Lüthi 1976, 21). Metaphorically, the haunted house represents the point of contact, the transition, the threshold between the legend and the folktale, between reality and fiction. Reality exists *outside* of the haunted house. It is upon entering into the confines of the haunted house that the psychological landscape shifts and exposes us to the other-worldliness of the supernatural and the paranormal.

Six

The Commodification
of Belief

DIANE E. GOLDSTEIN

In May of 2001 an advertisement of a home for sale in the
Scottish Borders was posted on escapeartist.com's international
real estate listings and simultaneously advertised in real estate
listings in Scotland. The ad, which was reposted in December
2003,[1] announced:

> Home for Sale or For Rent in Scottish Borders, United
>   Kingdom
> Historic (Friendly Haunted) Family Residence
> Sell Price: $240,000
> Rent Price: $2,000 Per Month
> Location: Woodville House
> Melrose Road
> Earlston TD4 6DP
> Berwickshire, Scotland
> Scottish Borders
> United Kingdom
> Property Type: Single Family home
> Property Details: HISTORIC "WOODVILLE HOUSE"
> Constructed Circa 1705 AND NOW BEING OFFERED
> AT THIS AMAZING FIRM PRICE IF AN OFFER IS IN
> AND CONCLUDED BY MARCH 2004. Two Fireplaces
> alone are worth around $18,000 and there are numerous

171

antiques and paintings included now. The Seller is VERY MOTIVATED due to pending relocation in October. A truly magnificent (HAUNTED BY FRIENDLY GHOST) and spacious five bedroom stone built family residence constructed on four levels, now being offered at an incredibly attractive firm price to attract a quick sale. The house is extremely well located in one of the most scenic and historic areas of Scotland on the main A68 tourist route from the city of Edinburgh.[2]

The advertisement went on to describe a house most of us would be delighted to call our own—well located, professionally restored, retaining historic features such as a sitting room with a Regency carved fireplace and yet also boasting modern conveniences including a fully tiled split-level designer bathroom with "selective lighting effects." Nothing more is said in the advertisement about the briefly mentioned "friendly ghost." While we are not given much information about the ghostly resident, we are given some inkling about the sellers. What we are told, or what we can extrapolate, is that the owners or the estate agents involved in the sale of the house believe a friendly ghost to be an attraction, a selling feature worthy of mention in a posting placed in an international real estate listing.

The sellers of Woodville House are not alone in their recognition of a ghost as a potential selling feature and, in fact, a number of cottage industries and small economic initiatives have come to depend on consumer interests in ghosts. Ghost tours, haunted hotel travel guides, ads for haunted restaurants, real estate, cars, and all manner of other places and things publicized as haunted attest to the importance of other-worldly visitors to the tourism and leisure industry and to contemporary consumer culture.

The academic understanding of the relationship between traditional belief and commodified forms, however, has not generally been as positive as the entrepreneurial view of that relationship. In her book *"Alas, Poor Ghost!"* Gillian Bennett writes, for example, "Where it is not campaigned against by religious groups or sneered at by rationalists, the supernatural is often trivialized by the mechanisms of commerce" and "officially demoted to the nursery, commercial or fantasy worlds" (1999, 1). Bennett is far from unusual in her assertion that commodification strikes at the heart of supernatural seriousness, eroding or mimicking the nature of folk tradition and making a joke of otherwise sincerely held folk beliefs. In fact, her comments echo Edith Wharton's early argument (1937) that the "ghost instinct" is "being gradually atrophied by those two world-wide enemies of the imagination, the wireless and the cinema" (Wharton [1937] 1973, 2); they also parallel Bridget Marshall's 2004 critique of Salem, Massachusetts's touristic marketing of itself as the "Witch City." Marshall argues that the marketing campaign "capitalizes on its haunted history at the same time that it distorts and evades that history" (Marshall 2004, 244).[3]

The views of Bennett, Wharton, and Marshall are consistent with standard notions of authenticity, cultural appropriation, and tourist consumption that emphasize the negative transformational impact of commercialization. Sack (1992), for example, asserts that places of consumption focus only on those activities directly related to the purchase and use of commodities or the consumption of vistas and experiences. But while the commodification of culture certainly has a transformational effect on the traditions it celebrates, the assertion that the results of the commodifying process are necessarily trivializing is perhaps a bit too dismissive. A closer look at the merchandizing of haunted real estate and ghost tourism suggests that to the contrary, commodified culture is multifaceted, complex, and as likely to be a site for social meaning as any other. With the goal of not simply dismissing commodified forms without consideration, this chapter will explore the reasons for and nature of scholarly distrust of the commercialization of belief and will also examine the role of commodification in the creation of new and different contexts for the serious exploration and expression of belief.

Ghost lore is, of course, commodified in a huge variety of forms: as part of the eBay haunted object frenzy and spirit bottles trend mentioned in the introduction; in literature, television,

movies, and electronic games; as images on greeting cards and
Halloween decorations; in theme park "houses of horror"; and
even on the images on candy wrappers and the shapes chosen
for children's cereals. While all of these items commodify ghosts,
they each do so in a slightly different manner, a manner largely
determined by their medium, their audience, and the messages
they wish to exploit. This chapter explores the notion of ghosts
as a commodity through consideration of ghost tours, haunted
hotel travel listings, and issues related to the commercialization
of haunted real estate. The forms discussed specifically here
create a somewhat unified group because all three forms commodify spaces based on their reputed association with ghosts.
However, unlike theme-park-type haunted houses that are spaces
originally constructed as paranormal commodities, the spaces
discussed here are real spaces that have been subsequently marketed as haunted. The sections below are intended to provide
an introduction to some of the unique issues that surround the
commodification of haunted real estate, ghostly hotels, and ghost
tours. These sections are followed by a discussion of commodification that contrasts academic concerns and assumptions with
vernacular understandings of haunted space commodification.

Haunted Real Estate

While ghost tours are a relatively new phenomenon, the advertising of haunted real estate is not. Leslie Shepard reports that
in 1919 a number of British newspapers carried an ad for several
consecutive weeks offering for sale a gothic mansion near Bath
known as Beckington Castle. After describing the idyllic location and the architectural splendor of the castle, the advertisement went on to say that "the place was [all] the more desirable
because it was reported to be haunted" (Shepard 1984, 585).

Such hauntings are not only advertised in relation to castles
and mansions. The Texas Real Estate Center Online News
(RECON) advertised in October 2002 the online auction of the
federal courthouse in Corpus Christi, Texas. Built in 1915, the
building was reported to boast "Classical Revival architecture,

decorative cast concrete, decorative wood brackets under its eaves and ghosts" (RECON 2002, 3). The courthouse was reputed to be haunted following the unexplained shooting deaths of the postmaster and his assistant in 1939. In a discussion of the potential impact of the ghostly stories on the sale of the building, real estate broker Cliff Atnip was quoted as saying "anything that will make people talk about your building is a good thing" (RECON 2002, 3). Eric Wade, who purchased an inn in Pennsylvania that had listed among its features two resident ghosts, agrees. He has reported that if he ever sells the property he will advertise the presence of the ghosts just as the former owners did. "Whether people believe the stories or not," Wade is reported to have said, "they give this place an added touch" (Hines 1991, 9).

But is having stories of ghosts associated with a building you are trying to sell always a good thing? Some sellers, buyers, and real estate commentators say no. One study done by two business professors, James Larsen and Joseph Coleman, found that supernatural notoriety almost always lowered a home's selling price. Homes reputed to be haunted take roughly 50 percent longer than comparable homes to sell, and haunting can lower the selling price by 15 to 35 percent (Christie 2001, 1). Larsen described one case where a broker showed a couple a home where a murder had taken place. "The broker was walking ahead of them about thirty feet into the house when he started telling them about the murder . . . and when the broker turned around, the couple had disappeared" (Christie 2001, 1).

So what determines whether or not a ghost associated with a property will be seen as a commodity? The positive or negative impact of assertions of the existence of paranormal residents on property value appears to hinge on a couple of primary issues: the scope of a tragedy, nature of a death, or reputed behavior of ghostly visitors associated with a property; and the manner in which that information comes to be known.

Some homes become completely unsaleable by virtue of the horrific nature of deaths or disasters associated with the property. The home of Sharon Tate, who was killed by Charles Manson's followers, became completely undesirable despite its placement in Benedict Canyon, just north of Beverly Hills. The home ultimately was demolished and replaced with a bungalow that itself took two full decades to recover market value. The Milwaukee apartment building that housed gruesome murderer Jeffrey Dahmer, and where he committed his atrocities, became so stigmatized that not only was the building's desirability severely diminished but so were property values in the entire neighborhood (Fleck 1997, 2). While the notoriety of these locations may turn away some potential buyers, most specialists in these types of "tainted" real estate agree that it is fear of paranormal activity that keeps buyers away.

The buildings implicated in the Tate and Dahmer murders are referred to in real estate and legal discourse as "stigmatized properties." The American National Association of Realtors defines a stigmatized property as one that "has been psychologically impacted by a suspected or actual event that occurred on the property, resulting in no physical impact of any kind" (Hofmann 1999, 2). Included in this category are crime scenes (particularly murder scenes), suicides, and stigmatized illnesses (especially AIDS) that render properties difficult to market and sell (Hofmann 1999). Stigmatized properties, in short, are properties where a real or rumored event occurred that didn't physically affect the property but nevertheless adversely impacts its desirability. In many states in the United States, real estate disclosure laws govern the sale of stigmatized properties.

Prior to the 1990s, real estate disclosure laws were rare with most states honoring the notion of "caveat emptor" or "let the buyer beware." Caveat emptor placed the burden of recognizing defects that might affect property value on the shoulders of the purchaser. Today, most state real estate laws require sellers to disclose *material facts* that might affect a purchase such as roof damage, soil erosion, hazardous substances, structural problems, or other defects that might affect the value of the property. Some states, however, also require the disclosure of information that might *psychologically* impact on purchase, including crime, death, disease, and—yes—the reputed presence of a ghost.

In the 1983 California case of *Reed v. King* the court held that a broker had a duty to disclose the fact that a woman and four of her children had been murdered in the house. The court ruled that "blemishes of real property which are not physical defects or legal impairments to use" can affect resale value and should be disclosed. However, subsequent California rulings suggested that psychological impacts on property should be time limited. The California legislature passed a law forcing brokers to disclose a murder at a property up to three years after the crime (Fatsis 1995, B16).

Perhaps the most interesting stigmatized property case involved the 1990 contested sale of an old Victorian mansion in Nyack, New York. The owner, Helen Ackley, sold her home to Jeffrey and Patrice Stambovsky for the asking price of $650,000. The Stambovskys put a payment of $32,000 down on the house but discovered shortly after they placed their down payment that the house was reputed to be haunted. Although the Stambovskys had heard about the hauntings from a local architect who was simply passing on the rumor, subsequent inquiries revealed that numerous articles had been published on the mansion's paranormal activity in a variety of local and national publications including *Reader's Digest.*[4] Ackley herself had been promoting the house as haunted. She had written a number of the published articles and had allowed her home to be featured on the haunted house walking tour of Nyack. According to Ackley, the home featured a "cheerful, apple-cheeked" ghost and a number of other ghostly visitors "dressed in Revolutionary period clothing" (Fatsis 1995, B16). When the Stambovskys learned of the alleged disturbances in their prospective home they tried to back out of the real estate deal, but Ackley refused to cancel the sale. The Stambovskys took the case to court and lost on the grounds that the doctrine of caveat emptor made it their responsibility to uncover defects before entering into a contractual obligation (McClelland 1991).

The Stambovskys persevered with an appeal to the Appellate Division of the State Supreme Court and subsequently won with a narrow three to two decision. Writing for the majority, Justice

Israel Rubin stated that he was "moved by the spirit of equity" to allow the couple to break the contract. Rubin argued that because the Stambovskys were from out of town they could not be expected

> to have any familiarity with the folklore of the Village of Nyack. Not being a local, plaintiff could not readily learn that the home he had contracted to purchase is haunted. Whether the source of the spectral apparitions seen by defendant seller are parapsychic or psychogenic, having reported their presence in both a national publication (*Reader's Digest*) and the local press, defendant is estopped to deny their existence, and, as a matter of law, the house is haunted. (Madigan 1995, 2)

Justice Rubin continued:

> A very practical problem arises with respect to the discovery of a paranormal phenomenon: "who you gonna call?" as a title to the movie *Ghostbusters* asks. Applying the strict rule of caveat emptor to a contract involving a house possessed by poltergeists conjures up visions of a psychic or medium routinely accompanying the structural engineers and Terminix man on an inspection of every home subject to a contract of sale. In the interest of avoiding such untenable consequences, the notion that a haunting is a condition which can and should be ascertained upon reasonable inspection of the premises is a hobgoblin which should be exorcized from the body of legal precedent and laid quietly to rest. (Madigan 1995, 2)

Justice Rubin's discomfort with the topic of ghostly stigma can be seen in his tendency to resort to comedic uses of virtually every cliché associated with the paranormal. Rubin's reach for comedy in the middle of a legal majority opinion on a precedent-setting case most likely reflects his discomfort with having to cast a public and official opinion on a topic normally kept hidden in very private belief. A review of legal and popular articles written about disclosure of stigmatized properties indicates the general extent of this discomfort, with many sporting humorous titles such as Marianne Jennings's "Buying Property from the Addams Family" (Jennings 1993) or Lee R. Sullivan's "Spooks Stay Free" (Sullivan 1993). Numerous articles also could not resist tongue-in-cheek warnings that buyers should recognize that they have a potential problem if they notice the seller wearing garlic around his neck or blood dripping from the side of his mouth (Jennings 1993).

This is what happens when commodity meets belief. The private nature of belief issues, when commodified, become no longer about the individual stance of a believer or disbeliever but rather about seller and buyer and occasionally (as in the disclosure debates) about agents, inspectors, specialists in contract, and even whole legal jurisdictions. Whether or not the buyer or seller even believes in ghosts, marketing value is dependent on community tradition, oral history, and narrative. Resale is tied to folk process through community traditions of belief and rumor. Jennings notes, "Indeed, part of the fear of buying a property where a death has occurred may be the fear of hauntings, as well as the fear that you will never be able to dump the property on some other unsuspecting fool" (Jennings 1993, 46 fn. 25).

Folk tradition, of course, also affects the two crucial issues that determine the positive or negative marketability of haunted real estate—the nature of the death and way that information comes to be known. Like Woodville House, most advertisements of haunted houses emphasize the friendly nature of the ghostly inhabitants. Malevolent ghosts or ghosts believed likely to be bent on revenge are not advertised and generally cause the most concern if narratives about them are discovered and not disclosed. In her study of death and real estate, Kelso notes that the important distinction that determines the extent of the psychological impact of death in a prospective home rests on the issue of accidental or natural deaths versus unnatural deaths (Kelso 1998, 78). Kelso observes, "A natural death is rarely problematic when it comes to living at the site" (1998, 78). Unnatural deaths including murder and suicide appear to be a different thing. One of Kelso's informants argued,

> Well I guess it has to do with some vague belief that . . . the
> negative energy accompanying such an act can be conta-
> gious. . . . Also, when I think about ghosts or hauntings,
> the idea of unhappy or fitful spirits seems more plausible
> to me than other explanations. Those would be more
> likely with suicide and murder victims. So, although
> I don't know that I can honestly say that I "believe" in
> ghosts, I would be afraid of actually encountering one in
> a building in which such an occurrence had taken place.
> (Kelso 1998, 87)

While many of Kelso's informants emphasize the concern
with residual energy,[5] there is also a concern about murdered
victims returning for ghostly revenge. This belief in a vengeful
ghost connected to a gruesome or unnatural death is common
in ghost tradition, and in fact Louis C. Jones found in his survey
of over five hundred ghost narratives from upstate New York that
roughly one-third had died violent deaths. Gillian Bennett, in
her book *Traditions of Belief*, discusses two opposed poles of belief
in the returning dead suggested in her interviews with women
in England—"the wholly evil and the wholly good" (1987, 36).
At the evil end of the pole exists belief in "the meaningless,
malevolent, disruptive phenomena that the women refer to as
'things in houses,' 'spirits,' 'ghosts,' 'poltergeists,' or 'haunted'/
'wrong'/'nasty'/'unhappy' houses" (37). This contrasts with the
good dead, "whose presence is felt or who are heard or glimpsed
around the family home [and] are loved, familiar, trusted,
needed and welcome" (50). When buyers knowingly purchase a
property believed to be haunted, they appear to wish to purchase
a friendly ghost, or in Bennett's terms, "the good dead."
    But knowledge of the ghost, and how that knowledge is
revealed, is also crucially important to the buyer. When buying
the ghostly presence is a matter of choice, the ghost is a commodity, but when the ghost is encountered by accident it becomes a
liability for both sellers and buyers. Another person interviewed
by Kelso indicated that

personally, I wouldn't want to live in a house where someone had died or not necessarily, no I think even just died a natural death. Which is probably crazy, but it's just, I personally, and probably those people are like me, you know you sort of feel, not that I believe in ghosts or anything, but that the presence of that person is still there, kinda thing, and you know you don't want to turn around some night when you're there all on your own and there's Great Aunt Clara sittin' in the chair, . . . right? (Kelso 1998, 83)

While encountering a surprise ghost may be disturbing, it does not appear to be so upsetting as encountering a surprise rumor of a ghost or other forms of paranormal notoriety. The vast majority of disclosure law cases have rested on issues of property reputation rather than events reported inside the house. Let's face it: discovering that your new home is displayed nightly on a ghost tour as one of the most frightening places in the country to live may not be entirely conducive to settling down happily in your new abode.

Haunted Hotels and Inns

In 1980, Frances Kermeen bought an old mansion in St. Francisville, Louisiana, known as Myrtles Plantation. Her idea was to live in the mansion, furnish it with period antiques, and turn it into a romantic inn. No one told Kermeen that the plantation had a reputation for being haunted—a reputation that went back over one hundred years. Although she did not believe in ghosts, Kermeen indicated that she began to see ghostly figures constantly on the property. According to Kermeen, when she called the police to investigate (thinking she was a victim of a hoax), the police chief himself encountered a hoop-skirted woman who vanished before his eyes (2002, 26). Much to her initial dismay the story of hauntings at the plantation was picked up by the popular press, resulting in numerous sensationalistic stories in magazines and major newspapers. The haunting was also reported on every major American TV news channel and

Kermeen was eventually interviewed on a variety of human interest shows including *The Today Show* (1952–2007), *A Current Affair* (1986–1996), and *Ripley's Believe It or Not* (1982). Kermeen reported that when the initial excitement was over she became distressed by the coverage. She wrote:

> It was the worst thing that could have happened, I despaired. My inn would be avoided like the plague. No one would ever book a room, or host a wedding. My dream would be crushed. I'd go bankrupt. How wrong I was. Rather than hurting the business, as I feared, stories of the hauntings brought people by the droves. Thousands of people overwhelmed me with room requests. Ghosts turned out to be the greatest possible attraction. People came from all over the world, hoping to experience the ghosts at the Myrtles. And experience them they did. Over the years I collected more than one thousand personal ghost accounts from guests. (Kermeen 2002, 2)

Kermeen took so much interest in what was happening that she eventually started to explore other inns and hotels that reported resident ghosts. She continued:

> I began to hear from other inn owners from all over the country who also had ghosts. Most of them harbored the same fears. I was fascinated by their stories and I began to visit other haunted inns. Wanting to share this information, I wrote a travel guide of haunted inns for people who'd love to have a ghostly encounter. (Kermeen 2002, 3)

Kermeen's haunted hotel guide, *Ghostly Encounters: True Stories of America's Haunted Inns and Hotels* (2002), is joined on the market by *Haunted Hotels: A Guide to American and Canadian Inns and Their Ghosts* (Mead 1995), *Dinner and Spirits: A Guide to America's Most Haunted Restaurants, Taverns and Inns* (Wlodarski 2001), *Weekend Haunts: A Guide to Haunted Hotels in the UK* (Mead 1994), as well as a huge number of regional guides. Web searches uncovered, in addition to books, a number of advertisements for haunted inns, a Forbes slide show guide to "most haunted hotels,"[6] a map of the United States where you can click into a state of your choice for a listing of haunted accommodations, and a series of ads for lifestyle documentaries on notorious haunted hotels and inns from around the world. Kermeen, like so many of her colleagues, had happened onto a ghostly gold mine. Apparently, some people, actually many people were willing to pay for the opportunity to stay in a haunted room in a hotel, and many hotels were willing to advertise that they had a ghost on their premises.

Ghost tradition associated with hotels is not uncommon. Joe Nickell suggests that as places which house large numbers of visitors overnight or for longer periods of time, hotels and inns "allow extended time periods for visitors to have unusual experiences" (2000). Hotels are also intricately linked to symbolic events typically associated with reasons for ghostly return—marriages, acts of infidelity, suicides, and natural deaths. Some hotels and inns are predictable in their linkages with ghost traditions. They have long histories or have been the location of major current events, and many look or even play the part. Most haunted hotels surround visitors with historical architecture and romantic decor. The high ceilings, arched windows, drapes, furniture, wall sconces, and long corridors are the stuff of film and theater. But not all. The Holiday Inn at Grand Island, New York, despite its 1970s Holiday Inn-type decor, boasts a child ghost named Tanya who is said to inhabit room 422.

Some hotels play up their ghostly connections, holding ghost tours, séances, murder mystery nights, or historical and paranormal theme parties. For example, the Grove Park Inn in Asheville, North Carolina—home of the ghostly "pink lady"—hosts a paranormal weekend every January. The Buxton Inn, a tavern built in 1812 in Granville, Ohio, has its staff dress in period costume making them hard to distinguish from the multiple spirits called "the townspeople" that are said to haunt the facility. The St. James Hotel in Cimarron, New Mexico, advertises that twenty-six men came to violent deaths within its walls during its history as a Wild West saloon and hotel. The hotel not only is known for the numerous ghosts said to inhabit the building, but also for its murder mystery nights when guests come in costume to re-enact the lives and deaths of the hotel's most notorious ghostly customers. But some hotels are quieter or more cautious about their haunted history.

A few years ago, we three authors of *Haunting Experiences* stayed in one of these hotels while attending a 1997 conference at the historic Hotel Boulderado in Boulder, Colorado. Built in 1909 and restored and remodeled numerous times over the years, the hotel still retains much of the Victorian elegance intended in its original design. The rooms were replete with four-poster beds and large elaborate wooden wardrobes and, as in most hotels, the table top was covered with literature on the accommodations, the area, and local attractions. Among this literature was a hotel guest services guide, which featured the following story entitled "Ghosts Continue to Haunt the Hotel Boulderado":

> On a recent visit to Boulder, a doctor and his wife checked into the hotel for the first time. The husband had a meeting to attend, so his wife entered the room alone at 10:30 a.m. She was given the same room that a few months earlier had been assigned to a spiritually-oriented Native American. He had refused to stay in it because of a feeling he had when it was shown to him. But many other guests had come and gone in the interim with no comments. The doctor's wife, however, was happy with the room and felt comfortable upon arrival. . . . "At noon I heard a woman's voice, and maybe a baby's in the room," she said later. "I wasn't scared and the thought crossed my mind that some presence might be there, but I decided not to tell my husband or anyone else about it."

The article continues:

> At 4:00 p.m., her husband arrived and switched the television to basketball. . . . No sooner had he started to watch the game, then he heard a woman's voice, and said to his wife, "I think this place is haunted." They both heard it again and could almost figure out what the voice

was saying. They laughed about the incident and weren't frightened. The doctor looked up and saw a "white filmy thing" in the mirror of the dresser. Shaken up, he decided to have his first drink of the day, and went into the other room of their suite to get some ice out of the refrigerator. As he opened the refrigerator door, a shadow crossed the coffee table in a place where no sun shone in. He tried to create a similar shadow with his body before going back to the bedroom to tell his wife. . . . They spent the night in the room. When they checked out the next morning and told a sympathetic desk clerk what they had seen, they were totally amazed that other guests had reported similar experiences in the same, and only the same, room. (Pettern 2004, 13)

While the desk clerk in the narrative indicates that others had similar experiences in the Boulderado—but only in that room— Roz Brown and Ann Alexander Leggett, authors of *Haunted Boulder: Ghostly Tales From the Foot of the Flatirons*, suggest a more pervasive Hotel Boulderado ghost tradition. They note:

Over the years, guests have reported doors opening and closing on their own, whispers and voices in seemingly empty hallways, and wispy apparitions seen, out of the corner of one's eye, disappearing through doorways and drapes. One guest reported feeling as though she was being followed, only to turn and find she was alone. If there are ghosts in the Hotel Boulderado, they've never managed to frighten away the multitude of guests that come and go each year. These phantom spirits seem to enjoy the plush carpets and overstuffed furniture along with the rest of us as they continue to haunt Boulder's historic hotel. (2002, 103)

Although Brown and Leggett emphasized in their book the multiple ghostly experiences of visitors throughout the hotel, especially on the third floor, the hallways, and at the sites of three separate suicides that occurred over the years in the building, the hotel services guide emphasized only one haunted room—"the same, and only the same, room" as Pettern wrote (2004, 13). This incongruity is instructive. As we saw in the previous section, while ghosts can be a commodity, not everyone wants to buy them. In fact, one guest at the Boulderado during our visit commented, "Did you see the story in the hotel guide about the ghost? I sure hope it's not my room." Advertising one room with a ghostly resident limits the attraction to those who might seek such an experience while simultaneously not driving away those who might be frightened by the possibility of such an encounter. Nevertheless, the haunted hospitality industry does have a consumer base. So much so, in fact, that thousands of ghost enthusiasts spend their holidays every year moving from one haunted hotel to another (Mead 1994).

GHOST TOURS

Perhaps the most popular type of ghost commodification is the ghost tour. Edinburgh, Dublin, London, Melbourne, Brisbane, Tasmania, Paris, Prague, Venice, Krakow, and Cape Town all advertise ghost tours, as do numerous other locations around the world. In North America and in the United Kingdom virtually every major tourist city advertises at least one ghost tour, and in many cities competing companies distinguish themselves by specializing in very specific kinds of ghostly phenomena. How widely popular and available such tours are is evidenced by the 1,530,000 Web site hits prompted by a 2007 Google search of the phrase "ghost tours." Retrieval of a significant number of those sites reveals that they are largely advertising pages for actual ghost tours—tours located far and wide, and involving everything from planes, trains, buses, and foot tours to ghostly overnights, and exploring everything from haunted houses to haunted streets, pubs, churches, graveyards, and even visits to locations associated with tragically deceased celebrities.

Ghost tours have been around for quite some time in the United Kingdom but are a fairly recent phenomenon in North America. Erik Seeman argues that the first North American

FiGURE 1: Reverend Zombie's Voodoo Shop, starting location for Haunted History Tours. New Orleans, Louisiana. (Photo by Diane Goldstein)

ghost tour was Richard T. Crowe's Chicago Supernatural tour, which began in the mid 1970s. The Chicago tour however, was well ahead of the real boom in ghost tours, which took place in the late 1990s (Seeman 2002, 2). Ghost tours typically follow a similar format. The tour guide meets patrons at an easily identifiable location (a statue, historic building, or a murder site), which usually will itself become the topic of an opening narrative (figure 1). After waiting for a critical mass of customers and collecting the fee (generally five to twenty dollars), the tour guide will begin strolling from location to location, narrating stories and pointing out markers of ghostly or grisly concern in the surrounding landscape. Typically ghost tours cover very little spatial ground. Nevertheless, most tours fill two hours, time spent largely engrossed in tales of local history and the supernatural. Many tours conclude the trip with a visit to a haunted pub or store, where visitors can continue to savor their experience through the purchase of ghost tour books, videos, and T-shirts.

FIGURE 2: A ghost tour guide in plain street clothes, Haunted History Tours. New Orleans, Louisiana. (Photo by Diane Goldstein)

Ghost tour guides often dress in period clothing for the occasion, and in many cases lead the tours "in character." In St. John's, Newfoundland, tour operator Dale Gilbert Jarvis appears on the steps of the Cathedral of St. John the Baptist as the Very Reverend Thomas Wyckham Esquire. He is dressed in black cloak and tricorn hat carrying a skull-tipped, bone-white cane in his hand. He begins, "This is not a tour for the faint of heart," and continues by informing the crowd that he would not be responsible for "shortness of breath, palpitations of the heart, melancholia or even sudden death" (Jones 2002). Despite his ghost tour character, Jarvis is in fact not a man of the cloth at all, but by day actually a mild mannered actor, author, folklorist, and expert on local architecture who works for the provincial Heritage Foundation.

It is also not uncommon for tours to have a number of hired actors involved in jointly hosting the walk, with each dressed as one of the ghostly figures. Some tours use what are known among

Scottish tour operators as "jumper ooters," individuals dressed as historical or ghostly figures that jump out at the tour party from unexpected doorways and alleys. Other operators believe that "jumper ooters" compromise the historical integrity of the tour and argue that the authenticity of the stories is at risk if too much drama is involved. Inglis and Holmes note, "Some tour operators are keen to give the impression that the past speaks for itself" (figure 2). They continue, quoting personal communication with the operator of Edinburgh's Mercat Tours, "It is 'the vivid detail of the stories' which makes the tour 'a lively spine-chilling and accurate portrayal of [a] . . . grisly past'" (2003, 58). Joy Fraser, writing about Scottish ghost tours (as were Inglis and Holmes), indicates that tour operators identify three key ingredients which together form a recipe for ghost tour success. "According to this emic recipe," writes Fraser, "a good tour is one which 'mixes history, humor and horror' to create a performance which is informative and entertaining and is also effective in scaring the audience" (Fraser 2005, 20).

In the "Popular Ghost Tours Reviews" Web site, a site that evaluates tours, Fiona Broome assesses ghost tours according to four criteria, all adding up to overall "value for your money." She lists these criteria as "presentation, location, history and ghost potential." Broome's description of each of these criteria is significant in terms of the values used in assessing ghost tours. She writes:

> Presentation means the personal style of the guide, and how well he/she interacts with the guests. This is where we rate how much fun the tour is, based on how we enjoy the tour, as well as how the other guests seem to enjoy themselves. Locations score extra points for being genuinely haunted, and not easily located by tourists on their own. We expect a mix of popular sights and off the beaten path locations. On most tours, we expect at least one cemetery or "morbid" location.
>
> *Ghost potential* indicates the likelihood of returning with "ghost photos" or a great encounter with something

chilling. We expect at least one genuinely haunted location on each tour.

> *History* is judged based on how authentic, unique and plentiful the stories are. We expect primary-source research from the average tour company. (2004, 4)

Broome distinguishes, however, between two different kinds of ghost tour audiences. She notes:

> Overall value for your money lets you know whether it's worth taking this tour, if you are a ghost hunter. If you are simply looking for a fun evening, base your choice on "Presentation" ratings. . . . (2004, 4)

Broome assumes the ghost hunter to be the target audience for her reviews, treating the ghost enthusiast as the normative audience, while those simply looking for a "fun evening" are treated as secondary. A review of ghost tour advertisements suggests that while tours don't often make this distinction explicit and certainly don't minimize the emphasis on fun, many companies nevertheless focus their advertising on the on the promise of visitors encountering supernatural phenomena while on the tour. Ghost Tours of Niagara, for example, headlines their Web advertisement with bold letters indicating the dead have been on 60% of the tours. In smaller letters underneath this headline, they boast:

> On two-thirds of the tours we have run since 1994, visitors have encountered something not of this world. Perhaps the next story we tell will be about you. . . .

The Sleepy Hollow of Gettysburg Candlelight Ghost Tours makes a similar claim.

> Many have experienced sightings of their own while walking with us. Will you be among those who have seen the ghostly form of a visitor from another time?

Mercat Tours Haunted Underground Experience walk advertises:

Since we first ventured into the dark chambers hidden within the south Bridge, many visitors and guides have experienced for themselves the residents of the vaults whose spirits linger.[7]

Many tours likewise use their Web sites to post photographs or testimonials of supernatural events that took place during their tours. The Haunts of Daytona Tour in Daytona Beach, Florida, posts photos of orbs floating in a cemetery that they say "seem to follow our guest on the first third of our tour." The City of the Dead Tour in Edinburgh, Scotland, posts a diary-style list of incidents reported to have occurred on their cemetery visit. Below is a short excerpt from the list.

7 June 2004: Joe Keohane from Boston woke the morning after his tour with three large puncture wounds on his side. 22 May 2004: Katie Baker from Leeds heard scratching sounds in the tomb and when she got home she found a large bruise on her leg. 21 May 2004: Markus Palmen and his friend heard low grumbling sounds emitting from the back wall of the mausoleum.

These advertisements suggest that it is not simply the promise of scary stories and historical locations that consumers seek in choosing a ghost tour, but also the potential for their own ghostly experience.

The Commodification of Ghosts

What weaves together ghosts in real estate, ghosts in hotels, and ghosts on walking tours is that all three cultural forms attempt to sell interest in a location through that location's association with ghosts. In these examples, ghosts are a commodity. But commodification of ghosts, it is worth noting, is not a new development in cultural history. Apart from the early advertising of ghosts as a selling feature for real estate (such as Beckington Castle in 1919), commodification in the form of ghost tourism has in a certain sense existed since the late eighteenth century. Following the dawning of the enlightenment, which focused so heavily on the banishment of all that was irrational, ghost beliefs began to become associated with cultural "otherness," especially among the elite. Based on Keith Thomas (1991), Inglis and Holmes argue that people in general and elites in particular had "stopped seeing ghosts" in their own lives and locales. According to Inglis and Holmes, "as rationalism became the primary mode of elite perception of the world and the entities that existed within it, the ghost was banished to the peripheries, both mental and geographic" (2003, 52). This marginalization sent eighteenth-century travelers in search of a mythical and mystical past and created a kind of literary tourism in which travelers followed romantic images fostered by works of fiction such as those of Sir Walter Scott. (Inglis and Holmes 2003; see also Clery 1995).

In North America, the real expansion period of ghostly commercialization occurred during the middle of the nineteenth century. The development of popular ghostly commodification followed the rise in popularity of American and British Spiritualism in the late 1840s. Two events occurring within a year of each other inspired these developments. In 1847, Andrew Jackson Davis, sometimes referred to as the John the Baptist of Spiritualism, published *The Principles of Nature: Her Divine Revelation; and a Voice to Mankind*, a book that introduced large numbers of Americans to the notion that the souls of the dead could communicate with and through men and women. The following year, Margaret and Kate Fox, two sisters from Hydesville, New York, claimed that they had contacted the spirit of a dead peddler. The Fox sisters began to offer séances in their home. Ultimately séances and other events associated with communication with the dead developed into hugely popular events. By the 1860s séances were considered to be a major form of popular entertainment involving large numbers of mediums who made their living by holding public demonstrations of "spirit communication" in theaters and auditoriums. Industrialism fueled this commercial interest in ghosts, promoting the creation of books on the supernatural, mediums' tracts and handbills, and even mass-produced Ouija boards.[8] Ghosts were not only a commodity, but they were wildly lucrative.

The current wave of popular ghostly commodification appears to have developed as a result of a number of cultural imperatives occurring simultaneously. As noted, ghost tourism began in North America in the mid 1970s and really bloomed in the 1990s. These developments coincided with the blossoming of baby boomer spirituality and New Age interest in the celebration of a diversity of belief traditions, but also occurred at the same time as a shift in focus in the media to increasingly violent and reality based television[9] and a shift in tourist consumer patterns. Thomas Blom argues that modern tourism has moved toward a focus on morbidity related events, evident in visits to celebrity grave sites and spontaneous shrines (such as that of Princess Diana or Jim Morrison), locations of famous disasters (such as submarine trips to visit the wreckage of the *Titanic*), and museum exhibitions focused on war, brutality, and genocide (such as the Holocaust museum in Washington D.C.). He calls the interest in these attractions morbid tourism,[10] which he defines as "on the one hand, the form of tourism that focuses on sudden violent death and which attracts large numbers of people and, on the other, an attraction-focused artificial morbidity-related tourism" (Blom 2000, 32). Blom considers numerous explanations for this shift, including the possibility that as we become more and more used to tourism we seek existential experiences and not just material physical experiences. He argues:

> New, different and seemingly strange experiences are in demand from the increasingly choosy tourist. Is it perhaps our relatively secure western existence that is creating a demand for the frightening, the unknown and even the supernatural? (2000, 32)

While Blom's comments are interesting, one could question the assumption that morbid tourism is new, especially if one considers the older forms of ghost tourism noted above, or for that matter the medieval taste for morbid public spectacles evidenced by commercialized pilgrimages to locations housing relics of saints (Geary 1986). Nevertheless, whether prompted by growing spiritualism or a modern obsession with the macabre or both

combined with an overwhelming need to experience more, tourist attractions focusing on death and the supernatural are being
produced and consumed in ever-increasing numbers. From a
commercial standpoint, ghost tours and other types of morbid
tourism are a godsend. They create new niches that keep tourism
markets exciting and they cost comparatively little to produce.

So where is the problem? Commodification occurs, according
to Cohen, when "things come to be evaluated in terms of their
exchange value" (1988, 381). As places, events, and activities
evolve to meet the needs of consumers, culture and tradition are
themselves redefined as commodities that can be bought and
sold. Selective image-making enhances certain aspects of culture
and removes other less desirable elements. The act of consum-
ing culture itself is a culture-creating and culture-altering force.
New meanings emerge that often conflict with the meanings
once ascribed by the local community. Tourism and cultural
commodification is "not just an aggregate of merely commercial
activities; it is also an ideological framing of history, nature and
tradition; a framing that has the power to reshape culture and
nature to its own needs" (MacCannell 1999, 1).

While the prevailing notion maintains that culture is threat-
ened by cultural commodification, concerns about that threat
take a particular shape when applied to what we can call "belief
tourism."[11] Belief tourism, like all tourism, is the marketing of the
experiences of cultural "others," but with a particular focus on
the images and traditions associated with spiritual, metaphysical,
or paranormal values. Belief tourism takes on a variety of forms
in addition to the marketing of ghost belief, including such
commercial ventures as voodoo museums in New Orleans; crop
circle tours in southern England; UFO exhibitions in Roswell,
New Mexico; and commercial promotions of the town of Salem,
Massachusetts, as the location of witch trials.

Like Bennett, Wharton, and Marshall, most folklorists and
other scholars of belief who bemoan the cultural commodification of ghosts do so in part because of a respect for belief and
believers and a concern with the lack of seriousness and potential for trivialization involved in the commercializing activities.

These concerns reflect the general worries with cultural tourism previously noted, including issues of authenticity, exploitation, and residual effects on cultural traditions. But our academic commitment to the importance of respect for belief, combined with our knowledge of the sacredness or at least seriousness of those traditions, orients our concerns in particular ways. What seems to make us most uncomfortable about the commodification of ghost belief can perhaps be summed up in three concerns: one, the trivialization of the tradition through stereotyping and sensationalism; two, the fragmentation of the tradition, resulting in blended forms and decontextualization; and, three, the dichotomization of induced or intentional versus spontaneous experience suggesting invented tradition.

Trivialization

Ghost tours certainly cash in on the wild and wonderful imagery of the paranormal. Rattling chains, skeletons that pop out at you as you are walking, and buckets of water thrown seemingly from nowhere during particularly chilling stories are not uncommon and neither is the extensive rewriting of traditional narratives to capitalize on entertainment value. In addition to costumed characters, piped-in sounds, and "jumper ooters," many ghost tours use only flickering candles for light and lock participants into small dark spaces. These stereotypical images combine the ghost tour with the imagery of Halloween haunted houses, moving what are often stories based on local tradition into the realm of what one person interviewed calls "popular silliness." For folklorists, this aspect of ghost tours creates problems of inauthenticity, at odds with what we know about traditional belief. Bennett notes:

> The full blooded ghost stories with howling storms and dogs, hollow voices echoing in cobwebby attics, white clad figures flitting through the gloom of old houses by the light of a single flickering candle are the stuff of literary fiction, not folklore. Fact is more prosaic. The strange experiences we have and talk about to others and which

FiGURE 3: A ghost tour guide in period costume, Haunted History Tours. New Orleans, Louisiana. (Photo by Diane Goldstein)

go to make up the belief-traditions which our group share are, as the women I spoke to said, just little things—less baroque but more believable, less flamboyant but more fascinating. (Bennett 1987, 11)

The Very Reverend Thomas Wyckham Esquire (aka Dale Jarvis) continually stresses that ghost tours are theater, and that he leads the tour in character to emphasize the theatrical nature of the presentation (figure 3). For Dale, the theater is what his clients want and expect. But what is the reaction from ghost tour patrons?[12] Dale's comments are interesting when placed next to those of Cindy, who calls herself "a ghost tour junky." Cindy said:

You know, I like all that dramatic silly stuff. Every time I go on one of these tours I'm scared, and I know the dramatic costume and scary noises stuff is supposed to scare us more—but it actually makes me feel better. You see when I go on these things I want something to happen,

but I don't. But I do. I figure as long as they are being so
silly nothing bad is going to get me.

. Writing about regular tourism, Dean MacCannell (1999)
asserted in his important work *The Tourist* that tourism is a quest
for authenticity. In their quest, tourists are constantly seeking
entrance into the "real" or "authentic" culture. They want to see
life as it is really lived. Using Goffman's notions of front and back
regions, MacCannell argues that the front region of tourist events
is the site of "staged authenticity" (1999, 92). The tourist, however, is always trying to catch glimpses of the back region where
real everyday life occurs. MacCannell asserts that tourists will not
be satisfied by attractions that are overtly staged or faked.

While MacCannell's notion of "staged authenticity" still
remains central in critical studies of tourism, others have built on
this notion and argued in recent years that we are perhaps now
seeing a new type of tourism that no longer strives for authenticity. Urry (1990) and Rojek (1998) discuss this new form of
"post-tourism," "which is characterized by the fact that the tourist
increasingly accepts the commodified world and therefore does
not seek authentic values; further, the tourist knows they do not
exist" (Blom 2000, 32). Postmodern tourists, according to Urry,
know they are tourists and that "tourism is a game, or rather a
whole series of games with multiple texts and no single, authentic tourist experience" (Urry 1990, 100).

In belief tourism the effects of post-tourism and the quest for
authenticity or inauthenticity is more complex. Like Cindy, most
of the people interviewed about ghost tours were ultimately in
search of an authentic experience, but weren't, but were. . . . The
sought-after authentic experience, however, for those interviewed
was not simply hearing the *real* story of a historical murder, not
being in the *real* tomb where the poltergeist is reported to have
been. In fact, those things appear to be interpreted as the play
part of the experience. The *real* sought- after experience was the
potential for one's own supernatural encounter. The informants'
desire to see a ghost or hear or feel something was rivaled only
by their fears that is exactly what would happen. The result is an

ambivalence that wants the inauthentic as much as the authentic (defined in their terms), but which also wants the two to be separate and identifiable. Karen contrasted the in-character tours to the more straightforward ones by saying:

> Where she was done up as a witch is kind of like, over-dramatizing it. Like making you think that a witch is leading us and telling creepy stories, even though you know she's not a witch. I did enjoy it, but it's a different kind of enjoyment. You don't get the hair standing up on the back of your neck, like [you do] when you hear of other people who might have seen something. . . . Being told that by a witch doesn't give you the same hair standing up on the back of your neck feeling. It is fun just to hear the stories though. A different kind of enjoyment.

The quest for the real, but in the form of a paranormal personal experience, was discussed by each of the people interviewed as one of the main reasons they seek out ghost tours. While responses to ghost tours are multivalent and multivocal, Eric Seeman, a historian and one of the few academics who has written on ghost tours, notes that skeptical customers are in the minority on most tours (Seeman 2002, 4). Further, the tour companies themselves are conscious of the desire of their clients for personal ghostly experiences and orient their marketing to stress that potential. One company was quite transparent about the boost in interest factor created by promoting ghost potential. They noted in their Web promotion:

> The chance that one of them [a specter] might glide gracefully across your path as you tour a palace or a stately home really puts the tingle into sightseeing. Bleak corridors and empty alcoves are a whole lot more interesting when . . . [a ghost] is a possibility. (quoted in Inglis and Holmes 2003, 57)

Inglis and Holmes respond to this type of marketing by saying:

> Nonetheless, there are problems with the deployment of irrational phenomena in the service of highly

rationalized and bureaucratized forms of generating income from tourists. On the whole, ghosts do not make reliable employees. It is reported that it is a standing joke among Scottish tourism officials that "real" ghosts are liable not to turn up "on cue" when a party of tourists is being guided around the putatively "haunted" locale. The lack of the revenant thus could potentially quite seriously spoil the experience. (Inglis and Holmes 2003, 57)

Because of the unpredictability of guests having or reporting an experience during tours, guides often work into their narrative stories of their own experiences or those of past patrons. Other operators narrate experiential testimonies on film (such as *Journey into Darkness*, a film by the New Orleans Haunted History Tours) or even phrases on T-shirts (such as the "I Saw Dead People" shirts available for purchase on the Niagara tour). Like legend trips[13] to neighborhood haunted houses, ghost tours and haunted hotel stays provide contexts for old narratives as well as new, emergent, tradition-maintaining beliefs and stories. Karen, for example felt she had an experience on the Niagara tour and has incorporated that experience into her narrative repertoire. She said:

> We were walking up past this one building and I said to my sister-in-law, "Ohhh, candle light in the window." We were joking around about it, laughing, and I looked back later, there was no candle in the window. And the leader of the tour, when I asked about it [said] all the buildings . . . all the lights are off in the building until we go in and turn them on and turn them off when we leave. So that was kind of weird, I saw a candle and I joked about it thinking, ohhh you know, how spooky and there was actually no candle there.

We should not be surprised that for tour patrons, character portrayals and over the top dramatization exist side by side with less trivialized, more serious aspects of belief and personal narrative. Such a combination mirrors traditional supernatural culture in which serious belief genres and personal experiences are held in repertoire and told together with humorous genres and more heavily fictionalized narratives. Tour patrons, like other audiences, make generic distinctions and adjust expectations accordingly.

FRAGMEПTATIOП

The trivialization factor that concerns academics in dealing with commodified forms is interwoven with concerns about fragmentation. In the re-creation of traditional culture for a market audience, tradition is by definition fragmented, re-engineered, and reinvented as experiences for visitors to enjoy. Most tour operators will admit that they alter the narratives, deleting confused or boring parts, and occasionally merging two or more narratives to heighten dramatic effect. Similar types of fragmentation are characteristic of all postmodern and commodified forms. Martin Laba (1986) and Henry Jenkins (1992) connect this process of fragmentation in "rituals of consumption" (Laba 1986, 14) to Levi-Strauss's concept of bricolage. The bricoleur, according to Levi-Strauss, is adept at performing a large number of tasks but does not subordinate them to the availability of raw materials and tools conceived of and procured for the purpose. He or she makes use of whatever comes to hand and elements are collected or retained on the principle that they may always be used somewhere for some project. As Laba uses the term, bricolage refers to the reordering and recontextualization of an object from an established context of meaning into a new context of meaning to communicate a completely different message. This process may involve the transformation of an item from an existing tradition into a market of commodities and then back into a subcultural artifact. In the recurrent exchanges in a small group context, the item of popular culture then takes on new meaning apart from the original producers of that item (Laba 1986, 14). Jenkins agrees. He discusses consumer "textual poaching" as "a type of cultural bricolage through which readers fragment texts and reassemble the broken shards according to their own blueprint, salvaging bits and pieces of the found material in making sense of their own cultural experience" (Jenkins 1992, 26). Ghost tour operators are certainly bricoleurs in Laba and Jenkins's sense of the term, piecing together stories that they identify as fragmented or which they themselves have fragmented into a new reordered, recombined whole. One caretaker of a historic masonic lodge indicated that lodge ghost narratives were on one ghost tour but that the tour operator had stuck a couple of the stories together into one story to "make it sound better." The caretaker, who is very proud and protective of his building, was not angered by the change, and if anything seemed to feel that it was amusing.

Of course, haunted real estate and haunted hotels rely on fragmentation as a way to exert greater control over the reputations of buildings. Hotels, as noted, will advertise ghost narratives as restricted to particular rooms or areas, and haunted real estate sales supply only enough information to attract a curious market. Fragmentation allows the entrepreneurs to manipulate motifs to fit their understanding of the market.

A couple of ghost tour fans, however, identified a different kind of fragmentation as the most worrisome part of ghost tours. Apart from the fragmenting and recombination of the content of ghost narratives, fans of the tours expressed concerns about the ripping of narratives from their original belief context. Janis said:

> I love the tours but can you imagine living on one or having them tell your story. Total strangers knowing the most horrifying, most intimate details of your home, your life, something you saw that so called "normal" people don't see.

Carl, who characterized himself as a fan of the tours, went on a tour during a work-related visit to another country. After the tour, which spent a great deal of time in a graveyard, he accidentally met a woman who told him that the cemetery was in her parish and was part of her church. Carl was embarrassed by the voyeurism involved and indicated that it had hit him that these were real places with real and perhaps sacred meaning for real

people and he didn't think he'd go on any more tours. Several
other tour fans indicated they were more concerned with ripping stories from their contexts and recombining them with new
contexts than they were about ripping narrative content apart
and recombining story elements. Their concern about context
was based on their concern for believers and a desire not to do
violence to something meaningful for tradition bearers. But
meaning, for those interviewed, rested more in belief context
then in content. This makes sense, because location was everything for these individuals. Carl said, "I go because I like to be
in spiritual places, places where you might feel something." Janis
said, "I don't really care what they say or do on the tours, I go so I
can get to those places, experience the space where things might
have happened."

INDUCED OR INTENTIONAL VERSUS SPONTANEOUS EXPERIENCE

The issue of induced or intentional versus spontaneous experience always makes academics uncomfortable. Going in search
of an experience—whether it be of a ghost or of a traditional
culture—appears always to be tinged with a sense of the artificial,
a sense that participation is about the fulfillment of expectation.
As David Hufford notes:

> The fact that an experience has been sought by no means
> proves that the seeker's intention caused the experience
> to be as it was (if I intend to get wet by jumping in the
> water, it is nonetheless the water that makes me wet, not
> my intention). But if prior knowledge and intention
> are always present, it becomes impossible to show that
> they did not cause it. This is especially true of percep-
> tual experiences which are well known to be influenced
> by expectation. . . . However, when the same perceptual
> pattern recurs in different subjects, those without prior
> knowledge of it, then prior knowledge and intention
> cease to be explanatory options. (2001, 34)

Belief scholars have tended to stay away from exploring induced experiences except in so far as they might venture to write about such events as invented tradition.[14] The tendency is to trivialize the subject, transforming serious vernacular concerns into artifacts of adolescent culture or events only worthy of academic consideration because of their role as popular entertainment. Seeking an experience suggests a predisposition to believe in that experience and, for belief scholars, that disturbs the delicate argument that believers do not jump to supernatural conclusions.

Asked if there was more of a likelihood of experiencing a ghost on the tours rather than simply encountering that experience in daily life, Linda responded by returning to the location issue. She said:

> I live in a ten-year-old bungalow in a new subdivision. I get in my car everyday and drive down new roads to my new office building. There is no place in my life where I am likely to see an old tree, let alone a ghost. So I go on tours—you know, it's like going to a museum to see old stuff. It's just that the old stuff I want to see happens to be dead.

Most of the tour patrons indicated that in addition to location, the presence of the group was important. For some, the group indicated safety in numbers. Unlike the privacy of a haunted hotel room or the seclusion of buying a haunted property, if "Great Aunt Clara is sittin' in the chair" on a ghost tour, there are others to share and confirm the experience. Like many tours, the San Francisco Ghost Hunt recognizes the attraction of communal experiences and includes in their ad the following lure, which directly articulates the support issue.

> Hopefully, as has happened to many other people on the San Francisco Ghost Hunt you may indeed meet a ghost in a safe and supportive way.[15]

Some ghost tour fans argued that paranormal experiences require confirmation. "If something happens," Carl indicated, "it is likely to be a shared experience and that would mean that

there would be others there to verify it." Carl's comments actually reverse our concerns about sought experiences as indicative
of an individual ready to jump to supernatural conclusions. The
tour group, for him, is a form of reality testing, a way to confirm
what really happened and why.

The comments of tour patrons suggest that ghost tours provide special contexts for belief, contexts that allow individuals
to pursue a desire for ghostly experiences in historic locations
where others have had the experiences they seek, and in the reas-
suring company of others. The exaggeration, silliness, and even
the tools of marketing (which make belief scholars so uncomfortable) appear to be central in creating a safe space to explore
both past and potential experience.

Likewise, induced experiences are crucial for both those who
commented on haunted real estate and those who commented on
haunted hotels as a way of managing the experience. Those who
visit a haunted hotel prefer to know what to expect, which room is
haunted, and what might happen there. The idea is attractive to
some consumers, but the likelihood of a spontaneous experience
frightens away other potential customers. Haunted real estate
is even more controlled by concerns about spontaneous versus
induced experiences. A building that one chooses as haunted is
a commodity—valued as both a home and an experience, but a
home that one spontaneously finds is haunted wrestles the sense
of agency from the consumer. While academics fear the study of
induced or sought-after paranormal belief, vernacular culture
embraces induced experience as manageable, controllable, safe,
and supportive.

Conclusion

Ghost tours, like haunted hotels and the haunted real estate
market, have rarely been written about by folklorists; when they
have, with very few exceptions, they are discussed in a scholarly
context of condemnation. But the 1,570,000 Web site hits on the
topic should tell us that our scholarly conservatism and disap-
proval of the commodification of traditional culture is unten-

able. Academic difficulties with commodification reduce consumers to passive receptors of cultural productions. However, closer study of ghostly commodified belief turns those passive receptors into creative individuals who seek personal meaning in texts created for mass consumption and express that meaning through their own interpretations. Trivialized texts don't arise intact into a vacuum and stay in a vacuum; they are integrated into pre-existing belief systems where they thrive or die out. While those who participate in ghost tours, haunted real estate sales, and haunted hotels are members of a multidimensional and multivocal community, it is clear by the passion of their discussion, the time and money spent on these undertakings, and the need (on occasion) to resort to legal recourse that haunted commodities are no trivial matter. Trivialization of tradition is perhaps instead exactly what scholars have done in their failure to see that belief doesn't turn and run when it sees a ten-dollar admission fee.

Conclusion

The "Spectral Turn"

Diane E. Goldstein, Sylvia Ann Grider,
and Jeannie Banks Thomas

It is indeed a remarkable cultural phenomenon that the para-
digms associated with scientific rationalism still pervade contemporary academic understandings of ghost lore in ways that: 1)
assert a dying tradition despite intense saturation into virtually all
areas of vernacular and popular culture and 2) stress decline as
society grows more educated and technological, despite ghostly
belief and experience professed at all educational levels and
engagement with the highest, most modern forms of technological development. In other words, we appear to be unable to
suspend belief in a paradigm that is centuries old, despite undeniable evidence of its insufficiency all around us. Our attitudes
about ghost lore are deeply disconnected and disengaged from
our actual traditions and practices. Where there is belief, the
rationalist tradition sees only spectres of cultural survivals. But as
many of the preceding chapters demonstrate, the blossoming of
ghost lore in contemporary folklore and popular culture demonstrates continuity of belief and continued fascination with ghosts
beyond fragmented survivals. With these caveats in mind, this
concluding section returns briefly to issues of popular culture,
mass media, and technology to address their role in creating or
maintaining contemporary ghost lore and their connection to
more traditional forms of folklore.

GHO8† LOR€ αη∂ POPULAR CUL†URE

As noted in the introduction to this volume, we have chosen
to view popular culture and folklore as "related rather than disparate" (Narváez and Laba 1986, 1), mutually interactive, and
employing different modes of communicative media to address
social groups of different sizes and shapes. Although definitions
of popular culture are highly disputed, the term is often understood to refer to the wide diffusion of a product and its acceptance, at least temporarily, by a portion of the population (Mazur
and McCarthy 2001, 7). For some, defining the "popular" in
popular culture is, as such, a politically charged act, implying as
Fluck notes "a facile populism that uncritically equates popular
cultural forms with the voice of the 'people' and disregards questions of ideology and social control"(1987, 3) . Certainly much of
popular culture is created, controlled, and manipulated by the
dominant culture, but as Henry Jenkins (1992) and so many others (Laba 1986; Buhle, 1987; Story 1998) have argued, audiences
are not passive consumers blindly accepting all that industry-
driven mass culture sends their way. While it is mass-produced
for mass consumption, its audience is not a mass of nondiscrimi-
nating consumers (Story 1998, 11). As popular culture theorist
John Story argues,

> To deny the passivity of consumption is not to deny that
> sometimes consumption is passive; to deny that the con-
> sumers of popular culture are not cultural dupes is not
> to deny that the culture industries seek to manipulate.
> But it is to deny that popular culture is little more than
> a degraded landscape of commercial and ideological
> manipulation, imposed from above in order to make
> profit and secure social control. Neo-Gramascian cul-
> tural studies insist that to decide these matters requires
> vigilance and attention to the details of the production,
> distribution and consumption of culture. . . . it is, ulti-
> mately, in "production in use" that questions of meaning,
> pleasure, ideological effect, incorporation or resistance,
> can be cogently decided. (1998, 228)

Although often exploitative, the popular culture industry is generally successful, like folklore itself, only to the degree to which it responds to the needs, expectations, experiences, aesthetics, and desires of its audience (Mazur and McCarthy 2001, 8). While some would argue that popular culture campaigns can create a need or interest that didn't exist until that interest was promoted by advertisers, it is hard to imagine that these campaigns would achieve any level of sustained cultural entrenchment unless they (on some level) complemented the beliefs and concerns of the targeted culture.

In recent years, technology and marketing practices have allowed niche marketing to become more feasible than in the past (see Anderson on the "long tail," 2006). This attention to niches means that marketing acts a bit more like folklore. Both folklore and mass culture have produced what can be called "blockbuster" narratives—stories that many people are familiar with (such as the vanishing hitchhiker and *Star Wars* (1977), respectively). However, folklore typically has been more nimble than mass culture because it is not generally constrained by a bottom-line mentality. That is, it travels happily among both large groups and small ones. For example, the Bloody Mary legends (see chapters 1, 3, and 4) are told across the United States and United Kingdom, while lesser-known ghost stories about debt can circulate among a smaller group of Cape Bretoners (see chapter 1). Today niche marketing techniques and the Internet are mirroring the folk process in their embrace of small groups as well as large ones. However, unlike some mass marketed items, a form of folklore (because it's not generally as constrained by profit) can survive regardless of whether its audience fills a football stadium or a living room. That ghosts thrive in both mass and folk venues is proof of their cultural durability, and one might even say immortality.

In 1991 the popular daytime television talk show *The Oprah Winfrey Show* explored the theme of ghost experiences in homes that had been built over cemeteries. Midway through the show, Oprah herself recounted:

Listen, I don't want to read about this in the tabloids, but
. . . I live very high up . . . next to some buildings with
lights. So [one night] I got up . . . [and] . . . I saw this
thing. I don't know if it was a ghost or what, in a shadow-
like white form, almost transparent, gliding across the
floor. So I think, am I crazy, am I asleep? No, I get up, I
go to the window, I look outside the window to make sure
no lights, no planes, no helicopters are flickering. I saw
the thing, so the next day . . . a friend of mine [who] was
staying at my house . . . my guest bedroom, she said, "Oh,
I had such a terrible evening. There was a spirit in my
room, and I was fighting it, I was fighting the spirit . . . ."
This was just like her . . . yeah [I said], you fought it—into
my room . . . ! So I think that maybe certain people maybe
attract this type of phenomenon. (quoted in Primiano
2001, 48)

Oprah's account demonstrates continuity with the tradition
of individuals telling narratives about encounters with rev-
enants, but the conduit of the mass media brings the story into
the homes of millions of people simultaneously. Incorporating
traditional motifs and narrative structures discussed throughout this volume, Oprah's story mass disseminates ghost belief
and ghost narratives. But the relationship between mass media
dissemination and belief (like the relationship between tradition and belief) is complex. Media studies of the relationship
between exposure to TV programs that depict paranormal phenomena, and beliefs in the paranormal, report contradictory
findings. An initial study done in 1994 by Sparks, Nelson, and
Campbell reported that paranormal beliefs are prevalent in the
population and that they are related to reports of TV exposure
to programs that regularly depict paranormal phenomena. A
second study done in the same geographic area several years
later found that the relationship between TV viewing and paranormal beliefs was contingent upon prior personal experience
with a paranormal event (Sparks and Miller 2001). These findings reflect similar observations made by folklorists concerning

the relationship between narrative tradition and paranormal belief that suggests that knowledge of a preexisting narrative tradition does not lead to the assumption of supernatural conclusions (Hufford 1982a).

Such a view, it might be argued, begs the issue of the ideological authority of mass distribution and popular culture heroes. After all, when Popeye ate his spinach, children did too. Do the "mass" and the "popular" quality of popular culture carry a voice of credibility and expertise that exerts a new kind of authority over folklore and belief? While Oprah's account highlights continuity with traditional beliefs related to the appearance and dispelling of ghosts, it also foregrounds the changing nature of narrative dissemination and contemporary assessments of narrative credibility and authority. After all, this is Oprah, voted by *Forbes* to be one of the nine most powerful women in the world—she has a net worth of more than $1 billion, an Academy Award nomination, a hit TV show which airs in 112 countries, a successful magazine (*O, The Oprah Magazine*), a cable channel (Oxygen Media), and two charitable organizations (Oprah's Angel Network and the Oprah Winfrey Foundation). She is a vocal and respected advocate for the education and well-being of women and children around the world (Hoppough 2005), and as one TV news host argues, "She tells us what to read, how to decorate, who to prosecute, and people listen" (Hammer 2005). And now, with all of the rationalist modifiers and cautions we associate with the tradition, Oprah tells her viewing audience that she not only believes in, but has also seen, a ghost!

The narrative authority accorded to popular culture and media gurus like Oprah is not new, nor is it very different from assessments of credibility or authority in narrators or witnesses encountered in traditional ghost lore. Like the extra credibility afforded traditionally to ghost accounts from clergy (thought in some cultural contexts to be powerful, skeptical, careful about jumping to supernatural conclusions, and trustworthy) (see Francis's narrative involving the priest in chapter 2) or innocent children (thought in some contexts to have little reason to lie, due to innocence and as-yet unformed cultural agendas), Oprah and many of her colleagues achieve special status as narrators, witnesses, and cultural experts. This is important. But it does not give popular culture authorities a power very different from that afforded other folk cultural authorities. It does, however, make that power accessible to huge numbers of people simultaneously.

While popular culture does, over time, feed into belief and tradition, as can be seen in chapter 5 on the development of images of the haunted house, it is clear that not *all* popular culture renderings of the supernatural are accepted and incorporated into tradition. Bennett's comment that "white clad figures flitting through the gloom of old houses by the light of a flickering candle are the stuff of literary fiction, not folklore" (1987, 11) points to a selective ghost tradition and one that does not appropriate whole from popular or literary culture. If such appropriation was automatic, ghosts in narrative tradition would be greener and slimier, inspired by the 1980s ectoplasm craze in box office hits like *Ghost Busters* (1984). Not typically a part of folk tradition, ectoplasm rarely figures into contemporary ghost narratives, even those highly impacted by other elements of popular culture.

Another area of significant divergence between narrative tradition and popular culture involves the merger process discussed in chapter 6. Popular culture has a tendency to draw its images from multiple supernatural traditions, combining elements, motifs, and supernatural beings that would rarely be found together in tradition. A classic example of this process can be seen in commercial Halloween kitsch yard art or greeting cards and decorations, which merge various supernatural figures into one scary melting pot of undifferentiated tradition. Ghosts, vampires, werewolves, witches, zombies, and monsters hang out together in popular culture in ways that tend to turn a blind eye toward history, cultural variation, and patterns of tradition and transmission. Supernatural films also tend to jump from tradition to tradition, merging elements that are likely to have the most horror impact. The film *American Werewolf in Paris* (1997)

for example, draws from zombie, ghost, and werewolf traditions simultaneously. As chapter 1 argues, the oral supernatural
repertoire is replete with the mundane; however, Hollywood's
supernatural is frequently hyperbolic. The practice of combining multiple traditions can up the dramatic ante. While similar
tradition-hopping might occur in some forms of material culture (see chapter 3 on the Winchester Mystery House) heavily impacted by popular imagery, in children's narratives (see
chapter 4 on children's merging of monsters, ghosts, and other
supernatural characters) or joke forms, it would be more of a
challenge to find such mergers in serious adult narrative genres
such as legend or memorate. This is not to say that supernatural
folklore is purist or static, but rather to assert that changes in
tradition are selective and occur in ways that make the greatest
cultural sense.

GHOST LORE AND THE MASS MEDIA

One of the significant concerns about the relationship between
folklore and the mass media is the extent to which the power of
media discourse will replace or dominate folklore. In ghost lore,
this concern rises to the fore because of the incredible popularity of ghosts in literature, TV, and movies in recent years. Media
scholars argue that widespread and frequent repetition of similar media texts can have a forceful impact on social consensus,
individual conviction, and worldview (Edwards 2001, 86). As
Edwards writes concerning this paradigm, "The assumption is
that if audiences consistently hear other people describe haunting experiences in documentaries and frequently see fictional
characters interact with ghosts in movies, the repetitions combine to shape a cultural insistence on the authenticity of ghosts"
(2001, 86). Such a position, while in some ways mirroring the
concerns of folklorists about domination of tradition by media
voices, neglects to recognize the already existing (and flourishing) folk tradition of belief in the authenticity of ghosts and
the reciprocal relationship of folklore and media culture. Our
discussion below explores the relationship between ghosts in

folk belief and narrative traditions and the popularity of ghosts in media culture.

As Jay Mechling notes, "The dialectical relationship [between folklore and mass media] reflects the fact that folklore and mass-mediated culture share the paradox of being simultaneously dynamic and conservative cultural forms" (1996, 462). He goes on to say that while mass-mediated culture seeks novelty, it often renders novel materials through conventional content, genres, or styles appropriated from traditional narrative. The use of giants to sell vegetables or UFOs to sell candy in commercial advertising are examples of such appropriation, but the "supernatural uptake" in mass-mediated texts can also be seen as feeding back into the tradition, strengthening some forms of cultural expression and weakening or transforming others. There is good reason to believe, for example, that while angel motifs have long been important in folklore, their presence in narrative and belief tradition was substantially strengthened by their popularity in TV, journalism, and other forms of media and popular culture in the 1990s. During this period we saw the release of best selling angel books such as Sophy Burnham's *A Book of Angels: Reflections on Angels Past and Present, and True Stories of How They Touch Our Lives* (1990), the enormously popular TV show *Touched by an Angel* (1994–2003), films such as *Michael* (1996) and *City of Angels* (1998), and the massively popular guardian angel lapel pin. During the 1990s and up to the present, the Gallup Poll has reported a significant increase in the percentage of Americans that report belief in angels, reaching a remarkable 78 percent in 2004 (Winseman 2004).

Some argue that the rise in angel belief is not tied to popular culture inundation but rather that both the belief and the mass-mediated culture forms are reactions to an increase of stress and crisis in the world and are linked to the appeal of New Age spirituality. While tabloid newspapers, literature, film, and TV clearly play an important role in shaping and transmitting images of the supernatural, assessing the impact of mass media on belief is complex. James McClenon and Emily Edwards, in their study "The Incubus in Film, Experience and Folklore," attempted to test the hypothesis that media images govern the incidence and content of supernatural accounts in folklore (1995). McClenon and Edwards compared incubus film motifs with the content of stories told as personal experiences and believed by narrators to be true, ultimately finding that their collected data failed to support the media source hypothesis.

Determining if the growing popularity of supernatural media is a result of, cause of, or indicator of growth in popularity in folklore is difficult, particularly because what is clear is that both mass media and folklore respond to similar cultural imperatives waxing and waning in accord with world events, new inspirations, experiences, perspectives, discoveries, and technologies. As Elizabeth Bird argues:

> We need to forget about whether or not popular culture "transmits" folklore. Rather, we begin to consider that certain popular culture forms succeed because they act like folklore. To some extent they may have replaced folk narratives, but not with something completely new. Thus popular culture is popular because of its resonance, its appeal to an audience's existing set of story conventions. (2006, 346)

While the chicken and egg issue of which comes first—the popularity of a particular theme in folklore or in popular culture and mass media—requires incredibly complicated research of massive scope to demonstrate true causality, mutuality of appeal and mutual use of themes can be demonstrated with greater certainty and raises equally interesting issues (see, for example, chapter 1 on bathroom ghosts).

Oprah's narrative, quoted above, and indeed the choice of theme for her show that day, is suggestive of what Luckhurst (2002, 527) calls the "spectral turn" in contemporary culture,[1] a turn toward interest in the spectral which, according to Luckhurst, has become "a master trope available for appropriation in a wide variety of contexts" (2002, 527). The proliferation of ghosts on TV and in film certainly suggests a flourishing mass media interest in the topic. A survey conducted by Grey and Sparks in 1996 found that over half of prime-time programs contained at least one mention or depiction of paranormal phenomena (unpublished data cited in Primiano 2001, 59). Nine years later, in 2005, supernatural shows made up nearly half of the new fall TV lineup (Bellmont 2005).

Some scholars have asserted that this "spectral turn" ebbs and flows over time in relation to historical moments and resulting cultural concerns, emphasizing the dialectical relationship between traditional culture and mass communication. Edwards, for example, asserts based on the compilation of a chronological filmography that the 1940s brought about a proliferation of media stories about departed spirits (such as the *Casper* series) in response to times of economic struggle and World War II; she calls it "the untutored response of a film industry to social needs" (Edwards 2001, 84). Edwards argues that there followed a general decline of ghostly characters during the 1950s and 1960s indicating a social shift away from metaphysical questions, but that by the end of the twentieth century the presence of ghostly characters in film and TV rivalled their popularity in the 1940s. Citing films such as *The Sixth Sense* (1999), *The Haunting* (1999), and *Restless Spirits* (1999) Edwards notes that the year 1999 brought a proliferation of new films depicting ghosts and disembodied spirits credited to "end of the millennium uneasiness" (2001, 84).

TV columnists and commentators suggest a different, though not necessarily competing, reason for the spectral turn. Citing a variety of hit shows, they argue that the success of a particular supernatural-themed show paves the way for networks to place similar shows in prime-time slots. Citing shows such as *Buffy the Vampire Slayer* (1997–2003), *The X-Files* (1993–2002), and *Lost* (2004–2007) as the impetus for the contemporary prime-time fascination with ghosts and ghouls, commentators nevertheless seem to agree that supernatural dramas such as *Ghost Whisperer* (2005–2007) and *Supernatural* (2005–2007), at least for the moment, rival cops, courtrooms, and operating rooms for viewer attention (Emery 1997; Bellmont 2005).

The spectral turn in contemporary mass media becomes more multidimensional if one explores the style of the television, film, and literary genres that have obtained popularity. While supernatural comedy and drama genres have come, gone, and returned as noted above, what really marks the current spectral turn is the movement toward experientially based genres depicted as nonfiction in reality TV, documentary and documentary-like film, Internet experience-sharing blogs and Web sites, and supernatural autobiography or "true narrative" book collections. All of these genres share with reality TV a presentation of unscripted situations, depicting what are supposed to be actual events, featuring ordinary people rather than professional actors or writers.

Although the reality genre of television has been around, in some form, for a long time and is often traced to the late 1940s show *Candid Camera* (1948–1950), the current explosion of popularity of the genre in North America dates from around 2000 (Murray and Ouellette 2004). Typically associated with shows such as *Survivor* (2002–2007), *Big Brother* (2000–2007), and *The Apprentice* (2004–2007), the last couple of years of reality TV have brought a number of ghost shows including *Ghost Hunters* (2004–2007), *Ghost Trackers* (2005–2007), the British cult hit *Most Haunted* (2002–2007), and spin-offs and follow-ups like *Antiques Ghost Show* (2003) and *Derek Acorah's Ghost Towns* (2006).

Though these shows are part of the preexisting wave of reality programming and fit most definitions of that genre, there appears to be a certain discomfort in popular TV commentary Web sites and tabloids with referring to these shows as reality TV due to their paranormal subject. Survey pieces on reality TV, which discuss a dazzling array of reality shows, rarely mention even one in the ghost hunting genre. While reality TV is based on the notion of ordinary people in extraordinary situations, ads for paranormal reality shows joke about the lack of ordinariness of their ordinary participants, with *Ghost Hunters*, for example, advertising that its participants are "Plumbers by day—ghost hunters by night" (for similar joking behavior by lawyers and judges involved in ghost disclosure laws see chapter 6). The discomfort evident in the advertising rhetoric and in dubbing these shows "reality" highlights the belief element required to establish the shows as such. While *Survivor* or *Project Runway* (2004–2007) require a certain suspension of disbelief to distract one from the highly controlled environment of filming and to think of the participants as in any way ordinary, paranormal shows add an extra layer of concern about the "real" nature of what is/might be captured on film.[2]

Ghostly reality TV came into a paranormal enthusiast market that was already primed for displays of ordinary people in extraordinary circumstances and seemingly unscripted action and dialogue, following the genre-changing release in 1999 of the film *The Blair Witch Project*. Presented as a documentary pieced together from amateur footage, *The Blair Witch Project* tells the story of three young student filmmakers who get lost in the woods while filming a documentary about the Blair Witch, a legendary character believed to haunt the woods near Burkittsville, Maryland. According to the story, the students were never seen again, but the film footage was found a year after the students set out on their adventure. The film consists of fragments that the students were intending to use in their documentary mixed with footage of their own experience after they get hopelessly lost and encounter a series of events which lend themselves to supernatural interpretation. The producers of *The Blair Witch Project* created the film by hiring three actors and turning them loose in the woods with film equipment to shoot a movie. The actors themselves did not know what was going to happen, following clues and instructions left for them with a Global Positioning Satellite system. Like the television series *Survivor*, directors built the movie mood by making things truly difficult for the actors, who walked far in the daytime over rough terrain, were harassed at night, and were deprived of food. The film moves in and out of color and black and white and is made to feel both amateurish and scary by shaky handheld camera movement and poor lighting. *The Blair Witch Project* grossed over $160 million in the United States and $248 million worldwide despite its $25,000 budget, making it the highest profit-to-cost motion picture ever (Telotte 2001).

The Blair Witch is, according to the film's treatment, the ghost of Elly Kedward, a woman accused of witchcraft in 1785 in Blair Township (which later becomes Burkittsville). Although an invented legend, the story is said to have been somewhat influenced by the Bell Witch legend of Tennessee; the legend of Moll Dyer, a woman accused of being a witch in Maryland; and motifs drawn from *The Crucible* (Aloi 1999, Blair Witch 2006). While other films prior to *The Blair Witch Project* used similar techniques of incorporating the camera and crew into the story, *The Blair Witch Project* made the story seem real by creating frightening situations in real locations, capturing unscripted dialogue and action, and by placing the camera in the hands of amateurs. Like paranormal reality TV, the movie's niche was that it took supernatural subjects and set them in unscripted or loosely scripted reality-like contexts, using individuals presented as "ordinary."

Additionally, the film's marketing employed the folk process of pseudo-ostention (hoaxing) in creating pre-release buzz by leading potential viewers to think that it was a "true" story (see Dégh and Vázsonyi 1983; Dégh 2001; Ellis 2001a on ostention and pseudo-ostention). One way this was accomplished was by placing a faux documentary about the movie on the Internet. This tactic was effective enough to cause many of the viewers attending the movie to believe that it was "real." Other viewers tried to disabuse the first group of their belief in the film's veracity. In this manner, the discourse about the movie also mirrored the debate over veracity and believability that often surrounds legends (supernatural and otherwise) in more traditional performance situations.

The move from dramatic supernatural TV and film productions to the extraordinary events in ordinary contexts of both reality TV and *The Blair Witch Project* mirror performance genre choices of traditional narration of supernatural events in folktale, legend, and memorate or personal narrative. Although primarily an intimate genre compromised by the constraints of rationalism, there is some evidence that personal supernatural narratives have become increasingly tellable in more public contexts in recent years. Book collections of traditional supernatural narratives increasingly include personal accounts, and contemporary deposits of supernatural materials in folklore archives suggest a similar flourishing of memorate. While changes in book and archival collections may suggest developments in the openness of collectors to personal supernatural narrative rather than shifts in tradition and performance, those disciplinary developments themselves are significant and may herald more general change. Oprah's personal ghost narrative and the informal exchange described in chapter 2 are not uncommon, and neither is the kind of personal narration associated with the Internet discussion described in chapter 2. The move to reality-based mass culture productions may both support and reflect a similar folk cultural change in popularity of first-person supernatural narration and a similar emphasis on ordinary people in extraordinary circumstances.

Building on Elizabeth Bird's work, Mikel Koven's analysis of folklore studies and popular film (2003, 179) argues that popular culture behaves like folklore in ways that go beyond motif borrowing or the transmission of traditional folkloric items to reflect other aspects of folklore styles, patterns, and performance contexts. As such, Koven has explored, for example, how films like *The Joy Luck Club* (1993) and *How to Make an American Quilt* (1995) reproduce women's speech patterns, narrative contexts, and structures (Koven 1999). A similar approach to supernatural popular culture suggests not only motif borrowing in film and TV, but perhaps also the borrowing and dynamism of generic conventions, reflecting characterization, performance style, and disposition toward reality.

While concerns about the impact of dominant media voices on tradition are not groundless or insignificant, they do move our attention away from reciprocal relationships. Those are missed chances for folklorists to understand more about the multidimensional tenacity of our subject.

Ghost Lore and Technology

The discussions of ghosts in popular culture and mass media above would be quite different if it were not for the enormous changes in technology of the last century. The preceding chapters demonstrate that traditional ghost lore has adapted relatively smoothly to new ways of communicating. While evolutionary arguments have asserted that technological development would create a decline in supernatural belief, it could be argued that in fact the opposite has occurred. Advancements in technology frequently prompt folk revivals in their flurry of new ways to pass on traditions. In ghost lore those revivals, especially as mediated by technology, reach out to involve film, television, literature, and the Internet and then feed back both into tradition as well as into new forms of interest in the paranormal. While many folklorists are concerned about the popularizing and melding impact of the Internet on traditional folklore (see, for example, Brunvand 2004), it has created a context for sharing, collecting, and archiving ghost lore as well as a context for dialogue about those traditions. Nevertheless, technology (like popular culture and the mass media) has significantly changed our sense of the communities that participate in the transmission and celebration of folklore. While virtual communities may create their own kind of "community life," informing and giving meaning to shared cultural expression, they are different than less technologically dependent communities. Members of virtual communities may never meet and may never share anything else in common other than the subject of their virtual communication. Interestingly though, much of the material on the Internet resembles interpersonal sharing of memorates and legends, with numerous sites set up to post commentary from individuals with relevant experiences or ideas to share. The Internet, TV, and movies have, however, brought about wider access to the perspectives of ghost enthusiasts and paranormal professionals. Just as in medicine and many other fields, the easy availability of information on the Internet and on TV has changed the relationship of the general lay public to enthusiasts and professionals, with issues of access, resource availability, information sharing, and authority simultaneously changing dramatically.

Technology, whether as a medium for ghosts to communicate, or as a medium for the living to communicate about ghosts, is and has always been central to ghost lore. As Kirby notes, "before there were ghostbusters, there was Thomas Alva Edison" (2005, 1). According to Edison's diaries and biographers, in the later years of his life he was intent on inventing a device that could record the voices of the dead. While Edison never did create his invention, his plan was to develop a machine that would allow two-way contact between the living and the dead. One biographer of Edison quotes an interview with a columnist from *Scientific American* in which Edison said:

> It is possible to construct an apparatus which will be so delicate that if there are personalities in another existence or sphere who wish to get in touch with us in this existence or sphere, this apparatus will at least give them a better opportunity to express themselves than the tilting tables and raps and Ouija boards and mediums and the other crude methods now purported to be the only means of communication. (Clark 1977, 235)

Edison was not alone in his beliefs about the possibility of using new technologies to communicate with the dead. Other well-known inventors, such as Guglielmo Marconi, were said to be working on similar communication instruments. The creative energy exerted by Edison and Marconi on their projects has been continually mirrored through the years in both folklore and artistic works exploring the use of technology for otherworldly communication. In 1899, John Kendrick Bangs wrote *The Enchanted Typewriter*, a story about a man who discovers that through the medium of his typewriter he can communicate with famous dead people (Bangs [1899] 2003; Harris 2005). His book presages numerous similar computer accounts such as Margret J. Anderson's *The Ghost Inside the Monitor*, a story about a ghost that lives inside a young girl's computer that ultimately finds a resting place inside a floppy disk installed in a computer in her old home (1990).

Like the ghostly associations with cell phones discussed in the introduction to this volume, Linda Dégh cites numerous forms of communication and household technology reported as used by the dead to communicate with the living. She summarizes a 1992 survey of the theme in tabloid newspapers by writing:

> A man tells that his ex-wife has called him on their wedding anniversary every year for 22 years; a woman tells how her dead husband talks to her on the lower end of the TV dial; a widow is contacted by her spouse over the dial tone of her cordless phone; another widow finds the message "I miss you" on the Xerox copy of her dead husband's will; a couple reports that their recently deceased son confronted them by telling them over the static between two AM stations that he is in a happy place; a concerned dead mother uses the toaster to burn the words "car port" on the bread when her son lost the key of the safe deposit box she willed him.
>
> Similarly classic ghost stories have been rejuvenated by the fax machine: Employees of one company report that the dead boss "still tries to run the company from beyond the grave!" His orders for shipping, invoices and money decisions arrive at random intervals on the company fax. Another story tells of a fax received from London by a travelling salesman who was killed on the way to London a week earlier. (1994, 26)

As can be seen from Dégh's mention of the toaster, technology that is believed to help facilitate communication with the dead need not be that which is normally associated with communication. The discussion of toilet ghosts in chapter 1 demonstrates the association of ghostly attempts to commune with the living through flushing toilets and other mysteries of plumbing. Discussions throughout this volume (chapters 1, 3, and 4) as well as in other studies (such as Tucker 2005b) demonstrate ghostly or paranormal associations with mirrors, exemplified by the Bloody Mary tradition. While the technology associated with communication with the dead changes with time, location, and social group, and while understandings of what is technologically complex may differ, the belief itself has remained relatively constant: death is a bridgeable gulf and technology can allow the living and the dead to remain connected in perpetuity. Ghostly communication through cell phone, fax, the Internet, or other trappings of contemporary culture suggest more than anything that this belief has adapted very nicely to the times.

A great deal of folklore concerning ghosts is centrally about disembodied spirits looking for embodiment (see chapter 3 on gender and ghostly embodiment). Machines, oddly enough, are also disembodied. If they work well, they are meant to run with little human interference. The notion of the "ghost in the machine" as metaphor and as a more literal topic of endless narratives, films, and literary productions, attests to our discomfort with the corporeal status of machinery. In the folklore of ghosts and technology, our disembodied spirits can use our technology for temporary embodiment to communicate, but the trick is to communicate and move on. As such, many of our stories are about ghosts becoming trapped in a liminal, insufficiently embodied location (like a mirror or a hard drive), metaphorically and literally stuck betwixt and between this world and the hereafter. Lingering in film, computer, or tape recorder contradicts the point, which is to contact loved ones and ultimately find a resting place.

In the late nineteenth century spirit mediums (see chapter 6 on Spiritualism) used photography to claim visual evidence of the existence of ghosts and radio waves as a way of contacting the dead (Grove 1997; Wicker 2003, 64–70). The notion that new technologies and recording instruments could document ghostly efforts at communication has stayed with us (Sconce 2000; Warner 2006) and began to flourish in the 1950s with new attention to what is now called "EVP"—or Electronic Voice Phenomenon. EVP is believed by some to be communication by spirits that can be detected through tape recorders and other electronic devices. In the current computer age, EVP messages are stored on thousands of Web sites for sharing by ghost communication enthusiasts (Roach 2005, 181–211).

While EVP communication is currently incredibly popular with numerous organizations created for its study and has created a flourishing market for the development and sale of specialized equipment, it mirrors other associations of technology with not only human but also ghostly communication. For Edison, Marconi, many of the nineteenth-century spiritualists, and current-day ghost hunters, technology is not just a means of communicating with loved ones but is crucial to capturing empirical evidence of the spirit world. Ghost hunters are hobbyists, or sometimes professionals, who investigate allegedly haunted places while attempting to gather empirical evidence of supernatural disturbances. While most ghost hunters will argue that the tape recorder is the most crucial and basic form of technology for capturing EVP, they hope that better evidence might be obtained through the latest equipment in sound, video, and still-image recording as well as various kinds of sensors for detecting changes in temperature and electromagnetic fields. Kirby argues that the emphasis on ghost hunting equipment was inspired by the display of technology in the film *Ghost Busters* (1984). Quoting an interview with Vince Wilson, author of *Ghost Tech: The Essential Guide to Paranormal Investigation Equipment* (2005), however, Kirby notes that any ghost hunter who wore the "proton pack" containing the particle accelerator depicted in the movie would actually be wearing gear the size of a tractor trailer and would develop several forms of cancer (Kirby 2005). Nevertheless, many ghost hunter Web sites suggest equipment necessary for the "ghost hunters' tool belt" including some quite expensive and expansive items: an electromagnetic field meter, digital sound recorder and audio software, camera or video camera, thermometer, infrared camera, night vision goggles, thermal-vision camera, and Geiger counter (see, for example, http://www.getghostgear.com/).

The equipment-heavy and technology-heavy work of ghost hunters does emphasize a different tradition than is normally found in ghost lore, one with documentation of experience through EVP, photographic and other evidence of ghosts posted on thousands of Web sites and TV, which is available for public scrutiny. In this sense, ghost hunting tradition presents a ghost with bells and whistles, twenty-four-hour video ghost watches, orbs, infrared pictures, and mechanically enhanced sound. But there are some similarities with traditional ghost lore. The work of ghost hunters in many ways mimics the tradition of legend tripping (discussed in chapters 1 and 6), exploring sites associated with legendary ghosts and legendary events in hope of having one's own experience. And no matter how technological the work of the ghost hunter is, their goal is to follow up on old stories, hopefully by adding new stories of their own to the tradition. As such, ghost hunters ultimately rely on narrative as the inspiration for their work, narrative as the goal of their work, and narrative as at least part of their evidence. In a paper on contemporary ghost hunting and the relationship between proof and experience, Lynne McNeil notes,

> Interestingly, despite the incredibly pervasive emphasis on the filter of technology and the insistence on objective proof, in almost all manifestations of ghost hunting in popular culture—the Internet, television shows, ghost books—personal experience narratives and memorates abound. Television shows, such as the Discovery Channel's *Real Ghosthunters* and Living TV's *Most Haunted*, regularly use people's own retellings of the events that have prompted the more scientific investigation as a means of introducing their topic, offering dramatic re-enactments of the events as the original participants tell the story in a voice-over, emphasizing subjective details along with the common reality-testing assurances. (2004, 7)

Just as McNeil ties the ghost hunter back to traditional ghost lore by recognizing the continued centrality of the memorate to ghost hunting tradition, Waren Bareiss reminds us that even the sounds and sights of ghost hunting Web sites and TV bear some resemblance to traditional narrative. His comments are tied to Susan Stewart's study of the horror story (1982). He notes,

> Ghost stories are immediate sensory experiences giving us "the creeps" and "goose bumps" . . . the discourse is turned into what it represents. Sounds thus endow

ghost stories with immediacy that directly implicates our
senses in an intimate knowing of what cannot be spoken.
(Bareiss 2002, 7–8)

Bareiss continues,

Technology of the Internet provides new means of
addressing us with sensory stimulation in keeping with
ghost storytelling traditions. Ghost hunters' use of multiple forms of presentation—EVP, photographs, and
video—along with written texts, creates a multi-sensory
experience, much in keeping with screeches, moans,
and screams inserted into traditional ghost-story performance. (2002, 14)

Despite commitment to both technology and scientific proof,
McNeil and Bareiss remind us that storytelling is still a central
aspect of the ghost hunters' work and that technology assists in
that process.

Regardless of the narrative-based work of ghost hunters, it
would be foolish to maintain that they are in any way average
contemporary tradition bearers. They are over-the-top professionals and enthusiasts, more a part of a fan community than
the average tale teller.[3] Nevertheless the work of ghost hunters
is all around us, on TV, in movies, all over the Internet, and
woven throughout tourism and presentations of local history.
Like nineteenth-century spiritualist mediums, they are on the
periphery of vernacular ghost tradition, but through communications technology their work is more accessible. They
are professional storytellers with a powerful rhetorical style
and a highly visible stage. Like TV, movies, greeting cards,
Halloween haunted houses, ghost tours, and spirit bottles sold
in stores, ghost hunters are part of our multidimensional, not-
traditional-but-more-traditional-than-we-thought, ever-evolv-
ing ghost culture.

In many ways scholars of ghosts in contemporary culture are
like the spirit caught in the mirror or the ghost caught in the hard
drive, betwixt and between, stuck in the liminal space between

past and future. But like the spirit that is caught, lingering between worlds contradicts the point, which is to figure out how to move on. Changes wrought by popular culture, mass media, and technology suggest a potential popularization of tradition and a levelling that some are worried will threaten the integrity of traditional folklore. Yet any survey of ghost tradition over the last several centuries reveals that commodification, popularization, technological change, culture brokering, fragmentation, and decontextualization have always been as much a part of the tradition as have the spirits themselves. Despite our worries, old spirits in new bottles shimmer before us every bit as brightly as they ever did.

Their persistence is due, at least in part, to the serious cultural meanings and issues they raise through time and over generations. In these pages, we've seen that ghost stories allow children to explore taboo subjects and their fears, while assisting in the development of cognitive skills. The narratives also mirror attitudes toward place and the environment, as well as affecting individual behaviors. Furthermore, some ghost narratives reflect and refract gender expectations and violence. Haunted sites, such as the Winchester Mystery House or a Halloween hell house, demonstrate the profitability of the presentation of extremes (such as the Deviant Femme or the Extreme Guy).

Despite their concern with these earthbound matters, ghost stories also remain one of our most democratic and accessible venues into Mystery. As any ghostly medium—whether a story, a movie, or a person who hosts séances—will reveal, ghosts remain with us in all these venues because they give voice to both the everyday and the extraordinary experiences that haunt us.

Notes

Introduction: Old Spirits in New Bottles

1. The famous cartoon character Casper the Friendly Ghost first appeared in a 1945 animated movie. Later a series of comic books about the character were published by Harvey Comics from 1949–1982. In 1963 the character was featured in a made-for-TV series of short cartoons. A live-action movie, *Casper*, was produced in 1995.

2. Amazon.com is an online mail-order store based in the United States with international sites located in Canada, the United Kingdom, Germany, Japan, France, and China. It advertises itself as having the earth's biggest selection of books.

3. In an effort to ease her son's fear of his dead grandfather's walking cane, Mary Anderson of Hobart, New Jersey, put the cane up for sale on eBay, the online auction house, as a haunted item for sale. The cane joined a large number of allegedly haunted dolls, jars, and other items submitted for sale on eBay. In December of 2004, the Anderson haunted cane sold for $65,000 to an online casino company that had previously purchased a grilled cheese sandwich believed to bear the image of the Virgin Mary.

Chapter 1: The Usefulness of Ghost Stories

1. Some folklorists, notably Jan Brunvand, devote much of their work to discerning hoaxes and truth (2001). Also, throughout the chapter, I often use the term "legend" to describe ghost stories. A legend is a third-person narrative about the unusual or supernatural; it is a story that is believed or believable (Dégh 1971, 2001). In contemporary popular culture, it is common to hear these "legends" called "myths." Such usage is incorrect and often demeaning. Although most people are unaware of it, the word "myth" actually means sacred narrative; therefore, the Bible is myth as is the Bhagavad Gita. When a folklorist calls a narrative a "myth," she is not saying that it is an untrue story, which is usually the deprecating connotation of the word in popular usage. Instead she is merely recognizing that the story is sacred and important to some group of people.

2. My discussion of ghost stories and culture, nature, and the personal is not synonymous with Hufford's "cultural source hypothesis," which he says posits that supernatural experiences are "fictitious products of tradition or imaginary subjective experiences shaped (or occasionally even caused) by tradition" (1982b, 14). Hufford's delineation of the "cultural source hypothesis" and the "experiential source hypothesis" works particularly well with the memorates that he studies and his research concern with demonstrating that "some significant portion of traditional supernatural

belief is associated with accurate observations" (1982b, xviii). My research focus is different. I'm concerned with discussing what the stories can reveal in relation to three specific realms when issues of fictitiousness or the accuracy of observation are not paramount. In other words, the story could present an account that is accurately observed and wholly true, inaccurately observed and fictitious, or any permutation of the preceding, and I would still be interested in what the story could tell me about culture, nature, or the personal. I don't argue that culture, nature, or the personal explains away the story—what I posit is that the story can tell us something more about culture, nature, or personal experience. I take a literary tack; I'm arguing that there's a varied interpretive wealth offered by different types of ghost stories to everyone, skeptics and believers included.

3. Many Internet narratives also detail haunted toilets and bathrooms. For example, one Web site posits that Britain's most haunted bathroom is at the Cock and Bottle Inn in Bradford, Yorkshire (VisitBritian 2003). Tabloid newspapers in the United States run headlines such as "Haunted Toilet Paper Leaps Off the Roll!" (Rivenburg 2002). In South Korea, a museum interprets the history of toilets and maintains that angry ghosts traditionally inhabited toilets, so some people customarily cleared their throats before entering in hopes that the hostile spirits would take the hint and vacate the area (Toilet Museum 2001). Sometimes tourist publications emphasize such supernatural manifestations and direct visitors to sites primarily because of their spectral merits. For example, a walking guide to "haunted London" mentions two haunted toilets. One story is reminiscent of Scott's story; it's in the Old Deanery, which was built by Christopher Wren—here the toilet paper holder acts "decidedly wonky." Martin Sullivan, the dean there until his retirement in 1977 and the person responsible for upkeep, disputes this claim: "Since I can't conceive of a haunted toilet-roll holder, I can only put it down to my skill at do-it-yourself" (Jones 1999, 112, 122).

4. This malevolent bathroom ghost goes by a variety of names, including Bloody Mary, Mary Worth, and Mary Whales. The story and the ritual play associated with it was the subject of a presentation by British play specialist Marc Armitage at the 2002 annual International Society for Contemporary Legend Research conference held at Sheffield, England (Armitage 2002, 1–2). An unpublished revision entitled "'All About Mary': Children's Use of the Toilet Ghost Story as an Mechanism for Dealing with Fear. But Fear of What?" (n.d.) was provided by the author. Two published studies of this legend are Dundes (2002) and Langlois (1980).

5. I discuss personal health issues under the heading of "culture" here because such health concerns are common. They're shared by large numbers of people and understood through culture.

6. Hufford calls these and several other things the cultural source hypothesis (1982b, 13–14). While I'm not wholly comfortable with his use of the term "cultural" to cover all the six areas he outlines (ranging from hoaxes to

natural phenomena to psychotic episodes, for example), I understand why
he chose this term. If I were to use his terminology, then, I would say that
the folk sometimes draw on the cultural source hypothesis to interpret
their own out-of-the-ordinary experiences.

7. In a personal communication in 2004, folklore film scholar Mikel Koven
    points out that Japanese films such as *Dark Water* (2005) often present a
    different view of the supernatural than films such as *The Amityville Horror*
    (1979, 2005). Incidentally, films that depict priests, such as *The Amityville
    Horror* and particularly *The Exorcist* (1973), caused an increase in the num-
    ber of phone calls requesting exorcism that priests get from people of
    all religious backgrounds (Brady 1995). Katherine A. Fowkes also points
    out that Hollywood employs supernaturally themed movies as vehicles for
    romance; she cites films such as *Heaven Can Wait* (1978), *Ghost* (1990), and
    Meet Joe Black (1998) as examples (2004, 186–87).

8. Bloody Mary has less benignly appeared in the horror film *Urban Legends:
    Bloody Mary* (2005).

CHAPTER 2: SCIENTIFIC RATIONALISM AND THE STRUCTURE
OF SUPERNATURAL EXPERIENCE NARRATIVES

1. Ghost ships (also called phantom ships) are boats that return, generally
    from the ocean bottom, and are reported to be seen in ghostly form, par-
    ticularly as a sign of bad weather or as a warning of impending disaster.
    Sailors and boats who return from a watery grave appear in tradition virtu-
    ally worldwide: the *Palatine* in Rhode Island; the *Young Teazer* in Lunenberg,
    Nova Scotia; the *Asiatic Prince* in Hawaii; the *Flying Dutchman* at the Cape of
    Good Hope; the *Violet* of Goodwin Sands; and the five-masted *Copenhagen*
    seen in Chile and Peru (Goldstein 1990).

2. As Hufford notes, "Perhaps because of the loose way the words 'empiri-
    cal' and 'rational' have been used with belief, there has been a tendency
    to overlook their technical meanings. They have developed connotations
    that make them almost synonymous with 'correct' or 'true'" (1982b, xvii).
    And in a different context, Hufford argues "the rationality and empirical
    grounding of a belief are separate from its 'truth'; many false beliefs are
    rationally held on empirical grounds . . . and many true beliefs are held
    without rational or empirical grounds" (Hufford 1995a, 18).

3. Bill Ellis, for example, discusses the embedded rational performance
    style of a ghost story narrator in his book *Aliens, Ghosts, and Cults* (2001a,
    117–41), emphasizing "fact heavy interpretations and descriptions of occa-
    sions" (2001a, 135).

4. The nature of scientific rationalism narrative structures prior to the eigh-
    teenth century still remains to be explored. Bill Ellis notes in a discus-
    sion of a fifteenth-century version of "The Vanishing Rape Victim" that
    the story begins with rationalist contextualization. The narrative begins,

"A well educated man, Cencio the Roman, frequently told me about something that's difficult to reject, which a neighbor of his, a person who was by no means a fool, narrated as having happened to himself" (cited in Ellis 2001b, 84).

Chapter 3: Gender and Ghosts

1. The chapter provides basic demographic information about the narrators when it was available.
2. Many folklore forms depicted social problems before they were recognized as such by the culture at large and institutionally addressed. For example, several traditional ballads depict young women being murdered by their boyfriends. Bill Ellis provides an excellent overview of how a legend about a man who murders his wife and child works "in female-female circles to discuss tensions surrounding the gender roles" (2001a, 25).
3. The ghostly gender patterns that I identify in this chapter are not meant to be exhaustive; these are just some patterns that are easily discerned.
4. See Thomas (1997, 175) for a discussion of stories about dangers within the family.
5. For more on La Llorona see Arora (1997), Candelaria (1993), Doyle (1996), Hawes (1968), and Limón (1990).
6. At the end of the nineteenth century, the Lakota were starving and dying because of the draconian conditions on the reservations where they were forced to live. Many turned to the Ghost Dance religion, which foretold a return of the bison and a better life. Their frequent ghost dancing with its religious and supernatural overtones severely unnerved many whites in the area, despite a few voices of reason such as Valentine McGillycuddy (1990), who said "the coming of the troops has frightened the Indians. If the Seventh-Day Adventists prepare the ascension robes for the Second Coming of the Savior, the United States Army is not put in motion to prevent them. Why should not the Indians have the same privilege?" On December 29, 1890, at Wounded Knee, South Dakota, Custer's old unit (the Seventh Calvary) killed approximately two to three hundred mostly unarmed Lakota men, women, and children (many of whom where Ghost Dance participants) who were returning to Pine Ridge Reservation.
7. See Lindahl (2005) for a discussion of the cultural importance of children in Latino legends. The manner in which children appear in ghost stories is beyond the scope of this chapter and a topic that offers possibilities for future research.

Chapter 4: Children's Ghost Stories

1. The etymology of "boo" is discussed at some length by linguist and folklorist John Widdowson (1971, 1977).

2.   Some of my published research on children's ghost stories includes "Gotcha! American Children's Ghost Stories" (1980); "American Children's Ghost Stories: Manipulation and Mastery of a Belief System" (2004); "Children's Telling of Ghost Stories" (1999); and "From the Tale to the Telling: A/T 366" (1980a).

3.   See, for example, Maria Leach (1959), Richard and Judy Dockrey Young (1990), and Alvin Schwartz (1981).

CHAPTER 6: THE COMMODIFICATION OF BELIEF in CONTEMPORARY CULTURE

1.   It would seem reasonable to assume that the reposting a year and a half later is either because the house did not sell or because any sales that might have been initiated fell through.

2.   Listed on escapeartist.com on May 1, 2004 (http://realestate.escapeartist.com/P-306/).

3.   Thank you to Janet Langlois for calling the Wharton and Marshall examples to our attention.

4.   Ackley had written and submitted the article entitled "Our Haunted House on the Hudson" to *Reader's Digest* (1977).

5.   The descriptions of ghostly stigma are similar to notions of contagious magic in which people and objects are thought to influence each other through the transfer of essential properties long after physical contact has ended.

6.   The *Forbes* slide show is available at http://www.forbes.com/2002/10/31/cx_cv_1031feat.html. The map of the United States is available at http://www.hauntedhouses.com/map.htm. An example of an advertisement for a haunted hotels documentary series can be found on the Cinamour Entertainment site (http://www.cinamour.com/haunted.html).

7.   For the full advertisements see http://www.ghrs.org/ghosttours/gt.htm (Niagra), http://www.sleepyhollowofgettysburg.com (Sleepy Hollow of Gettysburg), and http://www.mercattours.com/tours/haunted_underground.htm (Mercat Tours Haunted Underground Experience).

8.   For more on this shift in consumer patterns and literature see Schlereth (1991) and Kerr (1972).

9.   Seaton (1996) notes that visits to death sites were an integral part of tourism consumption long before the twentieth century, but that media and communications-driven tourism shifts the focus because these technologies make global events appear local.

10. Others call this "dark tourism." See, for example, Lennon and Foley (2000) and Seaton (1996).

11. As opposed to "morbid tourism," "dark tourism," or "ghost tourism," the phrase "belief tourism" highlights exactly that group of tourist venues that commodify the metaphysical, spiritual, and paranormal values and

traditions of cultural communities. While a part of this group overlaps with dark, morbid, and ghost tourism, belief tourism has its own set of shared characteristics and concerns, as discussed below.

12. These comments are taken from interviews with twelve ghost tour patrons in the United States and Canada. Individuals interviewed ranged from those who had attended one tour to those who go on ghost tours several times a year both in their own community and internationally.

13. Legend trips are journeys to sites with supernatural or scary stories associated with them. Ellis notes that legend trips have a three-part structure: 1) the introduction, 2) the enactment, and 3) retrospective personal narratives (Ellis 1983, 2001a). The latter part of this structure turns each legend trip into an additional or appended narrative that becomes part of the legend trip tradition.

14. For more on authenticity issues in light of sought experiences see Magliocco (2004).

15. The San Francisco Ghost Hunt, "Ghost Hunt Guarantee," (http://www. sfghosthunt.com/generic.html?pid=1).

Conclusion: The "Spectral Turn" in Folklore, Mass Media, Popular Culture, and Technology

1. This term is a play on the phrase "narrative turn," which refers to the proliferation of attention to narrative in the social sciences, generally thought to represent a shift in knowledge culture generated in response to poststructural and postmodernist attention to multiple realities.

2. And in fact, the TV show *Most Haunted* (2002–2007) has continually come under attack for fraud.

3. Interestingly, Bill Ellis writes of those typically involved in traditional legend tripping, "Most will engage in one or two ritual visits out of curiosity, but several folklorists have noted the role of small groups of 'experts' in publicizing and perpetuating the tradition" (2004, 114).

BIBLIOGRAPHY

Aarne, A., and S. Thompson. 1964. *The types of the folktale.* Helsinki: Suomalainen Tiedeakatemia Academica Scientiarum Fennica.

Ackley, H. H. 1977. Our haunted house on the Hudson. *Reader's Digest,* May:217–24.

Addams, C. 1991. *The world of Charles Addams.* New York: Alfred A. Knopf.

Aloi, P. 1999. Blair Witch Project—An interview with the directors. http://www.witchvox.com/va/dt_va.html?a=usma&c=media&id=2416 (accessed November 1, 2006).

Anderson, C. 2006. *The long tail: Why the future of business is selling less of more.* New York: Hyperion.

Anderson, M. J. 1990. *The ghost inside the monitor.* New York. Alfred A. Knopf.

Anson, J. 1977. *The Amityville horror.* New York: Bantam Books.

Arora, Shirley L. 1997. "La Llorona." *Encyclopedia of Mexico: History, society, and culture.* Chicago: Fitzroy Dearborn Publishers.

Armitage, M. 2002. From sticks and stones to toilet ghosts: An examination of story and character development in children's pretend play as they progress through school. *Foaftale News: Newsletter of the International Society for Contemporary Legend Research* 53:1–2.

———. n.d. All about Mary: Children's use of the toilet ghost story as a mechanism for dealing with fear—But fear of what? Unpublished manuscript.

Ascher, R. 1999. Tin can archaeology. In *Material culture studies in America,* ed. T. Schlereth, 325–37. Walnut Creek, CA: Altamira Press.

Baham, J. 2002. The secrets of Disneyland's Haunted Mansion. *Haunted Attraction Magazine* 30/31:32–51.

Bailey, D. 1999. *American nightmares: The haunted house formula in American popular fiction.* Bowling Green, OH: Bowling Green State University Press.

Baker, M. 1979. *Folklore of the sea.* London: David and Charles Inc.

Bangs, J. K. [1899] 2003. *The enchanted typewriter.* Boston: Indy Publishing Company.

Bassett, F. S. 1885. *Legends and superstitions of the sea and of sailors in all lands and at all times.* Detroit, MI: Singing Tree Press 1971.

Bassett, W. [1917] 1974. *Wander-ships: Folkstories of the sea with notes upon their origin.* Norwood, PA: Norwood Editions..

Bareiss, W. 2002. Ghost hunting, mystery, and the rhetoric of technology. Paper presented at the meeting of the Association of Educators in Journalism and Mass Communication, Miami Beach, Florida.

Baughman, E. 1966. *Type and motif index of the folktales of England and North America.* The Hague: Mouton.

Bauvier, J. 1914. "Evidence." *Bauvier's law dictionary,* Vol.1. St. Paul, MN: West Publishing.

Belk, R. 1994. Carnival, control, and corporate culture in contemporary Halloween celebrations. In *Halloween and other festivals of death and life*, ed. J. Santino, 105–32. Knoxville: University of Tennessee Press.

Bellmont, B. 2005. Supernatural shows haunt new TV season. http://www.mnsbc.msn.com/id8917696.html (accessed October 30, 2006).

Bennett, G. 1987. *Traditions of belief: Women, folklore, and the supernatural today*. London: Pelican Books.

———. 1999. *"Alas, poor ghost!" Traditions of belief in story and discourse*. Logan: Utah State University Press.

Berger, P., and T. Luckmann. 1966. *The social construction of reality*. Garden City, NY: Doubleday.

Bergland, R. L. 2002. *The national uncanny: Indian ghosts and American subjects*. Hanover, PA: Dartmouth College/University Press of New England.

Best, J., and G. T. Horiuchi. 1985. The razor blade in the apple: The social construction of urban legends. *Social Problems* 32:488–99.

Binkley, S. 2000. Kitsch as a repetitive system: A problem for the theory of taste hierarchy. *Journal of Material Culture* 5:131–52.

Bird, E. 2006. Cultural studies as confluence: The convergence of folklore and media studies. In *Popular culture theory and methodology: A basic introduction*, eds. H. E. Hinds, M. Motz, and A. Nelson, 344–56. Madison: University of Wisconsin Press/Popular Press.

Blair Witch. 2006. http://en.wikipedia.org/wiki/Most_Haunted (accessed November 10, 2006).

Blom, T. 2000. Morbid tourism—A postmodern market niche with an example from Althorp. *Norsk Geografisk Tidsskrift* 54:29–36.

Brady, E. 1995. Bad scares and joyful hauntings: "Priesting" the supernatural predicament. In *Out of the ordinary: Folklore and the supernatural*, ed. B. Walker, 145–58. Logan: Utah State University Press.

Briggs, K. 1976. *An encyclopedia of fairies, hobgoblins, brownies, bogies, and other supernatural creatures*. New York: Pantheon.

———. 1978. *The vanishing people: Fairy lore and legends*. New York: Pantheon.

Brogan, K. 1998. *Cultural haunting: Ghosts and ethnicity in recent American literature*. Charlottesville: University Press of Virginia.

Broome, F. 2004. Popular ghost tours. http://www.hollowhill.com/reviews/tours.htm (accessed July 13, 2005).

Brown, A. 2006. *Ghost hunters of the south*. Jackson: University Press of Mississippi.

Brown, R., and A. A. Leggett. 2002. *Haunted Boulder: Ghostly tales from the foot of the Flatirons*. Boulder, CO: White Sand Lake Press.

Browne, R. B. 1958. *Popular beliefs and practices from Alabama*. Berkeley: University of California Press.

Brunvand, J. H. 1961. Three more variants of the "tag" tale. *Journal of American Folklore* 74:146–48.

———. 1963. A classification of shaggy dog stories. *Journal of American Folklore* 76:42–68.

————. 1989. *The vanishing hitchhiker: American urban legends and their meanings.* New York: W. W. Norton.

————. 2001. *Too good to be true: The colossal book of urban legends.* New York: W. W. Norton and Company.

————. 2004. The vanishing "urban legend." *Midwestern Folklore* 30:5–10.

Buhle, P. 1987. *Popular culture in America.* Minneapolis: University of Minnesota Press.

Bunting, E. 1994. *In the haunted house.* New York: Houghton-Mifflin/Clarion Books.

Burnham, S. 1990. *A book of angels.: Reflections on angels past and present, and true stories of how they touch our lives.* New York: Ballantine.

Burrison, J. A. 1968. *The golden arm: The folk tale and its literary use by Mark Twain and Joel Chandler Harris.* Atlanta: Georgia State College.

Candelaria, C. 1993. Letting La Llorona go: Or re/reading history's tender mercies. *Heresies* 7:111–15.

Caplan, R. 2002. *Cape Breton book of the night: Stories of tenderness and terror.* Wreck Cove, Cape Breton: Breton Books.

Cartwright, C. 1982. To the saints which are at Ephesus . . . A case study in the analysis of religious memorates. *New York Folklore Quarterly* 8:57–71.

CastleofSpirits.com. 2005. Ghost in the mirror. http://www.castleofspirits. com/stories05/inthemirror.html (accessed July 6, 2005).

Celtic brew. 2002. Howie MacDonald, performer. Self-produced CD.

Charles Addams. n.d. http://westfieldnj.com/addams/index.htm (accessed October 13, 2006).

Chavez, J. 1997. *Haunted house Halloween handbook.* Jefferson, NC: McFarland's Company.

Chisholm, A. N. 2000. *As true as I'm sitting here,* eds. B. Sutcliffe and R. Caplan. Wreck Cove, Cape Breton: Breton Books.

Christie, L. 2001. Real estate's scary side: Three beds, two baths, one ghost, a haunting tale. *CNN Money* 31:1–4.

Clark, R. W.1977. *Edison: The man who made the future.* Oxford, UK: Putnam Publishing Group.

Clery, E. J. 1995. *The rise of supernatural fiction, 1762–1800.* Cambridge: Cambridge University Press.

Cohen, E. 1988. Authenticity and commodization in tourism. *Annals of Tourism Research* 15:371–86.

Corliss, W. R. 1982. *Lightning, auroras, and nocturnal lights: A catalog of geophysical anomalies.* Glen Arm, MD: Sourcebook Project.

————. 1994. *Science frontiers: Some anomalies and curiosities of nature.* Glen Arm, MD: Sourcebook Project.

Coventry, M. 2004. *Haunted castles and houses of Scotland.* Musselburgh, Scotland: Goblinshead Publishing.

Covington, D. 1995. *Salvation on Sand Mountain.* New York: Penguin Books.

Creighton, H. [1957] 1994. *Bluenose ghosts.* Halifax: Nimbus Publishing.

Crow, C. L. 2004. The girl in the library: Edith Wharton's "The eyes" and American gothic traditions. In *Spectral America: Phantoms and the national imagination*, ed. J. A. Weinstock, 157–68. Madison: University of Wisconsin Press.

Davis, A. J. 1847. *The principles of nature: Her divine revelation; and a voice to mankind.* London: John Chapman.

Dégh, L. 1971. Legend and belief. *Genre* 4:281–304.

———. 1994. *American folklore and the mass media.* Bloomington: Indiana University Press.

———. 2001. *Legend and belief: Dialectics of a folklore genre.* Bloomington: Indiana University Press.

Dégh, L., and A. Vázsonyi. 1983. Does the word "dog" bite? Ostensive action: A means of legend telling. *Journal of Folklore Research* 20:5–34.

Douglas, J., and M. Olshaker. 2000. *The cases that haunt us: From Jack the Ripper to JonBenet Ramsey, the FBI's legendary mindhunter sheds new light on the mysteries that won't go away.* New York: Scribner's.

Doyle, C. C. 1988. The avenging voice from the depths. *Western Folklore* 47:21–37.

Doyle, J. 1996. Haunting the borderlands: La Llorona in Sandra Cisneros's *Woman Hollering Creek. Frontiers* 16:53–70.

Dundes, A. 1996. *The walled-up wife: A casebook.* Madison: University of Wisconsin Press.

———. 2002. Bloody Mary in the mirror: A ritual reflection of pre-pubescent anxiety. In *Bloody Mary in the mirror: Essays in psychoanalytic folklore*, ed. A. Dundes, 76–94. Jackson: University Press of Mississippi.

Eberly, S. S. 1991. Fairies and the folklore of disability: Changelings, hybrids, and the solitary fairy. In *The good people: New fairylore essays*, ed. P. Narváez, 227–50. Lexington: University Press of Kentucky.

Edwards, E. D. 2001. A house that tries to be haunted: Ghostly narratives in popular film and television. In *Hauntings and poltergeists: Multidisciplinary perspectives*, eds. J. Houran and R. Lange, 82–119. Jefferson, NC: McFarland and Company.

Ellis, B. 1981. The camp mock-ordeal theater as life. *Journal of American Folklore* 94:486–505.

———. 1983. Legend-tripping in Ohio: A behavioral survey. *Papers in Comparative Studies* 2:52–69.

———. 1989. Death by folklore: Ostension, contemporary legend, and murder. *Western Folklore* 48:201–20.

———. 1991. Legend trips and satanism: Adolescents' ostensive traditions as "cult" activity. In *The satanism scare*, eds. J. T. Richardson, J. Best, and D. G. Bromley, 279–95. New York: Aldine de Gruyter.

———. 1993. Adolescent legend-tripping. *Psychology Today* 17:68–69.

———. 1994. "Safe" spooks: New Halloween traditions in response to sadism legends. In *Halloween and other festivals of death and life*, ed. J. Santino, 24–44. Knoxville: University of Tennessee Press.

————. 1996. Legend Trip. In *American folklore: An encyclopedia*, ed. J. H. Brunvand, 439–40. New York: Garland.

————. 2001a. *Aliens, ghosts, and cults: Legends we live by.* Jackson: University Press of Mississippi.

————. 2001b. Hæc in sua parochial accidisse dixit: the rhetoric of the 15th century contemporary legends. *Contemporary Legend* 4:74–92.

————. 2004. *Lucifer ascending: The occult in folklore and popular culture.* Lexington: University Press of Kentucky.

Emery, E. 1997. Season of the supernatural—Television shows centering on the supernatural. *Skeptical Enquirer*, March/April. http://www.findarticles.com/p/articles/mi_m2843/is_n2_v21/ai_19267321 (accessed October 26, 2006).

Erdrich, L. 1988. *Tracks.* New York: Henry Holt.

FarShores ParaNews. 2005a. Mobile phone radiation killing off ghosts. http://www.100megsfree4.com/farshores/phone2.htm (accessed June 28, 2005).

FarShores ParaNews. 2005b. Poll indicates Canadian belief in paranormal remains high. http://www.100megsfree4.com/farshores/pollcan.htm (accessed July 6, 2005).

Fatsis, S. 1995. Is that a haunted house you're buying? *Wall Street Journal*, 27 October.

Felton, D. 1999. *Haunted Greece and Rome: Ghost stories from classical antiquity.* Austin: University of Texas Press.

Fleck, C. 1997. Stigma or superstition? Appraisers weigh diminished value of tainted properties. *Realtor Magazine Online.* http://www.realtormag.com (accessed July 6, 2005).

Fluck, W. 1987. Popular culture as a mode of socialization: A theory about the social functions of popular cultural forms. *Journal of Popular Culture* 21 (3):31–46.

Forbes, B. 1997. Never seen a ghost? Then TV may be your teacher. http://www.purdue.edu/UNS/html4ever/971017.Sparks.survey.html (accessed July 5, 2005).

Fowkes, K. A. 2004. Melodramatic specters: Cinema and *The sixth sense.* In *Spectral America: Phantoms and the national imagination*, ed. J. A. Weinstock, 185–206. Madison: University of Wisconsin Press.

Fraser, J. 2005. Never give up the ghost: An analysis of three Edinburgh ghost tour companies. MA Thesis, Memorial University of Newfoundland.

Fraser, M. n.d. *Folklore of Nova Scotia.* Antigonish, Nova Scotia: Formac Limited.

Galdone, P. 1977. *The tailypo: A ghost story.* New York: Seabury Press.

Gallup Organization. 2005. American's belief in psychic and paranormal phenomena is up over last decade. http://www.gallup.com/poll/conmtent/login.aspx?ci=4483 (accessed July 13, 2005).

Garcia, C. 1992. *Dreaming in Cuban.* New York: Random House.

Gaudet, M. 1999. Robert Olen Butler's "A ghost story": Contemporary legend as literature. *Contemporary Legend* 2:8–17.

Gauld, A., and A. D. Cornell. 1979. *Poltergeists.* London: Routledge and Kegan Paul.

Geary, P. 1986. Sacred commodities: The circulation of medieval relics. In *The social life of things: Commodities in cultural perspective,* ed. A. Appadurai, 169–94. Cambridge: Cambridge University Press.

George, L. 1995. *Alternative realities: The paranormal, the mystic and the transcendent in human experience.* New York: Facts on File.

Georgetown Historical Society. 2005. The Brocklebank Museum. http://www.georgetownhistoricalsociety.com/index.html (accessed June 23, 2005).

Gillis, D. L., and N. MacDonald. 2004. *Inverness: Centennial 1904–2004: History, anecdotes, memoirs.* Nova Scotia, Canada: Donald Gillis-Ned Macdonald Publications.

God Destiny. 2006. http://www.godestiny.org/ (accessed October 13, 2006).

Goldstein, D. 1990. Modern rationalism and the structure of supernatural experience narratives. In *Papers II, SIEF Fourth Congress,* eds. B. G. Alver and T. Selberg, 211–26. n.p.

———. 1991. Perspectives on Newfoundland belief traditions: Narrative clues to concepts of evidence. In *Studies in Newfoundland folklore: Community and process,* eds. G. Thomas and J. D. A. Widdowson, 27–40. St. John's, Newfoundland: Breakwater Books.

Gordon, A F. 1997. *Ghostly matters: Haunting and the sociological imagination.* Minneapolis: University of Minnesota Press.

Gray, J. 1992. *Men are from Mars, women are from Venus.* New York: HarperCollins.

Greeley A. M. 1975. *The sociology of the paranormal: A reconnaissance.* London: Sage Publishing.

Grider, S. 1976. The supernatural narratives of children. PhD diss., Indiana University.

———. 1980a. From the tale to the telling: AT 366. In *Folklore on two continents: Essays in honor of Linda Dégh,* eds. N. Burlakoff and C. Lindahl, 49–56. Bloomington: Trickster Press.

———. 1980b. Gotcha! American children's ghost stories. *Center for Southern Folklore Magazine* 3:12.

———. 1984. The razor blades in the apples syndrome. In *Perspectives on contemporary legend: Proceedings of the conference on contemporary legend,* ed. P. Smith, 129–40. Sheffield, UK: Centre for English Cultural Tradition & Language.

———. 1999a. Children's telling of ghost stories. In *Traditional storytelling today: An international sourcebook,* ed. M. McDonald, 539–43. New York: Fitzroy-Dearborn.

———. 1999b. The haunted house in literature, tradition, and popular culture: A consistent image. *Contemporary Legend* 2:174–204.

————. 2004. American children's ghost stories: Manipulation and mastery of a belief system. In *From shaman to scientist: Humanity's search for spirits*, ed. J. Houran, 191–209. Lanham, MD: Scarecrow Press.

Grim Ghosts. 2004. http://www.grimghosts.com/ (accessed October 13, 2006).

Grimm, J. and W. Grimm. [1812–14] 1944. *The complete Grimm's fairy tales.* New York: Pantheon.

Grove, A.W. 1997. Roentgen's ghosts: Photography, X-rays, and the Victorian imagination. *Literature and Medicine* 16:141–73.

Guiley, R. E. 1992. *The encyclopedia of ghosts and spirits.* New York: Facts on File.

Hammer, A. J. 2005. The Power of Oprah. Transcripts to Showbiz Tonight, November 22. http://transcripts.cnn.com/TRANSCRIPTS/0511/22/sbt.01.html (accessed October 30, 2006).

Hand, W. D. 1964. Popular beliefs and superstitions from North Carolina. In *The Frank C. Brown Collection of North Carolina Folklore.* Newman Ivey White , General ed. Vols. 6 and 7. Durham, NC: Duke University Press.

Hand, W. D., A. Casetta, and S. B. Thiederman. 1981. *Popular beliefs and superstitions: A compendium of American folklore.* Boston: G.K. Hall and Company.

Harris, J. C. 1881. *Nights with Uncle Remus and legends of the old plantation.* Boston: Houghton-Mifflin.

Harris, M. 2005. Contemporary ghost stories: Cyberspace in fiction for children and young adults. *Children's Literature in Education* 36 (2):111–28.

Hauck, D. W. 1966. *Haunted places: The national directory: A guidebook to ghostly abodes, sacred sites, UFO landings, and other supernatural locations.* New York: Penguin Books.

Haunted Encounters Blog. 2005. Ghost story vs. haunted encounters. May 23, http://www.hauntedencounters.com/blog/2005/05/ghost-story-vs-haunter-encounters.html (accessed July 6, 2005).

Hawes, B. L. 1968. La Llorona in juvenile hall. *Western Folklore* 27:153–70.

Hawthorne, N. [1851] 1933. *The house of seven gables.* New York: Macmillan.

Hayden, J. K. 1987. Toward desacralizing secularization theory. *Social Forces* 65:587–611.

Hell House. n.d. http://www.hellhousemovie.com/hellhouse/index.html (accessed October 13, 2006).

Hell House Outreach Kit. n.d. http://www.godestiny.org/ministries/hellhouse/kit.php (accessed October 13, 2006).

Hendricks, R. D. 2001. GhostWatch: Hong Kong. http://www.weird-wi.com/ghostwatch/may2001.htm#hk (accessed March 10, 2005).

Hines, R. 1991. Selling a haunted house. *Missouri Realtor* June: 9–10.

Hofmann, J. V. 1999. When bad things happen to good properties: Taking stigma out of stigmatized. *Tierra Grande: Journal of the Real Estate Center of Texas A&M University* 6:1–6.

Honko, L. 1964. Memorates and the study of folk belief. *Journal of the Folklore Institute* 1:5–19.

Hoppough, S. 2005. The 100 most powerful women. *Forbes.* http://www.forbes.com/lists/2005/11/O0ZT.html (accessed October 30, 2006).

Houran, J. 2004. Introduction. In *From shaman to scientist: Essays on humanity's search for spirits,* ed. J. Houran, xi–xviii. Lanham, MD: Scarecrow Press.

Hudson, W. 1953. I want my golden arm. *Publications of the Texas Folklore Society* 25:183–84.

Hufford, D. J. 1982a. Traditions of disbelief. *New York Folklore Quarterly* 8:47–55.

———. 1982b. *The terror that comes in the night: An experience-centered study of supernatural assault traditions.* Philadelphia: University of Pennsylvania Press.

———. 1995a. Beings without bodies: An experience-centered theory of the belief in spirits. In *Out of the ordinary: Folklore and the supernatural,* ed. B. Walker, 11–45. Logan: Utah State University Press.

———. 1995b. The experience-centered analysis of belief stories: A haunting example in honor of Kenny Goldstein. In *Essays in honor of Kenneth S. Goldstein,* ed. R. D. Abrahams, 55–89. Bloomington, IN: Trickster Press.

———. 2001. An experience centered approach to hauntings. In *Hauntings and poltergeists: Multidisciplinary perspectives,* eds. J. Houran and R. Lange, 18–40. Jefferson, North Carolina: McFarland and Company.

Hyatt, H. M. 1935. *Folklore from Adams County Illinois.* New York: Alma Egan Hyatt Foundation.

Indiana State University Folklore Archives (ISUFA). 1993a. Bloody Mary legend. Uncatalogued legend text.

———. 1993b. Shiloh Cemetery legend. Uncatalogued legend text.

———. 1995a. Haunted house memorate. Uncatalogued memorate text.

———. 1995b. Mother's goodbye memorate. Uncatalogued memorate text.

———. 1995c. Sunken graveyard legend. Uncatalogued legend text.

———. 1996a. Haunted toilet seat legend. Uncatalogued legend text.

———. 1996b. Scary Mary legend. Uncatalogued legend text.

———. 1996c. Willow Hollow legend. Uncatalogued legend text.

Inglis, D., and M. Holmes. 2003. Highland and other haunts: Ghosts in Scottish tourism. *Annals of Tourism Research* 30:50–63.

Iwasaka, M., and B. Toelken. 1994. *Ghosts and the Japanese: Cultural experience in Japanese death legends.* Logan: Utah State University Press.

Jackson, S. 1959. *The haunting of Hill House.* New York: Viking Press.

Jenkins, H. 1992. *Textual poachers: Television fans and participatory culture.* New York: Routledge.

Jennings, M. M. 1993. Buying property from the Addams Family. *Real Estate Law Journal* 22:43–54.

Jones, G. 2002. Haunted hike entrances—An unusual guided tour of St. John's, Newfoundland. *Performing Arts and Entertainment in Canada Autumn.* http://www.findarticles.com/p/articles/mi_m1319/is_1_34/ai_96058393 (accessed July 6, 2005).

Jones, L. C. 1944. The ghosts of New York: An analytical study. *Journal of American Folklore* 57:237–54.

————. 1959. *Things that go bump in the night.* New York: Hill and Wang.

Jones, R. 1999. *Walking haunted London.* London: New Holland.

Jones-Baker, D. 1977. *The folklore of Hertfordshire.* Totowa, NJ: Rowman and Littlefield.

Joseph-Witham, H. 2004. Review of *Hell House. Journal of American Folklore* 117:462–63.

Kakrup, H. 1982. Conventional religion and common religion in Leeds: Interview schedule: Basic frequencies by question. In *Religious Research Papers.* Vol. 12. Leeds: University of Leeds.

Kelso, J. 1998. Death and real estate: A study of the impact of death beliefs on real estate values. MA Thesis, Memorial University of Newfoundland.

Kermeen, F. 2002. *Ghostly encounters: True stories of America's haunted inns and hotels.* New York: Warner Books.

Kerr, H. 1972. *Mediums, and spirit rappers, and roaring radicals: Spiritualism in American literature 1850–1900.* Urbana: University of Illinois Press.

Kimmel, M. S. 2000. *The gendered society.* New York: Oxford University Press.

Kirby, C. 2005. Ghost hunters utilize latest in technology, paranormal research has become a popular pursuit. *San Francisco Chronicle.* October 31, http://www.sfgate.com/cgi-bin/article.cgi/f=/c/a/2005/10/31/BUDGCFFS8Q1.DTL (accessed January 20, 2006).

Koven, M. 1999. Feminist folkloristics and women's cinema: Towards a methodology. *Literature Film Quarterly* 27:292–300.

————. 2003. Folklore studies and popular film and television: A necessary critical survey. *Journal of American Folklore* 116:176–95.

Laba, M. 1986. Popular culture and folklore: The social dimension. In *Media sense: The folklore-popular culture continuum,* eds. P. Narváez and M. Laba, 9–18. Bowling Green: Bowling Green State University Popular Press.

Labov, W., and J. Waletsky. 1967. Narrative analysis: Oral versions of personal experience. In *Essays on the verbal and visual arts,* ed. J. L. Helm, 12–44. Seattle: University of Washington Press.

Langlois, J. 1980. Mary Whales, I believe in you. In *Indiana folklore: A reader,* ed. L. Dégh, 196–224. Bloomington: Indiana University.

Leach, M. 1959. *The thing at the foot of the bed and other scary stories.* New York: Dell Publishing.

Leary, J. P. 1973. The boondocks monster of Camp Wapehani. *Indiana Folklore* 4:174–90.

Lennon, J. J., and M. Foley. 1999. Interpretation of the unimaginable: The U.S. Holocaust Memorial Museum, Washington D.C., and Dark tourism. *Journal of Travel Research* 38:46–50.

————. 2000. *Dark tourism: The attraction of death and disaster.* London: Continuum.

Limón, J. 1983. Legendry, metafolklore, and performance: A Mexican-American example. *Western Folklore* 42:191–208.

————. 1990. La Llorona, the third legend of greater Mexico: Cultural symbols, women, and the political unconscious. In *Between borders: Essays on Mexicana/Chicana history*, ed. A. R. del Castillo, 399–432. Encino, CA: Floricanto Press.

Lindahl, C., ed. 2004. *American folktales from the collections of the Library of Congress*. Vol. 2. Armork, NY: M. E. Sharpe.

———. 2005. Ostensive healing: Pilgrimage to the San Antonio ghost tracks. *Journal of American Folklore* 118:164–85.

Loftus, E. F. 1992. When a lie becomes memory's truth: Memory distortion after exposure to misinformation. *Current Directions in Psychological Science* 1:121–123.

———. 1997. Memories for a past that never was. *Current Directions in Psychological Science* 6:60–65.

Luckhurst, R. 2002. The contemporary London gothic and the limits of the "spectral turn." *Textual Practice* 16 (3):527–46.

Lüthi, M. 1976. Aspects of the folktale and the legend. In *Folklore genres*, ed. D. B. Amos, 17–34. Austin: University of Texas Press.

MacCannell, D. 1999. *The tourist: A new theory for the leisure class*. New York: Schocken Books.

MacDonald, H. 2002. *Howie's celtic brew*. n.p.

Madigan, T. 1995. Caveat spector. *Skeptical Briefs Newsletter* 5:1–3.

Magliocco, S. 1985. The Bloomington Jaycees' haunted house. *Indiana Folklore and Oral History* 14:19–28.

———. 2004. *Witching culture: Folklore and neo-paganism in America*. Philadelphia: University of Pennsylvania Press.

Marquez, S. 2004. Bottle tree creative way to decorate yard. October 30, http://www.mcherald.com/apps/pbcs.dll/article?AID=/20041030/HOMES/410300311/1011 (accessed June 24, 2005).

Marshall, B. M. 2004. Salem's ghosts and the cultural capital of witches. In *Spectral America: Phantoms and the national imagination*, ed. J. Weinstock, 244–63. Madison: University of Wisconsin Press.

Martin, J. 1988. Bottle trees. In *Encyclopedia of southern culture*, eds. C. R. Wilson and W. Ferris, 495–96. Chapel Hill: University of North Carolina Press.

May, A. 1993. *Haunted houses of California: A ghostly guide to haunted houses and wandering spirits*. Los Angeles: Publishers Group West.

Mazur, E. M., and K. McCarthy, eds. 2001. *God in the details: American religion in popular culture*. New York: Routledge.

McCain, G., and E. M. Segal. 1969. *The game of science*. Belmont, CA: Brooks/Cole.

McCelland, G. 1991. Stigmatized properties—Another court considers the issue. *Michigan Realtor*, June/July:6–7.

McClenon, J., and E. D. Edwards.1995. The incubus in film, experience and folklore. *Southern Folklore* 52 (1):3–18.

McGillycuddy, J. B. 1990. *Blood on the moon: Valentine McGillycuddy and the Sioux*. Lincoln: University of Nebraska Press.

McNeil, L. 2004. Ghost hunting and the relationship between proof and experience. Paper presented at the meeting of the American Folklore Society, Salt Lake City, Utah.

Mead, R. 1994. *Weekend haunts: A guide to haunted hotels in the UK*. Manassas Park, VA: Impact Books.

———. 1995. *Haunted hotels: A guide to American and Canadian inns and their ghosts*. Nashville, TN: Rutledge Hill Press.

Mechling, J. 1980. The magic of the Boy Scout campfire. *Journal of American Folklore* 93:35–56.

———. 1996. Mass media and folklore. In *American folklore: An encyclopedia*, ed. J. H. Brunvand, 462–63. New York: Garland Publishing .

Melani, L. 2005. The angel in the house. http://academic.brooklyn.cuny.edu/english/melani/novel_19c/thackeray/angel.html (accessed October 7, 2006).

Mikkelson, B. 2003. Urban legends reference pages: Horrors. http://www.snopes.com/horrors/ghosts/hndprint.asp (accessed March 10, 2005).

Mobile Phone Radiation Killing Off Ghosts. June 2005. FarShores ParaNews. <http://www.100megsfree4.com/farshores/phone2.htm> (28 June 2005).

Montell, W. L. 1975. *Ghosts along the Cumberland*. Knoxville: University of Tennessee Press.

———. 2000. *Ghosts across Kentucky*. Lexington: University Press of Kentucky.

———. 2001. *Haunted houses and family ghosts of Kentucky*. Lexington: University Press of Kentucky.

Moore, D. W. 2005. Three in four Americans believe in paranormal: Little change from similar results in 2001. http://www.gallup.com/poll/content/login.aspx?ci=16915 (accessed July 2, 2005).

Moran, M., and M. Sceurman. 2004. *Weird U. S.: Your travel guide to America's local legends and best kept secrets*. New York: Barnes and Noble.

Morgan, R. S. 2004. Tennessee spooklights. *Fortean Times* 188:74–75.

Morris, P., and D. Phillips. 1985. *How to operate a financially successful haunted house*. Charlotte, NC: Morris Costumes.

Morris, R. L. 1981. The case of the Amityville horror. In *Paranormal borderlands of science*, ed. K. Frazier, 170–78. Buffalo: Prometheus Books.

Morrison, T. 1987. *Beloved*. New York: Knopf/Random House.

Motz, M. 1998. The practice of belief. *Journal of American Folklore* 111:339–55.

Mullen, P. 2000. Belief and the American folk. *Journal of American Folklore* 113:119–143.

MUNFLA. 1963. *Manuscript* 63–DIT. The phantom weather ship of trinity bay. Memorial University Folklore and Language Archive. 100–103.

Murray, S., and L. Ouellette. 2004. *Reality TV: Remaking television culture*. New York: New York University Press.

Musick, R. A. 1965. *The telltale lilac bush and other West Virginia ghost tales*. Lexington: University of Kentucky.

———. 1977. *Coffin hollow and other ghost tales*. Lexington: University of Kentucky.

Narváez, P., and M. Laba, eds. 1986. *Media sense: The folklore-popular culture continuum.* Bowling Green: Bowling Green University Press.

Newell, W. W. [1883] 1963. *Games and songs of American children.* New York: Dover.

Nicholaisen, W. F. H. 1990. Space in folk narrative. In *Folklore on two continents: Essays in honor of Linda Dégh,* eds. N. Burlakoff and C. Lindahl, 14–18. Bloomington, IN: Trickster Press.

Nickell, J. 2000. Investigative files: Haunted inns: Tales of spectral guests. *Skeptical Inquirer,* September, http://www.csicop.org/si/2000–9/i-files.html (accessed July 13, 2005).

Norman, M., and B. Scott. 1994. *Haunted America.* New York: Tor.

NOVA. 1996. *Kidnapped by UFOs.* #2306. WGBH Boston Television.

O'Connor, B. B. 1995. *Healing traditions: Alternative medicine and the health professions.* Philadelphia: University of Pennsylvania Press.

Opie, I., and P. Opie. 1959. *The lore and language of schoolchildren.* Oxford: Oxford University Press.

———. 1985. *The singing game.* Oxford: Oxford University Press.

Pam's House Blend. 2005. I'm not shitting you, Halloween edition. http://www.pamspaulding.com/weblog/2005/10/im-not-shtting-you-halloween-edition.html (accessed October 13, 2006).

Paredes, A. 1960. Tag, you're it. *Journal of American Folklore* 73:157–58.

Patmore, C. K. D. 2003. Angel in the House, Project Gutenberg. http://www.GUTENBERG.ORG/ETEXT/4099 (accessed October 7, 2006).

Pettern, S. 2004. *Hotel Boulderado guest services guide.*

Philips, M., and L. Miller. 2006. Visions of hell. *Newsweek,* November 6:52–53.

Poe, E. A. [1839]1979. Fall of the House of Usher. In *The Norton anthology of American literature,* Vol.1, ed. W. H. Abrams, 1237–52. New York: Norton.

Potts, J. 2004. Ghost hunting in the twenty-first century. In *From shaman to scientist: Essays on humanity's search for spirits,* ed. J. Houran, 211–32. Lanham, MD: Scarecrow Press.

Primiano, L. N. 2001. Oprah, Phil, Geraldo, Barbara, and things that go bump in the night: Negotiating the supernatural on American television. In *God in the details: American religion in popular culture,* eds. E. M. Mazur and K. McCarthy, 47–64. New York: Routledge.

Puckett, N. N. 1931. Religious folk beliefs of whites and negroes. *Journal of Negro History* 16:9–35.

Pyle, R. M. 1995. *Where Bigfoot walks: Crossing the dark divide.* Boston: Houghton Mifflin Company.

Reality Television. 2006. http://en.wikipedia.org/wiki/Reality_Television (accessed November 10, 2006).

RECON: Real Estate Center Online News. 2002. It's kooky and spooky— Historic courthouse for sale. http://recenter.tamu.edu/news/recon1011.html (accessed July 22, 2005).

Religious Tolerance. 2004. http://www.religioustolerance.org/hallo_he.htm (accessed October 13, 2006).

Rivenburg, R. 2002. Off kilter: Waiting for a good punch line. http://www.offkilter.org/march202002.html (accessed March 10, 2005).

Roach, M. 2005. *Spook: Science tackles the afterlife*. New York: W. W. Norton and Company.

Rockwell, A. 1981. *Thump, thump, thump!* New York: E. P. Dutton.

Rojek, C. 1998. Cybertourism and the phantasmagoria of place. In *Destinations: Cultural landscapes of tourism*, ed. G. Ringer, 33–48. London: Routledge.

Ross, J., and P. Myers. 1996. *Dear Oklahoma City: Get well soon. America's children reach out to the people of Oklahoma*. New York: Walker and Company.

Rowling, J. K. 1998. *Harry Potter and the sorcerer's stone*. New York: Scholastic Press.

———. 1999a. *Harry Potter and the chamber of secrets*. New York: Scholastic Press.

———. 1999b. *Harry Potter and the prisoner of Azkaban*. New York: Scholastic Press.

———. 2000. *Harry Potter and the goblet of fire*. New York: Scholastic Press.

———. 2003. *Harry Potter and the order of the phoenix*. New York: Scholastic Press.

———. 2005. *Harry Potter and the half-blood prince*. New York: Scholastic Press.

Sack, R. D. 1992. *Place, modernity and the consumer's world: A relational framework for geographical analysis*. Baltimore: John's Hopkins University Press.

Sanday, P. R. 2000. The socio-cultural context of rape: A cross-cultural study. In *The gendered society reader*, eds. M. S. Kimmel with A. Aronson, 55–72. New York: Oxford University Press.

Sawin, P. 2004. *Listening for a life: A dialogic ethnography of Bessie Eldreth through her songs and stories*. Logan: Utah State University Press.

Schiller, L. 1999. *Perfect murder, perfect town: The uncensored story of the JonBenet murder and the grand jury's search for the final truth*. New York: HarperTorch.

Schlereth, T. J. 1991. *Victorian America: Transformations in everyday life 1876–1915*. New York: Harper Perennial.

Schmitt, J. C. 1998. *Ghosts in the Middle Ages: The living and the dead in medieval society*. Chicago: University of Chicago Press.

Schwartz, A. 1981. *Scary stories to tell in the dark, collected from American folklore*. New York: J. P. Lippincott.

Sconce, J. 2000. *Haunted media: Electronic presence from telegraphy to television*. Durham, NC: Duke University Press.

Scully, D. 1990. *Understanding sexual violence: A study of convicted rapists*. New York: HarperCollins.

Seaton, A.V. 1996. Guided by the dark: From thanatopsis to thanatourism. *International Journal of Heritage Studies* 2:234–244.

Seeman, E. 2002. Spooky streets. *Common-Place* 3:1–4.

Shelley, M. [1818] 1983. *Frankenstein, or, the modern Prometheus*. New York: Dodd, Mead.

Shepard, L. A., 1984. Haunted houses. In *Encyclopedia of occultism and parapsychology*, ed. L. A. Shepard, Vol. 2, 585–88. 2nd ed., Detroit, MI: Gale Research Company.

Siddons, A. R. 1979. *The house next door.* New York: Ballantine.

Smith, P. 1992. Read all about it! Elvis eaten by drug crazed alligators: Contemporary legend and the popular press. *Contemporary Legend* 2:41–70.

Sparks, G. G., and E. D. W. Miller. 2001. Investigating the relationship between exposure to television programs that depict paranormal phenomena and beliefs in the paranormal. *Communications Monographs* 68 (1):98–113.

Spetter, L. 2004. Lafcadio Hearn's legacy in Japan. Unpublished manuscript.

Stenhoff, M. 1999. *Ball lightning: An unsolved problem in atmospheric physics.* New York: Plenum Publishers.

Stewart, S. 1982. The epistemology of the horror story. *Journal of American Folklore* 95:33–50.

Story, J.1998. *An introduction to cultural theory and popular culture.* Athens : University of Georgia Press.

Sullivan, L. R. 1993. Spooks stay free. *Forbes,* Oct. 11.

Summers, M., trans. 1971. *The Malleus Maleficarum of Kramer and Sprenger.* New York: Dover.

Sutton-Smith, B. 1970. Psychology of childlore: The triviality barrier. *Western Folklore* 29:1–8.

The Tale. 2002. http://abc.go.com/primetime/movies/rosered/thetale.html (accessed June 2005).

Taylor, A. 1956. Raw head and bloody bones. *Journal of American Folklore* 69:175.

Taylor, H. 2003. The Harris poll: The religious and other beliefs of Americans 2003. http://www.harrisinteractive.com/harris_poll/index.asp?PID=359 (accessed July 13, 2005).

Taylor, T. 2002. Rose Red: The new Stephen King mini-series on ABC inspired by a real-life ghost story! http://www.prairieghosts.com/rosered.html (accessed June 24, 2005).

Telotte, J. P. 2001. The "Blair Witch project" project: Film and the Internet. *Film Quarterly* 54: 32–39.

Terrain Group, Inc. 2004. Population projections for Cape Breton municipal units—2001–2021. http://66.102.7.104/search?q=cache: A8hPfoJJk2gJ:www.cbrm.ns.ca/portal/civic/council/studies_reports/PDF/PopulationForcast_PNS (accessed June 3, 2006).

Thomas, J. B. 1991. Pain, pleasure, and the spectral: The barfing ghost of Burford Hall. *Folklore Forum* 24:27–38.

———. 1997. *Featherless chickens, laughing women, and serious stories.* Charlottesville: University Press of Virginia.

———. 2003. *Naked Barbies, warrior Joes, and other forms of visible gender.* Urbana: University of Illinois Press.

Thomas, K. 1991. *Religion and the decline of magic: Studies in popular beliefs in sixteenth and seventeenth-century England.* Harmondsworth, England: Penguin Books.

Thompson, S. 1946. *The folktale*. New York: Holt, Rinehart, and Winston.

Thompson, W. O. n.d. The dead still whisper, New England ghosts. http://www.invik.con/x519.html (accessed March 10, 2005).

Toilet museum in South Korea looks back at ghosts, pots, and candle light. 2001. http://www.planetsave.com/ViewStory.asp?ID=1566 (accessed March 10, 2005).

Tuan, Y.-F. 1980. The significance of the artifact. *Geographical Review* 70(4):462–72.

Tuchman, B. 1978. *A distant mirror: The calamitous 14th century*. New York: Alfred A. Knopf.

Tucker, E. 1980. Concepts of space in children's narratives. In *Folklore on two continents: Essays in honor of Linda Dégh*, eds. N. Burlakoff and C. Lindahl, 19–25. Bloomington, IN: Trickster Press.

———. 2005a. *Campus legends: A handbook*. Westbrook, CT: Greenwood Press.

———. 2005b. Ghosts in mirrors: Reflections of the self. *Journal of American Folklore* 118:186–203.

Twain, M. 1897. *How to tell a story and other essays*. New York: Harper and Brothers.

Urban Legends Reference Pages. Ring around the rosie. 2005. http://66.165.133.65/language/literary/rosie.htm (accessed October 13, 2006).

Urry, J. 1990. *Tourist gaze: Leisure and travel in contemporary societies*. London: Sage.

Virtanen, L. 1990. *"That must have been ESP!": An examination of psychic experiences*. Bloomington: Indiana University Press.

VisitBritian. 2003. Scare yourself senseless in England with Halloween ideas for big kids. http://www1.visitengland.com/visitengland/presscentre/press_releases/archive/oct_-_dec_2003/2003_10_21_01.htm (accessed March 16, 2005).

Vlach, J. M. 1971. One black eye and other horrors: A case for the humorous anti-legend. *Indiana Folklore* 4:95–140.

Von Sydow, C. 1948. *Selected papers in folklore*. Copenhagen: Rosenkilde and Bagger.

Walker, B., ed. 1995. *Out of the ordinary: Folklore and the supernatural*. Logan: Utah State University Press.

Wallace, A. F. C. 1966. *Religion: An anthropological view*. New York: Random House.

Walpole, H. [1764] 1966. *The castle of Otranto*. New York: Dover.

Ward, D. 1977. The little man who wasn't there: Encounters with the supranormal. *Fabula* 18:213–25.

Warner, M. 1998. *No go the bogeyman: Scaring, lulling, and making mock*. New York: Farrar, Straus and Giroux.

———. 2006. *Phantasmagoria: Spirit visions, metaphors, and media into twenty-first century*. New York: Oxford University Press.

Weaver, L. 2001. Who u gonna txt? Ghostbusters! IcCheshireOnline. http://iccheshireonline.icnetwork.co.uk/0100news/0200businessfarmingnews/page.cfm?objectid=11426498&method=full (accessed July 1, 2005).

Wecht, C.,and C. Bosworth.1998. *Who killed JonBenet Ramsey? A leading forensic expert uncovers the shocking facts.* New York: Onyx Books.

Wharton, E.[1937] 1973. *The ghost stories of Edith Wharton.* New York: Charles Scribners.

Wicker, C. 2003. *Lily Dale: The town that talks to the dead.* New York: HarperSanFrancisco.

Widdowson, J. 1971. The bogeyman: Some preliminary observations on frightening figures. *Folklore* 82:99–115.

———. 1977. *If you don't be good: Verbal social control in Newfoundland.* St. John's, Newfoundland: Memorial University of Newfoundland.

Wilgus, D. K. 1960. "Raw head" in Butler County. *Kentucky Folklore Record* 6:20.

Wilson, V. 2005. *Ghost tech: The essential guide to paranormal investigation equipment.* Alton, IL: Whitechapel Productions.

Winseman, A. L. 2004. Eternal destinations: Americans believe in heaven and hell. May 25, http://www.galluppoll.com/content/?CI=11770 (accessed October 18, 2006).

Wiseman, R. 2002. *Queen bees and wannabes.* New York: Three Rivers Press.

Wlodarski, A. P., and R. James. 2001. *Dinner and spirits: A guide to America's most haunted restaurants, taverns and inns.* Lincoln, NE: Universe Publications.

Woolf, V. 2004. Professions for women. http://etext.library.adelaide.edu.au/w/woolf/virginia/w91d/chap28.html (accessed October 7, 2006).

Yllö, K. A.[1931] 2004. Through a feminist lens: Gender, diversity, and violence: Extending the feminist network. In *Current controversies on family violence,* eds. D. R. Loseke, R. J. Gelles, and M. M. Cavanaugh, 19–34. Thousand Oaks, CA: Sage Publications.

Young, R., and J. Dockrey. 1990. *Favorite scary stories of American children.* Little Rock, AR: August House.

FiLMOGRAPHY

The Addams Family. 1964–1966. Dir. Stanley Z. Cherry et al. American Broadcasting Company.

The Addams Family. 1973–1975. Dir. Joseph Barbera and William Hanna. National Broadcasting Company.

The Addams Family. 1991. Dir. Barry Sonnenfeld. Paramount Pictures.

Addams Family Values. 1993. Dir. Barry Sonnenfeld. Paramount Pictures.

American Werewolf in Paris. 1997. Dir. Anthony Waller. Buena Vista Pictures.

The Amityville Horror. 1979. Dir. Stuart Rosenberg. American International Pictures.

The Amityville Horror. 2005. Dir. Andrew Douglas. Metro-Goldwyn-Mayer.

Antiques Ghostshow. 2003. Dir. David Lee. Flextech Television Limited.

The Apprentice. 2004–2007. Dir. Mark Burnett. National Broadcasting Company.

Because of Winn-Dixie. 2005. Dir. Wayne Wang. Twentieth Century Fox.

Big Brother. 2000–2007. Dir. Simon Hepworth et al. Channel 4 Television Corporation.

The Blair Witch Project. 1999. Dir. Daniel Myrick and Eduardo Sanchez. Alliance Atlantis Communications.

Buffy the Vampire Slayer. 1997–2003. Dir. Josh Whedon et al. Twentieth Century Fox Film Corporation.

A Bug's Life. 1998. Dir. John Lasseter and Andrew Stanton. Buena Vista Pictures.

Candid Camera. 1948–1950. Dir. Allen Funt. American Broadcasting Company.

Casper. 1995. Dir. Brad Silberling. Universal Pictures.

Casper the Friendly Ghost. 1945. Dir. Izzy Sparber. Paramount Pictures.

City of Angels. 1998. Dir. Brad Silberling. Warner Brothers Pictures.

A Current Affair. 1986–1996. Dir. Peter Shore. WNYW New York.

Dark Water. 2005. Dir. Walter Salles. Buena Vista Pictures.

Derek Acorah's Ghost Towns. 2006. LIVINGtv.

The Exorcist. 1973. Dir. William Friedkin. Warner Brothers Pictures.

Ghost. 1990. Dir. Jerry Zucker. Paramount Pictures.

Ghost Busters. 1984. Dir. Ivan Reitman. Columbia Pictures.

Ghost Hunters. 2004–2007. Dir. Jay Bluemke et al. The Sci-Fi Channel.

Ghost Trackers. 2005–2007. Dir. Wayne Moss. YTV.

Ghost Whisperer. 2005–2007. Dir. John Gray et al. Columbia Broadcasting System.

Halloween with the New Addams Family. 1977. Dir. David Steinmetz and George Tibbles. CBS Television.

Haunted History. 1999. Dir. Jim Lindsay and Scott Paddor. History Channel.

The Haunting. 1999. Dir. Jan de Bont. DreamWorks Distribution LLC.

Heaven Can Wait. 1978. Dir. Warren Beatty and Buck Henry. Paramount Pictures.

Hell House. 2003. Dir. George Ratliff. Plexigroup, Inc.

How to Make an American Quilt. 1995. Dir. Jocelyn Moorhouse. Universal
   Pictures.

Howl's Moving Castle. 2004. Dir. Hayao Miyazaki et al. Wild Bunch.

The Joy Luck Club. 1993. Dir. Wayne Wang. Buena Vista Pictures.

Lost. 2004–2007. Dir. Jack Bender et al. Buena Vista Televison.

Meet Joe Black. 1998. Dir. Martin Brest. City Lights Films.

Michael. 1996. Dir. Nora Ephron. Warner Home Video.

Monster House. 2006. Dir. Gil Kenan. Sony Pictures Entertainment.

Monsters, Inc. 2001. Dir. Pete Docter et al. Buena Vista Pictures.

Most Haunted. 2002–2007. Dir. Karl Beattie et al. Flextech Television Limited.

The Munsters. 1964–1966. Dir. David Alexander et al. CBS Television.

The Oprah Winfrey Show. 1986–2007. Dir. Joseph C. Terry et al. King World
   Productions.

The Others. 2001. Dir. Alejandro Amenábar. Dimension Films.

Pinocchio. 1940. Dir. Hamilton Luske and Ben Sharpsteen. Buena Vista Pictures.

Pirates of the Caribbean: The Curse of the Black Pearl. 2003. Dir. Gore Verbinksi.
   Walt Disney Company.

Pirates of the Caribbean: Dead Man's Chest. 2006. Dir. Gore Verbinksi. Buena
   Vista Pictures.

Pirates of the Caribbean: At World's End. 2007. Dir. Gore Verbinksi. Buena Vista
   Pictures.

Poltergeist. 1982. Dir. Tobe Hooper. Metro-Goldwyn-Mayer.

Project Runway. 2004–2007. Bravo Cable.

Psycho. 1960. Dir. Alfred Hitchcock. Paramount Pictures.

Ray. 2004. Dir. Taylor Hackford. Universal Pictures.

Restless Spirits. 1999. Dir. David Wellington. Canadian Broadcasting
   Corporation.

The Ring. 2002. Dir. Gore Verbinksi. DreamWorks.

Ripley's Believe It or Not. 1982. Dir. Richard Lyon. American Broadcasting
   Company.

Rocky Horror Picture Show. 1975. Dir. Jim Sharman. Twentieth Century Fox.

Rose Red. 2002. Dir. Craig R. Baxley. American Broadcasting Company.

Scooby Doo. 1969–1972. Dir. Joseph Barbera and William Hanna. American
   Broadcasting Company.

Scooby Doo. 2002. Dir. Raja Gosnell. Warner Brothers.

Scooby Doo 2: Monsters Unleashed. 2004. Dir. Raja Gosnell. Warner Brothers.

The Shining. 1980. Dir. Stanley Kubrick. Warner Brothers Pictures.

The Sixth Sense. 1999. Dir. M. Night Shyamalan. Buena Vista Pictures.

South Pacific. 1958. Dir. Joshua Logan. Twentieth Century Fox Film Corporation.

Star Wars. 1977. Dir. George Lucas. Twentieth Century Fox Film Corporation.

Supernatural. 2005–2007. Dir. Kim Manners et al. The WB Television Network.

Survivor. 2002–2007. Dir. Mark Burnett. CBS Broadcast International.

Texas Chainsaw Massacre. 1974. Dir. Tobe Hooper. New Line Cinema.

The Today Show. 1952–2007. Dir. Sylvester L. Weaver et al. National Broadcasting Company.

Touched by an Angel. 1994–2003. Dir. Armand Mastroianni. CBS Television.

Unsolved Mysteries. 1987–2002. Dir. Hank Capshaw. National Broadcasting Company.

Urban Legends: Bloody Mary. 2005. Dir. Mary Lambert. Sony Pictures Home.

The X-Files. 1993–2002. Dir. Chris Carter. Twentieth Century Fox Film Corporation.

Index

Illustrated matter is indicated by italics.

253

baby as hero, 127–28, 131
baby boomer spirituality, 193
Bailey, Dale, 146, 157
Baker, Margaret, 62
ball lightning, 48, 51
bandaids, 132
Bangs, John Kendrick, 221
basements in haunted houses, 36,
   126, 152, 153, 155, 156, 170
Bassett, Fletcher, 61, 62, 69
Bassett, Wilber, 61–62, 69
Bateson, Gregory, 120
bathroom humor, 134
bathrooms, haunted, 31–38, 43, 83,
   132–34, 229nn3–4. *See also* toilets,
   haunted
bats, 163
Beaton, Dan Angus, 42
Because of Winn-Dixie (movie), 1
Beckington Castle, 174, 191
behavior, transforming individual,
   52–53
beheadings, 84, 85–86
belief: empirical *versus* true, 67,
   230n2; phenomenological
   approaches to, 67; *versus* rationality, 19 (*see also* rationalism *versus*
   supernatural belief); traditions,
   collecting and preserving, 61
belief tourism, 194, 197, 232n11
Beloved (Morrison), 6
Bennett, Gillian, 15, 17, 30–31, 64,
   152, 172–73, 180, 194, 211
Berger, Peter, 73
Bergland, Renée, 6
Big Brother (television series), 216
Bigfoot, 8, 51, 52
"Big Toe, The" (story), 124–25
black cats, 147, 163
"Black Eye" creature, 129
Black Pearl (phantom ship), 164
Black Plague, 20
Blair Witch Project, The (movie),
   217–18

bleeding, 37, 38
blogs, 18, 70–71
"Bloody Fingers" (story), 131–32
Bloody Mary (ghost), 20, 37,
   58–59, 84–85, 86, 88, 95, 120,
   132–33, 229n4, 230n8
Bluenose Ghosts (Creighton), 10
Boccaccio, Giovanni, 114
bodily functions, 36, 37, 38
body: views of, 31; vulnerability in
   bathroom, 32, 36
bogeymen, stories of, 120
bogeys, 102
book burning, 59
Book of Angels, A (Burnham), 213
books, opening to key page numbers, 74–75, 76
"boo," 113, 118, 121, 122–23, 147,
   231n1 (ch. 4)
boots, kicking of, 103, 104, 105
Borden, Lizzie, 91
borrowed items, returning, 42
bottle trees, 1–2, 16, 58
boyfriend, murderous, 84, 231n2
boy protagonists in ghost stories,
   122
bricolage defined, 200–201
bridges, haunted, 8
Brizendine, Belle, 47–48
Broome, Fiona, 189–90
Brown, Roz, 185
Browne, Ray, 9–10
Brunvand, Jan, 25, 125, 135, 140,
   228n1 (ch. 1)
bubonic plague, 113–17, *115*
Buffy the Vampire Slayer (television
   series), 215
Bug's Life, A (movie), 133
buildings, ghosts associated with,
   175
Burnham, Sophy, 213
businesses, haunted, 147
Buxton Inn, Granville, Ohio, 183

dirty diapers as ghost story element, 129–30, 131

disembodied machines, 223

disembodied presence, impact of, 109

disembodied spirits, 122, 223

Disney, Walt, 133

Disneyland, 164

disobedience, 120, 122

displacement, fighting fear through, 58–59

distraction, fighting fear through, 58

DNA, ancestral, 25

dollhouses, 143

domestic violence in ghost stories, 20, 83, 85–87, 90, 231n2

door latches, lifting of, 36

doors, opening, 27–29, 185

doppelgangers, 102

Dracula, 112, 165

dramatic timing, 117, 119–20, 138

Dreaming in Cuban (Garcia), 6

drownings, 103, 104, 106

Dundes, Alan, 37

dungeons, 155, 165

Duomo of Siena, 114

duplication of experiences, 77

Dyer, Moll (legendary figure), 218

E

eBay, 16, 173, 228n3

eccentric's house, 100

economic stresses, 40–41

Edison, Thomas Alva, 221

education: concerns revealed through ghost stories, 18; *versus* supernatural belief, 19, 62, 66

Eldreth, Bessie, 92

electronic games, ghosts in, 174

Ellis, Bill, 13, 76, 230nn3–4

empirical, meaning of, 67, 230n2

Enchanted Typewriter, The (Bangs), 221

"Encounter with a Horrible Monster, The" (Shaggy Dog #100), 125, 126

endings, surprise, 130, 131, 132, 139–40

English novels, early, 145–46

enlightenment, 191–92

entertainment, ghost story as medium for, 112, 120, 124, 125, 126, 135, 138–39

environmental information, ghost stories as medium for, 26–27, 44–52

eradication, fighting fear through, 58–59

Erdrich, Louise, 6

escapeartist.com, 171–72, 232n2 (ch. 6)

ethnic boundaries, ghost story role in crossing, 56–57

ethnicity, ghost lore and, 18

ethnic literature, 6

ethnic minorities, stereotyped views toward, 62–63

ethnocentric bias, 63

ethnography, 12, 13

evidence, 71, 78

evil spirits, stories of, 111, 125

evolutionary theory, 61, 62

EVP (Electronic Voice Phenomenon), 223–24

existence of ghosts. *See* ghost beliefs

exorcisms, 36, 57, 158, 230n7

Exorcist, The (movie), 34, 57, 230n7

experience-centered hypothesis, 26, 46, 228n2 (ch. 2)

experiences, interpreting out-of-ordinary, 51, 230n6

extra-sensory perception (ESP), belief in, 4, 65, 66

extraterrestrial beings, belief in, 66

"Extreme Guy" (ghost type), 19, 81, 82, 83–91, 96, 107, 109, 110, 227

ᴨ

T

taboid newspapers: communication with dead, stories on, 222; haunted bathroom coverage in, 36, 229n3

tag game as ghost story theme, 125–26

"Tailypo" (story), 125

talking insects in toilets, 133, 134

Tanya (ghost), 183

Taro (ghost), 37

Tate, Sharon, 175–76

taverns, haunted, 105–6

technology: concerns revealed through ghost stories, 18; ghost lore and, 219–27; hoaxes exposed through, 134; relationship of supernatural to, 2–3, 19, 22, 109, 220

telepathy, belief in, 65, 66

telephone difficulties, 33

telephones, haunted, 3

television programs: ghost depictions in, 18, 173–74; ghost narratives in, 5, 208–9, 219; haunted houses in, 160–61; supernatural themes in, 3, 8, 214–15

Telltale Lilac Bush and Other West Virginia Ghost Tales, The (Montell), 11

temperature swings, 33

Terror That Comes in the Night, The (Hufford), 14–15, 58

Texas Chainsaw Massacre (movie), 161

Texas Real Estate Center Online News (RECON), 174

theme-park haunted houses, 174

Things That Go Bump in the Night (Jones), 11

thirteen (number), obsession with, 97

Thomas, Keith, 192

thought, transforming individual, 52

Today Show, The (television series), 182

Toelken, Barre, 15–16

toilets, haunted: on Internet, 36, 229n3; leaving up seats, 83; in literature and movies, 33; mysterious flushing of, 31–32, 36, 37; overview of, 59; voices from, 132, 133–34

torture chambers in castles, 155

Touched By an Angel (television series), 213

tourism: haunted locations in, 16; morbid, 193–94, 232nn9–11; publications, 36, 43, 229n3; supernatural themes in, 8

town and car lights, 50–51

toy haunted houses and model kits, 165

Tracks (Erdrich), 6

Tracy (27–year-old teacher), 90

tradition, contextual continuity and change in, 20, 227

Traditions of Belief: Women, Folklore and the Supernatural Today (Bennett), 15, 180

tragedy, impact on real estate sales, 175

trap doors, 165

trauma, views of, 31

treasure, buried, Nova Scotia stories about, 45

tree houses, 143

trick-or-treating, 136, 166

"triviality barrier," 139

trivialization of tradition: commercialization leading to, 194, 195–200, 205; and ghost stories, 22

Tuan, Yi-Fu, 169

Tucker, Elizabeth, 13

Twain, Mark, 124, 154